MANAGING THE NEW ORGANISATION

COLLABORATION AND SUSTAINABILITY IN THE

POSTCORPORATE WORLD

SECOND EDITION

Emeritus Professor David Limerick

Dr Bert Cunnington

Associate Professor Frank Crowther

A&U

First published by Allen & Unwin in 2002
First edition published in 1993
Second edition published in 1998

Allen & Unwin
83 Alexander Street
Crows Nest NSW 2065 Australia
Phone: (61 2) 8425 0100
Fax: (61 2) 9906 2218
Email: info@allenandunwin.com
Web: www.allenandunwin.com

National Library of Australia
Cataloguing-in-Publication entry:

Limerick, D.C. (David C.)
        Managing the new organisation: collaboration and sustainability
        in the postcorporate world.

        2nd ed.
        Includes index.
        ISBN 1 86508 995 8.

Organisational change - Management. 2. Strategic alliances (Business).
        I. Cunnington, Bert. II. Crowther, Frank. III. Title.

658.4012

Publisher: Tim Edwards
Edited and indexed by Helena Klijn at hexpress
Text designed by Sylvia Witte
Cover design by Maria Miranda
Printed by PMI Corporation

10 9 8 7 6 5 4 3

CONTENTS

INTRODUCTION

This book is the result of a long odyssey that started in 1984. In that year, together with our colleague Brian Trevor–Roberts, we were asked by the Australian Institute of Management (AIM) to undertake a study of what was coming down the road for management. We worked on Naisbitt's assumption that the best way to see the future is to understand what is happening now, and so we launched a study of 50 high-performing business and government organisations in Australia. The results of that study were published by the AIM in a monograph entitled *Frontiers of Excellence* (Limerick, Cunnington & Trevor–Roberts, 1984).

The timing of that study was serendipitous. As Louis argues, if you want to understand a culture, you need to see it under conditions of change (Louis, 1985). At the heart of our study was a series of in-depth interviews with the Chief Executive Officers (CEOs) of those organisations. We found them right in the middle of transforming their organisations into the new organisational form that lies at the heart of this book. They were downsizing, chopping away at their corporate headquarters, decentralising, attempting to move into global markets, forming alliances with overseas organisations, and trying to get more proactivity from their internal units.

Their cultures were changing too—they were becoming more *individualistic*, and yet more *collaborative*. The CEOs themselves were deeply involved in what we call in this book *metastrategy*, in attempting to put together a new configuration of strategy, structure and culture. They spent much of their time wrestling with the problem of managing *meaning*—of communicating their new vision to others in the organisation, and of managing a new corporate culture. CEOs of government departments and organisations were going through very similar processes, although some of their priorities were different. But they, too, were struggling to create a new organisation.

The Frontiers study gave us abundant evidence that massive change was afoot. Yet, back in 1984, the broad outlines of the new organisation were still somewhat blurred. Australian organisations—and Western organisations in general—were still evolving into the new organisational form. In 1988 Cunnington undertook a similar study of spin-off organisations in California's Silicon Valley and Oregon's Silicon Forest. He brought back with him interview and other data on organisations facing very high levels of discontinuous change. They were experimenting with different forms of organisation that had vital entrepreneurial capacity, organisations that in later chapters of this book we call *dual organisations*.

Moreover, the extent of internal and external *networking* among these organisations was impressive. The picture of the new organisation began to come into focus, and the extent of the new challenges to management became more obvious.

During the next few years we undertook four further lines of development. First, we began to workshop our findings and our ideas extensively with managers and other academics in Australia, Canada, the UK and the US. We were somewhat startled and very reassured by their responses. It seemed that we were echoing many of their own experiences and analysing many of the same new challenges and opportunities.

Second, we wrote a series of articles on our findings and ideas, and found that they were readily accepted and published in UK, US and Australian journals (Cunnington & Limerick, 1987; Limerick & Cunnington, 1987; Cunnington & Trevor–Roberts, 1986; Limerick & Cunnington, 1989; Limerick, 1989; Cunnnington, 1990; Limerick, 1990; Cunnington, 1991a; Cunnington, 1991b). The comments these publications stirred up from both managers and academics helped us to further refine our picture of the new organisation, and brought us opportunities to look at more organisations. We found that deliberate, consistent workshopping turns research into part of an ongoing process of 'action learning', involving spirals of action–reflection–discussion–action.

Our third task was to undertake an ongoing survey of the emerging literature on organisations. Here we found something very curious. Much of the experimental and academic literature was still lodged in the older conventional paradigm. It explored notions such as 'organisational commitment' within the older paradigms of the integrated organisation (eg Bateman & Organ, 1983; Bateman & Strasser, 1984).

But there was a number of studies (such as those of Kanter and Pascale) that we found scattered throughout the literature that came from more direct and recent observations of management in practice. These tended to reflect the different elements of our own experience. What we were observing was the emergence of a very new blueprint for organisations—the *network organisation*.

In 1991 Cunnington spent a six-month period at the IC^2 Institute at the University of Texas, Austin, investigating specific instances of network structures such as consortia, joint ventures, flexible manufacturing networks, business incubators and strategic alliances. This research gave us further insights into the special skills required for the management of network structures.

In 1993 we published the first edition of this book. Our challenge was to find a framework that pulled together all of the insights provided by our own research as well as those from the literature and from workshopping. The publication of the book provided us with further feedback and with further opportunities to workshop our ideas. It also gave us access to more organisations that were working at the edge, pioneering the design of 'Fourth Blueprint' organisations. This has helped us refine and extend our thinking. We have been able to take a closer look at the processes of changing towards and managing loosely coupled organisations. We also became acutely aware of the difficulties being experienced by large bureaucracies, particularly in the public sector, in moving towards Fourth Blueprint organisational forms. David Limerick was able to conduct a series of in-depth interviews with managers in the 50–60 year-old age group who were working in these bureaucracies, and was struck by the extent to which these managers were psychologically disengaging from the management of their organisations.

Thus in the revised edition of this book we have been able to introduce the notion of 'neocorporate bureaucracies'—organisations that have not become Fourth Blueprint, postcorporate organisations at all: they have evolved, instead, into newer forms of corporate bureaucracy. As we observe in this book, this is in many ways a sinister movement, for such organisations can (and often do) kill their members, albeit unintentionally.

This, in turn, has brought us to reframe our discussion of two primary aspects of our thesis. First, we have reframed our discussion of leadership, drawing on Limerick's previous doctoral work on shared leadership, and launching a more stringent attack on the academic managerial ideology of charismatic transformational leadership.

Second, we have revised our final chapters and extended them into a discussion of the *socially sustainable* organisation. We are convinced that organisations that do not build upon and contribute to the fabric of their society are simply not sustainable. Organisations cannot continue to ravage the planet, nor can they continue to destroy some of their finest participants. We argue that the remedy lies in our own hands: we construct the very organisations that kill. Why do we not build organisations around the contributive values about which we feel most passionate?

We have also extended our work into a fuller discussion of service organisations, in the light of the rapid growth of such organisations to the extent that some 70% of employees are now in this sector. Indeed, there are strong calls for a 'third sector' which rebalances private, public and nonprofit activity (van Biema & Greenwald, 1997; Lovelock & Yip, 1996; Paquette, 1997).

Finally, we have included a chapter on microstrategic management: this has enabled us to take a more considered view of the values that underlie operational management in Fourth Blueprint organisations. This, in turn, has provided a stronger platform for our final chapter, in which we tease out the emerging shape of a new paradigm for management theory, research and practice.

This new work has taken place in a time of great opportunity and devastating tragedy for us. The opportunity was afforded by our growing friendship with Frank Crowther, who in 1996 joined Bert and David in the venture of revising this book. Frank brought with him wide experience in educational administration, a closeness to the processes of metastrategic management, a sensitivity to social issues in the new management, and what he calls 'microstrategic management', that many of our readers will find both useful and refreshing. He also shared Bert and David's growing scepticism about transformational leadership and growing concern for the social sustainability of organisations.

The tragedy was the untimely death of Bert Cunnington last year, after a long illness. Despite being racked by pain, blinded, and eventually deafened, by his illness, Bert was extraordinarily brave—and productive. He bombarded us with insights and ideas almost to the end. He was particularly concerned with the centrality of love in social action, and drove us to be more out-spoken in our critique of neocorporate bureaucracies. We hope that, somehow, we have allowed Bert's braveness to emerge in this new edition of our book. Bert has gone. But his thinking and his impact on us have not. So from now on, when we write in the first person plural—when we write about 'we'—we mean all three of us, Bert, Frank and David. Our contributions to this book are inseparable.

Perhaps we should be talking about an even wider 'we', for we have drawn on so many resources for this book. We are desperate to acknowledge them. Where we draw on our previous research we attempt to cite those studies directly, without being overly cumbersome. Where we use the views of those with whom we have workshopped, we cite them directly, without giving a further source reference.

Some (especially those in government organisations) were reluctant to be directly cited on the more controversial issues. In such cases we have left their quotations anonymous. Wherever possible, we have attempted to quote our managerial sources directly and to let them speak for themselves. Of course, we take responsibility for the way in which we have put their views together, and for the interpretive framework of this book.

We are deeply indebted to the many managers who have contri-buted to this book. The medium is the message—this book on managing the new collaborative organisation has itself been a collaborative effort. And just as network organisations are quint-essentially designed to innovate, so this book is more than just an interpretation of events. It pushes at the boundaries of manage-ment theory. It attempts to offer new insights into new strategies of managing organisations and to suggest ways in which managers in business and government enterprises, large and small, can revitalise their organisations.

We are also deeply indebted to our wives and families—to Brigid, who was a fellow-traveller, who opened up new horizons to us, and whose influence on the book has been profound, and to Joy, Edwina, Tracey, Robin, Michael, Louise, Jennifer, Justin, Warren and Cameron—all of whom have helped us to remain sensitive to the social implications of our emerging thesis. They have consistently thought the unthinkable and said the unsayable: they have been our most outspoken critics and our bravest supporters. Finally, our three research assistants, Julie Mundy, Janette Tegg and Bronwyn Herbertson, were ideal partners in this strategic alliance: their insight and vigilance has added greatly to the richness of our material.

The book as a whole sets out to understand the new, post-corporate, network organisation and to map its implications for management. It does not assume that all organisations have experienced changes of the kind described here, and it does not set out to colonise everyone's working world. There are many who work in organisations, especially in neocorporate bureaucracies, that are based on different mindsets. Yet this book is for all managers—for those who work in network organisations and for those who do not. Those who do will find in this book much with which they are intimately familiar. The chapters that follow will give them an opportunity to share the experiences, problems and approaches of others who are exploring similar new managerial worlds.

Those who work in the more familiar territory of conventional corporate organisations will find many of the ideas in this book, and many of the experiences of the new generation of managers, strange and somewhat disturbing. But in reading this book they will glimpse a world that is very important to those other managers with whom they often relate. The new world, moreover, may creep up on them. Forewarned is forearmed.

THE STRUCTURE OF THIS BOOK

The structure of this book reflects the general logic of our overall argument. In essence, we argue that:

- the 1980s and 1990s have been a period of sharp, discontinuous change in the economic, social and interpersonal features of the Western world;
- these changes have led to new organisational strategies, structures and cultures—a new organisational configuration;
- this new organisation demands different strategic management processes, and new ways of managing change;
- these new processes, in turn, require new sets of managerial competencies;
- the new organisation presents a host of emerging social problems that will have to be addressed; and
- it also suggests a very different paradigm of management.

Figure 1.1 shows diagrammatically the essential elements of the new organisation. These elements form the foundation of what this book is about.

In more detail, the structure of the book is as follows:

- *Chapter 1: The emergence of the new organisation.* We start by looking at the social, economic and interpersonal changes of the 1980s, drawing briefly on the perspectives of major schools of thought such as postmodernism, neohumanism, and disorganised capitalism. We show that these changes are leading to new organisational strategies, structures and cultures, and require a different managerial mindset. We contrast these strategies with the emergence of the neocorporate bureaucracy.
- *Chapter 2: Organisational choice: corporate organisations.* This chapter looks at conventional ways of managing organisations. It shows how each of the previous mindsets or 'blueprints' was related to the key problems of its times, and how, with the rapid and discontinuous changes of the 1980s, it became inadequate. It teases out the model of organisational choice that still dominates most Western managerial thinking, and shows how it presents managers with a dilemma that cannot be resolved,

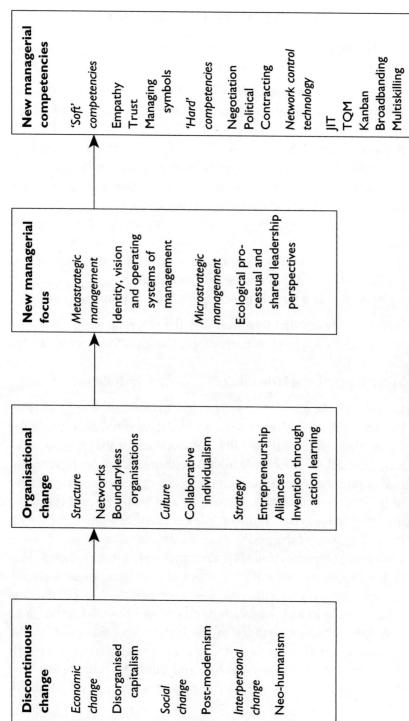

Figure 1.1 The essential elements of the new organisation

and that results in pendulum swings between centralised and decentralised organisations.

- *Chapter 3: Postcorporate organisations: networks and strategic alliances.* This chapter gets to the heart of the new organisation. As change becomes more discontinuous, organisations need more entrepreneurial cultures. Contemporary organisations are therefore experimenting with different kinds of organisational configurations, including internal networks and a range of external networks such as regional clusters, industry clusters, global alliances and temporary networks. These new configurations manage beyond hierarchy, and are fast becoming the dominant organisational form of the 1990s. There are also organisations that are stalled on the cusp of change: we argue that attempts to marry the Third Blueprint paradigm with the rhetoric and ideology of the Fourth Blueprint have led to the emergence of the conflicted, troubled, neocorporate bureaucracy. The 1990s solution transcends this dilemma. Finally, this chapter looks at how to manage network organisations. It brings together international experiences in a description of the nine basic managerial principles adopted by successful networks.
- *Chapter 4: Collaborative individualism and the end of the corporate citizen.* The corporate culture of the new organisation is very different from that of the conventional organisation. The good, loyal corporate citizen is being replaced by the autonomous collaborative individual. This chapter discusses the characteristics of the new individual, explores the conflict between the new managerial cohort and the older one, and suggests ways of developing the new skills and values of collaborative individualism.
- *Chapter 5: Metastrategy: beyond strategic management.* The new organisation demands high-order skills from its strategic managers. It pushes them beyond strategic management to *metastrategic management*, which focuses on managing the very *identity* of the organisation. It looks at the challenges of managing the key stages of the metastrategic cycle during periods of both continuous and discontinuous change. It introduces the concept of self-transcendence—the capacity of the new manager to envision the organisation as a whole and to grasp its

potentiality to become something different. It also examines the creation of the action learning organisation, and looks at the use of approaches such as appreciative inquiry in designing more satisfying organisations.

- *Chapter 6: Microstrategy: workplace management in the Fourth Blueprint.* This chapter looks at the values that underlie operational management in the Fourth Blueprint. It shows how postcorporate managers can take an ecological view of the nature of work, and can begin to develop socially sustainable organisations. It examines the way in which the Fourth Blueprint mindset reframes views on collaborative resources, examining, in particular, knowledge technology as a key organisational resource. Finally, it shows that postcorporate organisations take a very different view of leadership and focus on the development of multiple leadership roles—on what we term leadership diversity.
- *Chapter 7: Towards a participant based paradigm of organisational management.* The final chapter pulls together the themes developed throughout the book into a more coherent paradigm for theory, practice and research in organisational management. It argues that underlying postcorporate management is a paradigm that turns on its head the assumptions underpinning current management theory. The new paradigm starts with the participant as its focus, not the needs and activities of an élite group of managers. It looks at the ways in which participants create social realities, and argues for the creation of social systems that actualise the values about which we feel most passionate. It argues that research and theory are good to the extent that they provide more provocative ideas for social invention.

We hope that you enjoy this odyssey as much as we have, and that you find a new excitement and a new promise in the new organisation.

CHAPTER 1

THE EMERGENCE OF THE NEW ORGANISATION

> *We can say without hesitation that almost every single good thing that has happened within this company over the past few years can be traced to the liberation of some individual, some team, or some business.*
> [John Welch Jnr, Chairman and CEO of General Electric Company, cited in Thompson & Strickland, 1990: 70]

A NEW FORM of organisation is set to take us into the twenty-first century. It will have strategies, structures and cultures which are quite different from those with which we have been experimenting for the past decade and which are dramatically different from those that served us so well during the previous 20 years or more. It will offer new opportunities as well as new problems for management, and it will demand new mindsets, skills and competencies from those within it. This new organisation is with us now.

The period from the beginning of the 1980s to the mid-1990s was a period of remarkable change in Western organisations. People at all levels in organisations realised that traditional conceptions of capitalist organisation were frequently inefficient, unresponsive, cumbersome and demotivating. Responses were numerous and varied—moves from larger to smaller organisations; industrial awards that recognised workplace democracy; management training programs that cut across traditional barriers such as positional authority and gender; quality assurance initiatives; enterprise agreements; competency standards based on 'world-class' quality rather than cost; demolition of hierarchies and the chopping out of entire levels of management; inter-institutional linkages across corporate, service and government sectors—these are but a few of the more striking examples of the emergence of new organisational forms throughout the Western world. There is no shortage of evidence to indicate that, in turn, people in their organisations responded by taking the initiative in working together to provide new products and services, without waiting for commands from above. They began to manage beyond hierarchy to develop horizontal, collaborative forms of organising. From there, it was not a big step towards dissolving organisational boundaries and to networking and collaborating with people outside the organisation as well.

The emergence of this new way of organising has nevertheless brought with it a whole host of unforeseen managerial problems and challenges. It presumes a managerial capacity for global thinking, decision-making and acting that stands in stark contrast to our narrow 'anchors' of cultural, religious and political orient-ation. It is predicated on an aptitude for working across different sectors—private, public, social—while also competing with other sectors for scarce resources. It presumes an ability to assume responsibility for the ongoing redesign of the workplace while at the same time handling personal trauma when confronted with, for example, fellow human beings facing burnout, alienation and retrenchment. Particularly for those in the senior public service, the blurring of boundaries between the private and public sectors has been accompanied by workplace reforms that some regard as a threat to their traditional political independence and others regard as a destruction of an important leadership capability. In the public sector, perhaps most notably education, health and law enforce-ment, there is growing evidence that traditional structures in both management and unionised activity have experienced serious difficulty in facilitating authentic workplace empowerment and in letting go of their traditional authority base. Not surprisingly, strong evidence has emerged that workplace morale has not improved to the extent that had been hoped for or anticipated in some of these contexts.

But success stories also abound in which new organisational forms have liberated unprecedented levels of initiative and energy. Indeed, it seems fair to say that we are no longer about to make a quantum leap but are already mid-stride in every aspect of our organisational lives. We are clearly riding what Maxcy (1995) has called 'the cusp of a new wave', the timing of which catches us between two eras, one passing (which we call late-corporate), and one which has just begun (and which we call postcorporate). It is the problems, challenges and opportunities that are associated with our transition from late-corporate to postcorporate organisations which form the focus of this book.

That there are problems associated with postcorporatism is absolutely clear. Postcorporatism and globalisation go hand in hand. But Greider (1997), for one example, is concerned that the losers in a global economy will far outnumber the winners, and that this could lead to widespread social upheaval. Rodrik (1997) has similar fears:

> The process that has come to be called 'globalisation' is exposing a deep fault line between groups who have the skills and mobility to flourish in global markets and those who either don't have these advantages or perceive the expansion of unregulated markets as inimical to social stability and deeply held norms. [Rodrik, 1997: 30]

We can, nevertheless, be confident that the revolution that has begun, and in which we are all participants, has the promise of carrying Western organisations into strong competitive positions in the twenty-first century—as long as postcorporate managers recognise the social dangers that lie ahead, and attempt to build socially sustainable organisations. Managers, as we will show in later chapters of this book, cannot side-step responsibility for their impact on the social fabric.

This book will show that, in contrast to conventional organisations, the new, postcorporate, network organisation:

- has evolved to deal with a new era of change;
- reflects broader patterns of social change;

- has a radically different pattern of organisation;
- has a subtly different corporate culture;
- requires a new, strategic mindset; and
- is participant focussed, not manager focussed.

Clearly, organisations that have these characteristics also have new forms of management. To us, management in the new organisation is process oriented rather than structurally oriented; it is ecologically driven rather than hierarchically driven; it is value-added rather than competitive; and it is holistic rather than functional. This opening chapter traces the evolution and emergence of the new organisation. In subsequent chapters we examine the new management forms that seem to us to be critical to organisational success and health in the emerging postcorporate world.

AN ERA OF DISCONTINUITY

The changes that swept through Western organisations and society in the 1980s and early 1990s—and that still buffet them today—are not unconnected events. They form a single coherent pattern. Consider first of all the following more or less randomly selected events of the 1980s:

- the 1982 recession;
- the collapse of the stockmarket;
- Bob Geldof's *Band-Aid*, providing famine relief for Ethiopia;
- the rapid development of information technology;
- the increasing use of off-shore manufacturing;
- the rise—and fall—of television evangelists;
- the rise of 'people power' in Eastern Europe, and the fall of the Berlin Wall;
- the emergence of broadbanding and multiskilling;
- the principles of 'user-pays' applied to public-sector organisations;
- the focus on vision, mission and corporate culture;
- the emergence of multinational corporate strategic alliances;
- the focus on transformational leadership;
- the popularity of New Age thinking; and

- the emergence of Young Urban Professionals ('yuppies').

Now consider the following trends, also more or less randomly selected, from the mid-1990s:

- the reduction in government spending in areas of social welfare;
- the widening of the gap between the rich and the poor, to the extent that predictions of 'snaps in democracy' are becoming common;
- the rise of the 'new tribalism' in the Balkans and in Africa;
- the deterioration in relations between some superpowers, raising questions about the meaning of existing 'strategic friendships';
- a tendency towards rejection of rationalist thinking in relation to level playing field competitiveness and industry tariffs;
- the immense growth of the service sector as a result of factors such as the increasing grey proportion of our population;
- the government abandonment of policies to protect cultural and social minorities;
- the fragmentation of the socioeconomic middle class;
- a youth unemployment level of at least 30% in countries like Australia, with one likely long-term scenario being that of an 'unemployed generation';
- growing cynicism about multinational takeovers, particularly in the entertainment industries;
- the destabilisation of the 'knowledge sector', particularly in universities, but also in systems of school education;
- evidence of the unworkability of traditional notions of intellectual property in a world of 'virtual' communications;
- a youth generation for whom rapid change and its destabilising effects on society are simply 'the way the world is', not a source of anxiety; and
- a new concept of civic responsibility and courage—one of the 'hero within', learning to live with pervasive stress, fragmentation and minimal job prospects, rather than of heroes 'out there'.

These two sets of developments show that the issues of the mid-1990s are not the same as those of the 1980s and early 1990s (and will not be the same as those of the 2000s). But they are nevertheless part of a single paradigm shift and require a corresponding shift in the cognitive maps or mindsets we use to understand the world. One of the keys to achieving such a shift is the idea of *accepting discontinuity*. That is, each one of these developments represents discontinuous change, or a response to it. Development-ments such as these cannot be understood in the context of tradit-ional economic theory (which Peter Drucker described in a 1996 interview with Peter Swartz as 'obsolete'), nor can they be under-stood through reference to the values underlying political and social institutions (values held by people which Drucker describes as essentially 'conservers' rather than 'innovators'). Indeed, the first question with which we must come to grips in accepting discontinuity is 'Can they be understood at all?'.

Western managers have certainly begun to recognise that the changes that rocked their organisations in the mid-1980s and early 1990s comprised an organisational revolution that is part and parcel of discontinuous change, as we move from an age of mass production to an age of brainpower (Thurow, 1996). We have begun to accept the principle of discontinuity, if not yet to live it or be guided by it. Perhaps we have not learned to live with change in the way that our children seem to find second nature, even though some of its manifestations—information revolution, drug culture, unemployment, divorce—are readily apparent to us. How then can those of us involved in organisational management prepare ourselves for life in this new era?

In considering this question, and following Brigid Limerick and Crowther (1997), we find it useful to turn to McKinney and Garrison's 'third wave' metaphor of reform. The first wave of reform, they argue, stressed accountability within formal hier-archical systems. Without doubt, most traditional approaches to management development have been firmly centred in this first wave. The second wave, which focused on decentralisation and empowerment, overran the first and led to conditions of turb-ulence and organised anarchy. In recent years, many of us in-volved in management development have attempted to adjust our approaches to accommodate the demands of this second wave. Our revised approaches have incorporated recognition of principles of the learning organisation, and of equity and social justice, for example. But McKinney and Garrison assert that a third wave is about to break. Indeed, it could be argued that the third wave is already upon us:

> It is into this turbulence that the third wave washes. … there are no clear images of what the third wave of administrative alternatives may look like. Our suggested image is, needless to say, poststructuralist and postmodern. [McKinney & Garrison 1994: 82–3]

A number of earlier authors had recognised this discontinuity (eg Drucker, 1969; Toffler, 1981). In 1982 Naisbitt produced perhaps the best overview of this train of thought when he diagnosed 10 'megatrends'—10 'major transformations taking place right now in our society' (Naisbitt, 1982: 1). These changes consisted of moves from:

- an industrial society to an information society;
- a forced technology to a high-tech/high-touch (humanised) technology;
- a national economy to a world economy;
- the short term to the long term;
- centralisation to decentralisation;
- institutional help to self-help;
- representative democracy to participatory democracy;
- hierarchies to networking;
- the ageing 'rustbelt' industry of the northern US to the revitalised south; and
- either/or thinking to multiple options.

Naisbitt saw these as trends in the US, but the book was adopted as a manual for the future by managers and other readers in most Western countries. It proved to be reasonably prophetic—most of the themes listed above recur in the following chapters. Yet interestingly enough, Naisbitt's book seemed to have very little immediate impact on management. While there was change, the fundamental shape of the world seemed to be staying the same.

Each new event of the 1980s, from the drive towards decentralisation, through the middle-management wipeout, to global markets, seemed to be an unrelated example of that now familiar shadow, change. Managers accepted at face value Peters and Waterman's exhortation that if they were to achieve excellence they were to 'go back to basics' (Peters & Waterman, 1982). If the only constant was change, what was necessary was to refine the basic art of current managerial practice.

A rapid shift in the overall shape of organisations nevertheless began to take place in the mid-1980s. By the end of that decade there had been an unseen transformation in the worlds of their managers. Whether or not they recognised the total pattern, they were learning to manage a new organisation in a different world. They were developing an innovative configuration of strategy, structure and culture that offered new performance capabilities, and that demanded new managerial skills. They had begun to arrive at what, in this book, we call the *Fourth Management Blueprint*.

Perhaps it required the benefit of a few years' experience, of a little hindsight, to see a new world in the making, and to see the shape of a new, superior form of organisation. Several authors and researchers attempted to help managers with that process. Naisbitt, with Aburdene, attempted to show that the corporation was being reinvented 'from the bottom up' by a new generation (Naisbitt & Aburdene, 1985). What was management doing? Still going back to basics, evidently. By 1987 Peters had recanted. He had decided that if managers were to thrive on the chaos of the new world, they had to emphasise a set of *new* basics:

> If the word 'excellence' is to be applicable in the future, it requires wholesale redefinition. Perhaps: 'Excellent firms don't believe in excellence—only in constant improvement and constant change.' That is, excellent firms of tomorrow will cherish impermanence—and thrive on chaos. [Peters, 1987: 4]

The end of the decade was marked by wave after wave of writers, like Hickman & Silva (1987), Modic (1988), Rothschild (1988), Peters (1988), Coates et al (1989), Ulrich & Wiersema (1989), Drucker (1989a), Doyle (1990), and Naisbitt & Aburdene (1990) who attempted to capture the essence of the newly emerging world. They developed similar themes of globalisation, turbulence, social change, technological discontinuity, transformed organis- ational and management practices and cultural individualism.

Overall, what *did* this era of discontinuity imply for manage- ment in the 1990s? Perhaps two books stand out in their attempts to bring these changes together into a more coherent picture of the new management. The first is Kanter's *When Giants Learn to Dance*, published in 1989. In it she argued that winning the new game:

> [R]equires faster action, more creative manoeuvring, more flexibility, and closer partnerships with employees and customers than was typical in the traditional corporate bureaucracy. It requires more agile, limber management that pursues opportunity without being bogged down by cumbersome structures or weighty procedures that impede action. Corporate giants, in short, must learn to dance. [Kanter, 1989a: 20]

The second is Pascale's *Managing on the Edge* (1990), which also describes 'dedicated efforts by companies to be big and yet to act small'. Both tend to focus on larger organisations. Yet these changes were not merely part of the world of the larger corporation. Big, medium and small organisations alike found themselves competing—and collaborating—in a changing world, and they were forced to develop new managerial responses to it.

By the mid-1990s the meanings of globalism and knowledge technology were becoming clearer. Kanter once again offered a penetrating commentary. In discussing her 1995 publication, *World Class: Thriving Locally in the Global Economy*, she introduced dimensions to organisational management that tell us yet more about the nature of discontinuity. Consider, for example, her assertion of a qualitative relationship between local and global conditions in organisational competitiveness (Hodgetts, 1995: 57–60):

> Global competence is something every organisation needs, even to hold its local business. That's the bottom line and the main message of *World Class* for every organisation. You have to be world-ready even if you don't operate in international markets. [Hodgetts, 1995: 59–60]

> I've found that in order to fully understand multinational businesses, one also has to look at the places in which they operate, the countries from which they emanate, and the interactions they have with suppliers, customers, venture partners, and a work force, which is usually inherently local. [Hodgetts, 1995: 57]

Kanter's point about the new meaning of globalisation for every organisation and every manager was matched in importance by insights contained in Drucker's publication, *Post-Capitalist Society*

(1996). Drucker has extended earlier concepts of 'knowledge worker' and 'knowledge society' to a new level: that of knowledge as 'the one critical factor of production'. Knowledge, he argues, has two incarnations. Applied to existing processes, services, and products, it constitutes productivity; applied to new processes, services and products, it constitutes innovation. We neglect either form at our peril. (He argued that the Germans and the Japanese in the post-war period, and continuing today, have neglected innovation just as the Americans have tended to neglect productivity. The result in each case is immense organisational and societal stress.) To Drucker, the response that must be forthcoming is obvious: it is to work across political, economic, educational and social boundaries. He offers this advice in a recent article (*The Age of Social Transformation*, 1994):

> We will have to think through education—its purpose, its value, its content. We will have to learn to define the quality of education and the productivity of education, to measure both and to manage both.

> We need systematic work on the quality of knowledge and the productivity of knowledge—neither even defined so far.

> Increasingly, the policy of any country—and especially of any developed country—will have to give primacy to the country's competitive position in an increasingly competitive world economy. Any proposed domestic policy needs to be shaped so as to improve that position, or at least to minimise adverse impacts on it.

> We are beginning to understand the new integrating mechanism: organisation. But we still have to think through how to balance two apparently contradictory requirements. Organisations must competently perform the one social function for the sake of which they exist— the school to teach, the hospital to cure the sick, and the business to produce goods, services, or the capital to provide the risks of the future. They can do so only if they single-mindedly concentrate on their specialised mission. But there is also society's need for these organisations to take social responsibility—to work on the problems and challenges of the community. Together these organisations are the community. The emergence of a strong, independent, capable social

sector—neither public sector nor private sector—is thus a central need of the society of organisations. [Drucker, 1994: 18]

Globalisation, knowledge and social sustainability—these themes will reverberate in this book. So too will the challenge of developing world-class management in a world economy that will assume forms in the next decade that are not yet clear. Thus, discontinuity and planning must be thought of in the same moment. In a recent address to an Australian audience, Robert T Jones, President and CEO of the American National Alliance of Business, related this challenge specifically to education and training in Australia. He cautioned:

Just like companies you must redefine your product. You must re-organise. You must forget how you did things in the past. You have to realise that the product you deliver—education and training—will be the hottest commodity in the future. And that those who succeed in delivering it will have enormous positive impact on people and companies.

Educators and trainers must forever drop the arrogance of academic isolation. Your challenge is to:

Build a partnership with business

Develop a culture of continuous change and improvement

Adopt new training technologies

Focus on portability and credentialling

Form new strategic alliances

Most importantly, you must become an integral part of the constantly evolving economic environment. [Jones, 1996: 119]

The challenge, with the benefit of insights such as these, is to begin to internalise the full meaning of discontinuity as we will experience it in our organisational lives in the next decade. This daunting task may be made easier by reflecting upon three streams of thought that are part and parcel of the emerging postcorporate world.

THE POSTCORPORATE WORLD

The new approach to management described in this book is a response to the development of a new world—a new set of social, economic and political issues, particularly in the West. There have been many attempts to describe that new world, and we will not attempt to cover them all here. Generally, however, there are three broad streams of thought:

- postmodernism;
- neohumanism and the new millennium; and
- disorganised capitalism.

These schools of thought all take a look at the same kinds of issues that are beginning to plague managers of the new organisation, but each takes a different societal perspective. It is worth looking briefly at each of them in turn.

Postmodernism

Postmodern theory in general refers to the writings of a number of European authors such as Barthes (1986), Derrida (1973), Foucault (1973), and Lyotard (1984), who have been attempting to reconceptualise the processes of everyday life. It is not a unified homogeneous body of theory, and it has within it a number of conflicting forces, arguments and 'particular' forms of discourse (Hassard, 1994).

Any manager who ventures into the area of postmodernism is bound to find its ideas abstruse and to suspect that its arguments are irrelevant for the practitioner. It is partly a philosophical position that argues that 'reality' and language are inseparable. We construct 'realities' between us with the language we use (Hassard, 1994). Thus, truth and order are not immutable—they are based on a contract between individuals.

We will not go into the heady heights of that debate here. But it does create a picture of the world that is very important for managers. What is crucial for the manager is the postmodern view that social structures have no existence outside of the symbols and conventions used by interacting individuals. There are thus in the postmodern view, 'no absolute constraints in life or nature' (Cooper & Burrell, 1988: 105).

Postmodern theory is emancipatory. Individuals are freed from the imperatives and restrictions of structures, because these have been discredited and demolished:

Rather than introduce imperious guidelines to regulate order, postmodernists illustrate that persons are able to approach one another freely through the *recognition of difference*. [Murphy, 1988: 611–12]

In other words, individuals are free in every sense. They are free of constraints imposed by their recorded social and cultural history, free of artificial hierarchies and structures, and free to be different, to be themselves. Lyotard, in particular, is one theorist who stresses the role of information technology in allowing persons to be free, to create their own local knowledges (Lyotard, 1984).

A *Fortune* magazine study of the under-25s came to the same conclusion: these are 'the employees who can say no' to organisations (Deutschman, 1990: 23). In other words, this is the postmodern generation. The important issue for managers is this: if individuals are now free, especially from hierarchies, how can they be 'managed'?

The picture that emerges from postmodernism is one of an atomistic decentralised society composed of individuals who cherish their differences and resent attempts to control them through artificial social and organisational structures. There are negative as well as positive aspects to such individual freedom. There is often something quite pessimistic and haunting in postmodern literature—the lost, reactive individual in a society that has lost order and meaning. 'Nothing in man—not even his body—is sufficiently stable to serve as the basis for self-recognition, or even for understanding other men' (Foucault, 1977: 153).

A second picture that emerges from postmodernism is one of values confusion. Australian social anthropologist Hugh Mackay (1993) summed this up with an assertion that undoubtedly has meaning in most other cultures in the late 1990s:

The so-called Age of Anxiety is in reality nothing more than a symptom of the fact that what we are really living in is the Age of Redefinition. Since the early 1970s, there is hardly an institution or a convention of Australian life which has not been subject to serious challenge or radical change. The social, cultural, political and economic landmarks which we have traditionally used as reference points for defining the Australian way of life have either vanished, been eroded or shifted.. ... The Australian way of life is now being challenged to such an extent that growing numbers of Australians feel as if their personal identities are under threat as well. 'Who are we?' soon leads to the question 'Who am I?'. [McKay, 1993: 17–19]

Some commentators have found this situation so challenging that they have concluded that one of the primary tasks of management is to make life more predictable for employees. Stevenson and Moldoveanu (1995), for example, argue that:

In addition to making few promises and keeping the ones they do make, managers can help maintain predictability during a time of change by establishing the rules by which people can succeed and then playing by those rules themselves. [Stevenson & Moldoveanu, 1995: 142]

In the later chapters of this book we will take a very different tack: we will argue that it is the participants themselves who must set the rules—and who can renegotiate them when appropriate.

For good or bad, pictures such as these present enormous challenges to managers who are accustomed to controlling people through corporate hierarchies, or through controlling information flows. On the other hand, as Rouleau and Clegg point out, the very *acceptance* of postmodernism can provide opportunities for managers to help '...a less crippled human condition intellectually, physically and mentally, to flourish within organisational spaces' (Rouleau & Clegg, 1992: 19).

In the postmodern society, alternative means—that is, alternative organisational forms and structures—will have to be found that allow autonomous individuals to generate new forms of identity and to work together in collaborative effort.

Neohumanism and the New Millennium

On May 29, 1996, two days before he died, Timothy Leary, the 1960s radical and prophet of LSD, decided that he wanted his ashes spread throughout space. Watching a videotape of a satellite blazing its trail of light while plunging into Earth's atmosphere, he is reported to have said, 'That's me. I'm that light... I'm finally going to be a space pioneer.' (Michelle Koidin, 'Leary takes final trip—inner to outer space', *Associated Press,* June 3, 1996). This statement epitomised Leary's view of both the vastness of the human spirit and its essential freedom. It also epitomises a fascination with individual autonomy that has characterised the past 30 years but which organisational managers are only now beginning to understand.

In 1980 Marilyn Ferguson, in her book *The Aquarian Conspiracy,* wrote that: 'We are entering a new millennium of love and light' (Ferguson, 1980: 19). She argued that the US was in the midst of a paradigm shift, a revolutionary change from one world view to another. She wrote:

> The paradigm of the Aquarian Conspiracy sees humankind embedded in nature. It promotes the autonomous individual in a decentralized society. It sees us as stewards of all our resources, inner and outer. It says we are *not* victims, not pawns, not limited by conditions or conditioning. Heirs to evolutionary riches, we are capable of imagination, invention, and experiences we have only glimpsed. [Ferguson, 1980: 29]

These sentiments bear some remarkable similarities to the views of the postmodernists. The world is moving into an epoch of decentralisation and individual autonomy. But Ferguson's views lay at the endpoint of a long, respectable line of humanistic thought. It had its philosophical origins in Liebnitzian and Kantian philosophical traditions, with their emphasis on the proactive individual who is not just a puppet of the environment. She notes that others, particularly humanist philosophers, had 'premonitions' of the impending change:

> Carl Rogers described the Emerging Man: Lewis Mumford, the New Person, the age that would 'make the Renaissance look like a stillbirth'. Jonas Salk said that humankind was moving into a new epoch. [Ferguson, 1980: 57]

Ferguson the new (neo)humanist is broader than her philosophical mentors. She draws on an eclectic range of philosophers, psychologists, sociologists and anthropologists to support her contention of a new millennium. She acknowledges a particular debt to the writings of Teilhard de Chardin, a Jesuit priest, philosopher and scientist who is seen by many to be one of the greatest thinkers of the twentieth century (see, for example, Zonneveld & Muller, 1985). In his key work *The Phenomenon of Man* he developed the thesis that humankind has been moving through evolution towards a 'noosphere'—a unified sphere of the mind. Years after writing *The Aquarian Conspiracy*, Ferguson wrote:

> A deep change of vision is happening in the world today, that underlies all of the social changes. It came about because of all the millions of individuals who, one by one by one, have gone through their personal changes of vision and values and experienced almost a change of reality, of perception. ... this particular movement amounted to people simply wanting other people to take their own power, to participate in their awakening ...
>
> It had been Teilhard, who had prophesied the phenomenon central to my book *The Aquarian Conspiracy*. He forecasted a conspiracy of men and women whose new perspective would trigger a critical contagion of change; it was the idea of a paradigm shift, which gave an insight into the anatomy of the process of changing. [Ferguson, 1985: 162–3]

While both the postmodernists and the neohumanists see the present as the beginning of a new epoch of decentralised individuality, the latter are far more optimistic than are the former. For the postmodernists, individual empowerment is problematic, and may derive from, and contribute to, a 'me' generation narcissism that creates untold hardship, particularly for disadvantaged sectors of society. For the neohumanists, the new millennium is upon us; we need merely grasp it and join the conspiracy to empower others.

There is something quite seductive in the concept of the new millennium, of an irrevocable move towards freedom and harmony. In neohumanist thinking, the challenges presented by these moves also turn out to be unprecedented opportunities for managers. In developing the new organisation, it is suggested, managers find that they have access to resources and energies that were rare in the conventional hierarchy. Consider again the comment of John Welch Jnr, CEO of General Electric, with which we opened this chapter:

We can say without hesitation that almost every single good thing that has happened within this company over the past few years can be traced to the liberation of some individual, some team, or some business. [cited in Thompson & Strickland, 1990: 70]

But a decentralised, emancipated, autonomous society is strewn with problems, particularly problems of protecting its weaker members. As Ehrensal noted:

> I am concerned that 'postmodern management', like so many humanist management interventions, can easily be turned on its ear and utilised not to emancipate, but to further control... . [Ehrensal, 1995: 4]

Thus, emancipation can lead to vulnerability. On the other hand, the basic tenet of the neohumanists is tenable: *we are moving into an era of decentralisation which, used properly, can also lead to emancipation. This era will require a new kind of organisation, based on a different paradigm that can bring together the contributions of autonomous individuals in a socially sustainable way.*

Disorganised Capitalism

After the dizzying heights of neohumanism, it is almost comforting to get back to the more prosaic writing of economic and social analysts. But in these traditions, too, a number of authors argue that the 1980s and early 1990s constituted a period of unprecedented change, and who glimpse a similar decentralised world in which the corporation and corporatism are becoming less relevant. This is, they argue, the era of disorganised capitalism.

One of the first books to paint a picture of a viable alternative to the large hierarchical organisation was Piore and Sabel's *The Second Industrial Divide* (1984). Piore and Sabel demonstrated that, in areas such as Italy's Emilia–Romagna region, rapid economic growth has been generated by small, autonomous companies networking with each other, and subcontracting for each other. Such a system of decentralised flexible specialisation, they argue, marks a second 'industrial divide', a new point in industrialisation that stands in sharp contrast to the large integrated organisations of the past. The book attracted a great deal of attention from academics, but managers in the larger corporations did not really pick it up.

Nevertheless, they were to fall over the same divide: shortly after it was published, managers throughout the West came under enormous pressure to downsize as they witnessed the destruction of the large centralised, integrated corporations.

By 1987 two British researchers, Lash and Urry, had amassed evidence to demonstrate that a number of Western countries, including Germany, Britain, France, Sweden and the US, were moving into an era of 'disorganised capitalism'. They identified a number of characteristics of this era. Central to them is a decon-centration of economic activity into world markets consisting of smaller, fragmented, decentralised business units that engage and compete with each other through flexible specialisation. They document a move towards smaller business units and plant sizes in these five countries, a move towards service industries, and the emergence of more flexible forms of production. The end of organised capitalism, they argue, is also the end of corporatism in other sectors. Organised corporatism in government and politics, too, is coming to an end. Not only are business units becoming smaller, but trade unions and political parties are also suffering dwindling memberships, as society itself becomes more decentral-ised and disorganised.

Although the mass of evidence produced by Lash and Urry gives their basic thesis strong support, they have been taken to task on a number of points. Some have argued that they should also have looked at Asian economies and societies; others that they were observing a temporary phase of economic downturn in the West. (This counter-argument, though, has lost popularity since the fall of the Berlin Wall demonstrated so clearly that permanent changes are afoot.)

A more serious and consistent charge, though, is that what Lash and Urry were observing was not the *dis*organisation of capitalism, but its *re*organisation. *There is indeed a move towards smaller, auto-nomous, fragmented organisations—but what is emerging from these moves is a new form of organisation based not on hierarchy but on flexible, collaborative networks.*

The Postcorporate World

In this book we will use the term *postcorporate* to cover all these basic themes of postindustrialism, postmodernism, poststructuralism and neohumanism. We are aware that we are taking considerable liberties with the finely textured theories and paradigms of the latter schools of thought. But the term 'postcorporate' has considerable advantages for our purposes, for it underlines the move away from tightly integrated hierarchical systems of organisation towards the loosely coupled boundaryless systems that are the focus of this book.

The postcorporate world, then, is one that is characterised by a move towards smaller, autonomous, interdependent, collaborative units made up of empowered individuals. It is a global world of both emancipation and interdependence, as well as one of potential social upheaval and exploitation of the disempowered. We will describe this world in the chapters that follow. To cope with it, we are learning to manage beyond hierarchy and to move beyond conventional organisational boundaries into the creation of collaborative networks. The drive is for efficiency, flexibility and creativity. Australian Prime Minister John Howard summed up the impact of such change in February 1997 arguing that 'Globalisation of the economy ... has altered forever the sort of pressures and the sort of circumstances in which both the private and public sectors interact with each other. It is no longer an option for any part of the governance of this country to be inefficient' (Steketee, 1997: 23).

The developments of the mid 1990s lead us to this conclusion, but it would be wrong—and contrary to our principle of accepting discontinuity—to view the reorganisation that is under way as either inherently rational or necessarily good. As the postmodernists have pointed out, it is also a period of values confusion and of an elusiveness of personal, professional and organisational identity that is both unsettling and difficult to cope with. Moreover, the pursuit of efficiency, flexibility and creativity comes at a huge cost. The late historian Christopher Lasch, in *The Revolt of the Élites and the Betrayal of Democracy* (1995), argued that Americans are much less sanguine about the future than they used to be, and for good reason:

> The decline of manufacturing and the consequent loss of jobs; the shrinkage of the middle class; the growing number of the poor; the rising crime rate; the flourishing traffic in drugs; the decay of cities—the bad news goes on and on.

No one has a plausible solution to these intractable problems and most of what passes for political discussion doesn't even address them. Fierce ideological battles are fought over peripheral issues. Élites, who define the issues, have lost touch with the people. [Lasch, 1995]

Indeed, Australian national affairs commentator Peter Charlton, in discussing Lasch's description, notes that it applies in almost every respect in nations like Australia (*The Courier Mail*, March 15, 1997: 23). In Australia, for example, the restructuring of the economy across the past quarter century has been associated with increases in unemployment from 1.5% in 1970 to 5% in 1980 to 11% in 1990. The immense significance of these statistics is only apparent when viewed in the context of the fundamental importance of work to human well-being. As we observed earlier, 60% of new jobs are in the service sector (McCune, 1995), and social change (temporary employment, the greying population, etc) partly accounts for this. While governments of all political persuasions seem prepared to acknowledge 'the unemployment problem', for the most part they have a narrower focus, namely to redress budget deficits. Managers are thus confronted with some problems that are unique to our times. Whether to accept responsibility for social issues associated with the human need for meaningful work is prominent amongst these challenges.

Nor can managers avoid the broader context in which this specific issue is located. For example, sociologist John Carroll has been quoted (by commentator Peter Charlton, March 15, 1997) as saying that the vast mass of middle Australia—and this would include postcorporate managers—is in revolt against previously held ideas of class, status and power. Fellow Australian sociologist Michael Pusey has been similarly quoted by Charlton as believing that middle-class Australia is waking up to economic rationalism. ('It's very, very bad for you,' Pusey is reported to have written.) *Moves toward new organisational forms will not in and of themselves address the arguments articulated by Pusey, Carroll and Lasch. The disorganisation and reorganisation of capitalism poses far greater challenges for the management of postcorporate organisations. It poses issues of quality of life and social sustainability that historically have been the territory of politics, religion and social welfare agencies.*

A NEW MINDSET

All in all, a consistent picture emerges from all of these views. The world—especially the Western world—has undergone a transformation in the last decade and a half. It has been a time marked by rapid, cataclysmic change that produced a new configuration of social, economic and organisational forces. Individuals and business units alike sought autonomy and freedom so that they could deal with discontinuity after discontinuity.

The result has been a set of unprecedented challenges to managers as they edge towards new kinds of organisational forms—organisations that can bring autonomous units together to provide a quick response to discontinuous change. This book describes those challenges and those responses, and looks at the kinds of competencies required to deal with them.

As the book progresses, it will become clear that the new, postcorporate organisation is different from its predecessors in myriad ways. What ties all these characteristics together into a coherent managerial strategy is an underlying paradigm—a mindset—that gives them immense potency.

One of the most articulate proponents of the new mindset is Pascale:

> We must break the chains of the old mindset if we are to grapple successfully with the task of managing adaptive organisations. Recall Konusuke Matsushita's chilling observation: 'We are going to win and the industrial West is going to lose out: there is nothing you can do about it because the reasons for your failure are within yourselves.' The enemy 'within ourselves' is the old mindset. [Pascale, 1990: 88]

Pascale makes two important points. First he argues that this mindset gives direction to a host of managerial actions: 'That invisible force is a managerial mindset that, among other things, ignites a lot of little fires, and then harnesses their thermal energy' (Pascale, 1990: 28–9). Second, he gives strong support to Matsushita's argument that the industrial West has been slow to develop this mindset. The same point is made by others (eg Modic, 1988), who argue that Japanese managers are much more comfortable with the notion of strategic partnerships, which are central to the network organisation.

The new mindset, however, has to go further than a mere imitation of the Japanese approach, for as we observed earlier, writers like Drucker have argued that the latter have been slow to innovate. The new mindset must embrace individualism, collaboration and innovation. In other words, management in the postcorporate era implies a total strategic commitment based on 'entirely new ways of thinking about organisations' (Peters, 1988: 103). It implies a mindset that is oriented to process rather than to structure; that is ecologically driven rather than hierarchically driven; that is value added rather than competitive; that is holistic rather than functional; and that is collaborative and innovative.

The difficulties of understanding this mindset, and of implementing it even if it is understood, should not be underestimated. In the following chapters we will argue that many managers in large corporate bureaucracies, particularly in the public sector, are deeply aware of the new postcorporate mindset and its newly emerging ideology of devolution. But they are plagued by problems of accountability and are reluctant to let go of the apparent certainty of hierarchical control. So they have developed an uneasy hybrid form of organisation in which hierarchy is retained but which also attempts to implement some of the precepts of postcorporate organisation. The result is a new form of corporate bureaucracy that we call *the neo (new) corporate bureaucracy*, which is fundamentally not postcorporate at all: it is still based on the corporate mindset.

In order to understand this kind of difficulty, we need to have a sharper understanding of the internal coherence of different kinds of managerial mindsets and of their impact on managerial action. It is to this issue—that of evolving managerial mindsets or 'blueprints'—that we now turn.

CHAPTER 2

ORGANISATIONAL CHOICE: CORPORATE ORGANISATIONS

> *We must break the chains of the old mindset if we are to grapple successfully with the task of managing adaptive organisations.*
> [Pascale, 1990: 88]

THIS CHAPTER examines the mindsets that underlie different organisational patterns or configurations. It argues that the patterns of organisation adopted by managers and others within them and the mindsets on which they are based, are intimately related to the environment, or context, in which they are embedded. At the same time we argue that participants have real choice in the matter of which configuration to adopt, and that they will be held responsible for the choices they make. The move towards the new, postcorporate organisation reflects this blend of both agency (choice) and context. We begin with three examples to demonstrate this point.

CHOICE AND RESPONSIBILITY

The first example is one of failure to adopt a postcorporate mindset in recognising the boundaryless nature of the postcorporate world, and was described at the 1997 Conference of the Institution of

Engineers, Queensland Division. University academic Cynthia Mitchell told how the Institution had presented an engineering excellence award in 1993 to the third runway project at Sydney's Kingsford-Smith Airport at Mascot after it was completed under-budget and ahead of schedule. She told the conference:

> These are positive attributes when considered in isolation. However, a broader view shows that this project led to some of the most bitter and vocal community campaigns against a major infrastructure project in Sydney's history.
>
> The ensuing fracas and political fallout—with mass rallies and block-ades of the busiest airport in Australia, the demise of federal and state politicians, a new tax on all air travellers using Mascot airport and so forth—are compelling evidence that social factors should have played a much larger role in the planning of the development. [Mitchell, 1993]

What this brief account illustrates, of course, is that many of the decisions that managers—in this case an airport management authority—make in a postcorporate world have implications that extend well beyond their own boardrooms, systems or markets. Thus, they must ensure that their own structures, culture and processes will facilitate decisions that are not only economically sound but meet a range of other criteria, including, in this case, ecological responsibility. *They can accept this responsibility because of their opportunity to shape their own value frameworks, policy parameters and decision processes. In other words, they have organisational choice.*

As a second example of the need to make deliberate organis-ational choices, and to assume the responsibility that goes with such choice, consider the crisis that is said to threaten the future of the Royal Academy of Arts in London. Arts critic Giles Auty (1997) has linked the crisis to organisational vision and choice in des-cribing it this way:

> On my recent trip to Europe I first became aware of a crisis that threatens the entire future of the Royal Academy of Arts in London .... The national art gallery of England, from which the present royal institution derives, was founded in 1768, exactly 101 years after the first official exhibition held of works by members of the comparable institution in France, the so-called French Salon. ...

Yet the proof that institutions that take centuries to mould or perfect can be destroyed or changed irrevocably in months became increasingly evident as changes in personnel and emphasis first placed the Royal Academy on its present and rocky road. ...

[T]he Royal Academy has apparently accumulated a $4.5 million overdraft to add to a $4 million pension fund deficit. ...

As well as being responsible for financial failure, I contend that the recent, effective rulers of the Royal Academy in London have been untrue to that institution's founding principles. ...

[A] strong Royal Academy, dedicated to the principles for which it was founded, could have provided a beacon and rallying point for those sensibly unimpressed by non-stop artistic change. Traditions themselves do not have to be static, but artistic changes should be led by reason rather than by modishness. ...

The process of renewal it needs now is moral and aesthetic no less than financial. Sadly, I fear the chances of any such renewal happening in our current artistic climate are slim at best. [*The Weekend Review*, January 25–6: 13]

Of course, we do not wish to comment on the validity or otherwise of the debate about the vision or goals of the Royal Academy of Arts. But this venerable institution will influence, or cease to influence, the world of art through the way it shapes itself as an organisation, and Auty is holding its managers responsible for making (or for not making) responsible organisational choices. Its approach to planning, its internal relationships, its external networks, its view of leadership—these are aspects of its organisation about which it must make choices. This example also illustrates another theme we wish to develop with regard to the postcorporate world. Responsibility is not, fundamentally, something you *take*: it is something you have given to you by others. In a world of interdependence, you are *held* responsible by others: you have it whether you take it or not! *Indeed, what we call organisational choice presents both responsibility for interdependence and opportunities for influence which extend well beyond the organisation itself.*

As a third example of the importance of organisational choice, consider the restructuring of public education that has taken place in much of the Western world during the past decade or more. With state-based systems under increasing competition, for both students and finances, from independent educational institutions, and in the face of research evidence that restructuring of education workplaces can significantly improve student achievement (Newmann & Wehlage, 1995) the question of organisational choice is of obvious relevance and importance to education managers. But countervailing forces, including entrenched management structures, intransigent industrial brokers and some evidence of misuse of the concept of devolved authority in some parts of the world where it has been attempted, make the reality of choice in large centralised systems and organisations more complex than it need or should be, even in the face of crisis. *It is our view that managers in education systems are only now beginning to appreciate that organisational choice goes with the territory of management in the postcorporate era. Indeed, it is perhaps their greatest responsibility if they are to transform their organisations.*

Agency v Context: Responsive Agency

Of course, it is a primary principle of natural justice that you can only be held responsible for something if you have choice in that matter. If organisations are related to context, how much choice do you have?

This question raises a debate that has raged for decades in the social sciences: to what extent are you an agent (that is, you do have choice), and to what extent are you determined by your context (environment)? The position we take in this book is based on the concept of *'responsive agency'*, developed by Burgess-Limerick (1995). She argues that the debate is broadly characterised by false oppositional dichotomies. Traditionally, you either assert 'constrained agency' (your agency is limited by the environment) or 'unmitigated agency' (your agency is absolute, and unaffected by the environment). Burgess-Limerick, in a study of women who owned small businesses, noted that her participants accepted neither position. They asserted both their agency, and the importance of context. In exercising their agency, she argues, they *used* context, rather than being constrained by it. This point of the coming together (or 'coadunation') of context and agency she called 'responsive agency'—the responsive, agentic person using context to compose new ways of being.

Organisational choice is a matter of responsive agency. It will be readily apparent from our comments on the three case studies above that managers in postcorporate organisations have to make organisational choices that are far more complex than was the case in earlier, bureaucratised times. But they have capabilities of education and rationality, as well as access to education and widespread diverse resources, that *enable* them to conceive of different organisational designs and to choose responsibly and intelligently amongst them.

The four 'blueprints' that we describe below manifest myriad organisational choices. They are related to their times and contexts, but they also reflect rational, responsive, proactive choices and the use of context to mould new forms of organisation to stimulate and take account of change. It is to this issue—that of the evolution of managerial mindsets or 'blueprints'—that we now turn, in order to provide a perspective for the new ways of thinking that underlie the postcorporate organisation.

THE CONCEPT OF MANAGERIAL MINDSETS AND BLUEPRINTS

The notion of a 'mindset' that lies behind managerial action is not a new one. Management scholars have long recognised various 'schools' of management thought, such as the 'classical', 'human relations' and 'systems' schools, and have spent a great deal of time and effort debating and offering critiques of such schools (eg Etzioni, 1964; Silverman, 1970). Perhaps the most important aspect of the more recent debates has been the increasing realisation that it is not only academics and consultants who are members of schools of thought. Managers, too, carry in their heads 'cognitive maps' (Borys & Jemison, 1989) or 'mindsets' that profoundly affect their managerial actions.

We have come to call these mindsets managerial 'blueprints' in order to stress that they are not just passive ways of understanding the managerial world—they are images of the way organisations *ought* to be managed, and they directly affect managerial choice. They are partly descriptive, partly normative sets of beliefs and assumptions, organised into coherent cognitive and affective frameworks, which influence managers' perceptions of their worlds and frame their managerial actions. Such managerial blueprints or mindsets are not written down in a cut and dried form anywhere, or even expressed in their entirety by any one person. They are constructions of worlds of meaning shared by many of the managers and commentators of their time. Each blueprint is deeply related to a set of social and economic conditions and tends to be associated with different eras of social and economic development in the Western world.

As we look back over the history of Western management, it is possible to discern three previous blueprints of management—and a fourth blueprint that lies at the heart of the network organisation, and which this book is all about.

THE IMPACT OF
AMERICAN MANAGERIAL THOUGHT

Before we examine these blueprints, it is important to understand at the outset the enormous impact of the US on the development of managerial thinking. Heller, for one, argues that:

> Management is an American invention. With almost no exceptions every significant advance in management has come from the States, and so has almost every management writer worth reading. [Heller, 1984: xiii]

The Harvard historian, Robert Reich, goes further and asserts:

> Management emerged around 1920 as a philosophy, a science, and a pervasive metaphor which would dominate the way Americans viewed themselves and their institutions for the next fifty years. Management was America's own creation. No other industrialized nation so fully embraced it or experienced its spectacular capacity to generate new wealth. [Reich, 1971: 47–8]

That philosophy was not a constant, however—it changed over time. American management theory set out principles for controlling large organisations dedicated to the high-volume production of standardised goods. To achieve high levels of efficiency and economies of scale, the technical core of the organisation was buffered from the impact of external forces. Inventories of raw materials and finished goods allowed production to proceed unhindered by concerns of supply and demand. Specialisation separated the management of the technical core from the overall general management of the organisation. At the workplace, jobs became highly specialised and fragmented. In such a context, the worker came to be regarded as a form of machine. As expressed by Drucker, 'The great innovation of modern industry is a vision; a vision of the worker as an efficient, automatic, standardised machine' (Drucker, 1942: 79).

This initial view of the worker, and techniques for achieving high-volume production through large organisations, were to be challenged by successive waves of thinking, and ultimately vanquished by the philosophy of empowerment that underlies the Fourth Management Blueprint—the network organisation.

THE FOUR MANAGEMENT BLUEPRINTS

Table 2.1 summarises the major features of each of the four blueprints. In the discussion that follows, we take a look at the shape of the organisation prescribed by each blueprint, the organising principles of management central to each, their focal managerial processes, the skills demanded of managers in carrying out those processes, and the values that underlie them.

The First Blueprint

The traditional classical approach to management, which dominated Western thinking from the turn of the century to well into the 1930s, was a child of the Industrial Revolution. It was born in a society concerned with increasing productivity and industrial output.

Table 2.1   The four management blueprints

	First Blueprint	Second Blueprint	Third Blueprint	Fourth Blueprint
	Classical	Human	Systems	The collaborative organisation
Organisational forms	Functional Mechanistic	Inter-locking group Organic	Contin-gency Matrix	Loosely coupled Divisional networks and alliances
Management principles	Hierarchy	Supportive relation-ships	Differen-tiation and Integration	Collaborative individualism Empowerment
Managerial processes/forms	Manage-ment functions	Demo-cratic leadership	Open systems analysis	Management of meaning
Managerial skills	Person-to-person control	Goal setting, facilitation	Rational/diagnostic	Empathetic Proactive
Managerial values	Efficiency Productivity	Self-actual isation Social support	Self-regulation	Soc. sustainability Ecol. Balance

As the inventions of the nineteenth century were translated into consumer goods in the twentieth, so there was a need for specialised efficiency-oriented systems of management. This need was met by the First Blueprint, with its intellectual roots in the work of Adam Smith, and drafted in detail by Fayol (1956), Gulick & Urwick (1973), and others. Not surprisingly, with its focus on controlling and structuring human behaviour in such a way that increased efficiency and productivity would result, many of its initial progenitors were engineers, like Taylor (1947), Gantth (1910; 1916; 1919), and Emerson (1911; 1913).

Efficiency was maximised by grouping specialised tasks within specialised departments and by formally assigning responsibility according to such principles as delegation and span of control. Job specialisation was held together by a strong *hierarchical* system of authority and control that coordinated the activities of an unskilled, uneducated, disempowered workforce. Even if workers were not seen to be disempowered, they were at least seen to be rational and economic—to rationally understand that their own economic good was served by compliance with the hierarchy.

In sum, the mass production systems of the First Blueprint were based on internally consistent, mutually reinforcing principles of specialisation, centralisation and formality. They were fundamentally hierarchical systems, and their managers were concerned with the principles, processes and skills that made the hierarchy work.

There have been a number of devastating critiques of classical theory in the management literature (see Etzioni (1964), Rose (1975), and Reich (1983) for just a few examples). At the heart of it all is a trenchant attack on the impersonal, dehumanising autocracy of such a system, and on its manipulative assumption of congruence of interest between management and the worker. One could be forgiven for wondering why it existed at all, and why its managers gave it a ghost of a chance of success in practice.

The answer, of course, is that the First Blueprint was a child not only of the technology of the Industrial Revolution, but also of its legacy of nineteenth century social stratification. Britain, and to a certain extent the US, were characterised by a class structure, an acceptance of hierarchy as a normal way of life (reinforced by World War I), and largely uneducated, disempowered workers. Moreover, attitudes are a function of needs. The system, from a consumer point of view, worked: it produced organisations that made a wide range of consumer goods available to the public. One could at least buy a car—even if one could only choose between black and black.

The real cracks in the First Blueprint began to show during the Great Depression, which produced very different needs, and which radically challenged the underlying logic of the then-accepted capitalist model of society. Nevertheless, shades of the First Blueprint remain in many organisations, and in some instances they dominate.

The Second Blueprint

In the Second Blueprint the focus shifted from the formal organisation to the informal work group. The famous Hawthorne studies conducted at the Hawthorne works of the Western Electric company from 1922 to 1933 brought about a revolution in the way human nature and the work situation were thought about. Baritz has termed it 'the single most important social science research project ever conducted in industry' (Baritz, 1977: 77).

In the Hawthorne studies, Mayo (1933) and his colleagues showed that the group played an important role—perhaps even more important than that of management—in determining the attitudes and performance of individual workers. The scene was set for the emergence of a new conception of people, expressed in the doctrine of 'social man'. Money and economic motivations were now seen to be of secondary importance to how workers felt about their jobs, fellow workers and supervisors. Managers would henceforth be faced with the task of meeting the *social* needs of individual and group members, and would need social skills such as listening and communicating in order to do their jobs properly.

These events did not lead to management seeing the worker as an independent individual, or to workers developing a spirit of self-control. They led instead to a focus on collectivity—on groups. The demoralising effect of the Great Depression brought with it a sense of helplessness and dependency on others. Wren comments:

> Man was a creature caught up in a focus he could not control and therefore someone else must help. The self-help doctrine was obsolete and the economic, social and political climate was changing to offset the human dislocations of economic catastrophe. [Wren, 1972: 519]

Three decades later, David Riesman suggested that it was in this period that the transition from the 'inner-directed man' representative of laissez-faire capitalism, the Protestant work ethic and self-direction to the 'other-directed social, man' took place (Wren, 1972: 519).

The new social ethic was centred upon the collective nature of humans, and was reinforced by an explosive interest in group dynamics during World War II. By the early 1950s, with the advent of writers like Barnard (1948), managers began to understand the 'fact' that authority flows upwards (Wren, 1972: 316). Managers were taught about groups, informal organisation, social motivation, ascribed authority, democratic leadership, flat hierarchies, and other concepts and techniques aimed at a recognition of the 'human factor' in work.

The human relations philosophy and its concern for 'social man' lasted until the recession of 1957–58. The emphasis then shifted from human relations to human resources in which economic efficiency returned to be given equal recognition with respect for the personal dignity of each human being (Wren, 1972: 443).

Adherents of the latter movement see it as a new paradigm, a new blueprint. We have no strong objection to that view, but as it shares so many of the basic assumptions of the Second Blueprint, we have preferred to see it as an extension of that paradigm and a bridge to the Third.

The human resources movement expanded the focus of the Second Blueprint from a concern with social group-level phenomena to a concern with the interface between individual and organisational effectiveness. It still located the individual firmly in the group context, however. Thus one of its major proponents, Rensis Likert, after surveying a decade's work by the Michigan Institute for Social Research, developed a central 'principle of supportive relationships', which became in many respects the slogan of the movement:

> The leadership and other processes of the organisation must be such as to ensure a maximum probability that in all its interactions and all relationships with the organisation each member will, in the light of his background, values, and expectations, view the experience as supportive and one which builds and maintains a sense of personal worth and importance. [Likert, 1961: 103]

This captures well the concern of the movement for the well-being of the individual. Its axiom, however, identifies it clearly with the key assumptions of the Second Blueprint:

[M]anagement will make full use of the potential capability of its human resources only when each person in an organisation is a member of one or more effectively functioning work groups that have a high degree of group loyalty, effective skills of interaction, and high performance goals. [Likert, 1961: 104]

Thus the Second Blueprint began to depict organisational form as a flat hierarchy of 'interlocking groups'. Managers were brought to focus on distant supervision of such groups, the effectiveness of linking-pin roles, and like group-level constructs.

Through the work of Maslow, McGregor, Argyris, Bennis and others, the human resources movement came to incorporate some of the basic tenets of humanist psychology. Managers became concerned with problems of integrating the 'self-actualising' individual with the organisation. The problem was still conceived at the group level, though Self was to be found through the group, and the technology of self-discovery and self-acceptance came to centre around T-groups and sensitivity groups. The issues of organisational effectiveness and interpersonal competence were seen as inseparable (Argyris, 1964).

In their general form, the major tenets of the Second Blueprint are given in Table 2.1. Like the First Blueprint, they too represent a coherent, internally consistent set of beliefs and principles. Their general argument is basically this: if people are motivated by self-actualisation, and are essentially social beings, then they need to be located in supportive groups, given autonomy, and assisted by managers as facilitators.

This implies a flat organisation, consisting of a hierarchy of interlocking groups, integrated by linking-pin roles. The integrating principle is that of supportive relationships, which implies group support, wide spans of control, and a managerial focus on supportive leadership. Supportive, democratic leaders, in turn, are mainly concerned with the processes of democratic leadership that lead to effective groups—the heart of the effective organisation. They are concerned with setting objectives, facilitation of personal and group growth, and the evaluation of performance by end results. Finally, in order to accomplish these processes, managers require skills in process leadership and objective setting, and in the interpersonal skills of confronting, giving and receiving feedback, and team development.

Testimony to the stability of the Second Blueprint is the fact that it persisted until well into the 1970s, when it eventually became overwhelmed by the increasing popularity of the Third Blueprint, the systems model. For the very reasons that it persisted for so long, it continues to have a degree of appeal and can be discerned as a distinctive feature of some organisations even in the late 1990s. *We do not suggest that all aspects of the Second Blueprint are unworkable or inappropriate in postcorporate contexts, but we do suggest that if they are to be useful they have to be taken into a different mindset and transformed by it.*

The Third Blueprint

The Second Blueprint persisted for such a long time because it seemed to work, particularly in the United States. For the majority of middle-class Americans, the 1950s was a time in which the 'American dream' came true.

College enrolment, automobile ownership, foreign travel, longevity, the paperback boom, home ownership, social mobility—by most known measures, American life reached a new high in the fifties (Jones, 1965: 348).

This prosperity was based upon a number of interrelated causes: the enlargement of the domestic market through expanded population growth, large government expenditure on scientific and military needs, and extraordinarily high family incomes.

Challenges to the Second Blueprint

It seemed as if the dawn of a golden age based upon the mass production and mass consumption of largely standardised goods had arrived. Yet sometime in the decade between 1960 and 1970, the strategy of the mass marketing, production and distribution of standardised products encapsulated in the First and Second Blueprints, as applied by the US, began to fail. Reich puts it dramatically: 'The management era ended for America around 1970' (Reich, 1983: 117).

Dramatic changes in the world economy from the 1960s onwards allowed first Japan and then a number of newly industrialised countries to apply the principles of standardised mass production and move quickly into world markets as outlined previously. Korea, Hong Kong, Singapore, Brazil and Spain began specialising in simple products that required unskilled labour, such as clothing, footwear and simple electronic assembly. Japan, which had initially specialised in these products, also shifted into processing industries such as steel and synthetic fibres, which, while requiring substantial capital investment, were relatively stable through the use of mature technologies. The philosophy of mass production was being applied against the US by countries whose labour costs were a fraction of those of the US.

In addition, US culture was becoming increasingly self-absorbed. The very prosperity of the 1950s and early 1960s led to a questioning of the pursuit of attainment in the outer world and an assertion of the importance of self-fulfilment. In the 1960s this questioning was confined to the campuses of US universities. But the philosophical questioning spread far and wide during the 1970s. As reported by the social analyst and researcher Daniel Yankelovich:

> Our surveys showed that new questions had arisen. Instead of asking, 'Will I be successful?', 'Will I raise happy, healthy, successful children?'—The typical questions asked by average Americans in the 1950s and 1960s—Americans in the 1970s came to ponder more introspective matters. We asked, 'How can I find self-fulfilment?', 'What does personal success really mean?', 'What kinds of commitments should I be making?', 'What is worth sacrificing for?', 'How can I grow?', 'How can I best realize the commitment I have to develop myself?'
>
> In the 1970s all national surveys showed an increase in preoccupation with self. By the late seventies, my firm's studies showed more than seven out of ten Americans (72 percent) spending a great deal of time thinking about themselves and their inner lives—this in a nation once

notorious for its impatience with inwardness. The rage for self-fulfilment, our surveys indicated, had now spread to virtually the entire United States population. [Yankelovich, 1981: 405]

Such concerns and questioning seemed to considerably threaten the competitiveness of the US and her allies.

Contingency theory: Towards an open systems model

It is not surprising that in the midst of such turbulence and change there should emerge a new managerial paradigm. Whereas the First and Second Blueprints had largely concentrated upon looking within the organisation, the crisis confronting Western enterprises had largely been caused by changes in the competitive *environment*. What was required was a blueprint that focused on what was going on *outside* the organisation. The open systems paradigm was ideally suited to this purpose.

The emergence of the open systems model of management (we will call it the 'systems model' in the interests of brevity) as the dominant paradigm of the 1970s was in many ways a reaction to the one-eyed inadequacies of both the traditional and the human relations models. Both claimed a universal set of prescriptions for 'good' management. The problem was that, as evidence began to accumulate, the universality of both models began to look vulnerable. Perhaps the most devastating first shots at the systems model were fired as early as 1962, when two Scots, Burns and Stalker, after a study of electrical firms attempting to move into the electronics industry, argued that there was no one optimum system of management. They concluded instead that any system adopted should be *contingent* on the degree of change or stability in the environment of the organisation. They distinguished between two polar systems:

- *mechanistic* (which bore remarkable likenesses to organisations associated with the First Blueprint), suited to stability, and
- *organic* (which looked like Second Blueprint organisations), suited to change (Burns & Stalker, 1961).

The major features of organic and mechanistic systems, as identified by Burns & Stalker, are summarised in Table 2.2.

Table 2.2   Features of organic and mechanistic systems

Mechanistic system	Organic system
Abstract specialisation	Substance is people, not tasks
Centralised control	De-emphasis of the hierarchy
Formal and hierarchical structure	Interlocking, flexible, group structure
Utilitarian psychological contract	Shared norms, beliefs and values
Person-to-person control	Self-control, mutual adjustment

These organisational types form basic patterns: each aspect is congruent with and reinforces every other aspect. When conditions are stable, the *organisation* achieves the basic demand for efficiency by specialising. Specialisation has to be tied together by hierarchical centralisation because specialists tend to be concerned only with their own parts of the process. The authority of the central figure to control the operations is reinforced by a formal culture and formal processes such as job descriptions, schedules and the like.

Under such a culture 'lower' participants tend to be treated as 'employees' (not members) and to develop a calculative relationship with the organisation. In contrast, when things are changing, the organisation cannot be governed by job descriptions (they would become outdated too quickly) or by commands from a person at the top (things are happening too quickly for that person to keep pace with all the details).

Therefore, people have to organise themselves. This means that the emphasis has to be on the people themselves (jobs cannot be defined with any precision) and have to be located in flexible group structures where they can adapt and coordinate. What integrates them in such a structure are not the commands of a superior, but shared norms, beliefs and values. These, in turn, are sustained by an informal egalitarian culture.

In each system, each facet supports every other facet: within each configuration there is 'systems congruence', as Likert (1961) terms it.

An open systems model

Within contingency theory lay the main features of what can be called an 'open systems' model of organisations. There are three key aspects to such a model:

- The organisation is a system: it is a set of interrelated parts, and the way in which they interrelate defines the system.
- It is an open system: it operates in a dynamic environment, and the nature of that environment determines the nature of the system and its survivability.
- The managerial task is therefore one of rational diagnosis— managers should diagnose the nature of the environment, and then choose an organisational form appropriate to it.

This model, in its essential form, seemed to offer hope to troubled Western management. It gained in popularity in the 1960s and dominated the 1970s. That period saw the emergence of management schools as a major force in management education in the West. A generation of managers learned of systems concepts, as expounded by such innovators as Johnson, Kast and Rosenzweig. As they put it: 'the aim of systems theory for business is to facilitate better understanding in a complex environment' (Johnson et al, 1967: 13).

The job of the strategic manager became the job of the rational analyst–administrator, a vision ably popularised by Andrews and Christensen at Harvard. As they wrote:

> General management skills center intellectually upon relating the firm to its environment and administratively upon coordinating departmental specialities and points of view. [Andrews & Christensen in Learned et al, 1969: 9]

Prior to this, business policy had been conceived mainly in terms of the integration of the functional areas of the firm. External relationships, to the extent that they were considered, were treated as relatively stable and therefore predictable.

Complex organisations

The very complexity of the environment demanded the continuous elaboration of the systems model into an intricate, complex contingency theory. Lawrence and Lorsch (1967) fine-tuned the contingency model in the mid-1960s by demonstrating that organisations may consist of subsystems that could be organic or mechanistic, depending on the sub-environments they faced. (Such 'differentiation', they argued, left problems of integration that had to be resolved by management.)

By the early 1970s, researchers had discovered that subsystems themselves, or even organisations as a whole, may face requirements of adaptability and efficiency as equal priorities, and may require mixed, or matrix systems of management.

The primacy of the team

We will explore a number of variants of matrix systems below. All of them offer some opportunities for handling both stability and change. Their success rests heavily on the ability of members to come together quickly into a smoothly working team, and to overcome the basic conflicts of the functional areas from which they are drawn. Thus the emphasis in the Third Blueprint was placed on the development of an approach that emphasised the unity of the team and downplayed the importance of individual differences within it.

The full technology of team building as it is implied here was brought to bear on the development of team skills and the enhancement of team spirit. The ideal became the successful sports team—exemplified in its ultimate form by the Australia II team that wrested the America's Cup from its possessors:

> I did not have a single Olympic Yachtsman with me. And we were off to face the inevitable boatload of them in America. In the absence of stars there was but one commodity we could develop, and that was team spirit. In every walk of life, a tightly grouped, determined, well trained team will so often overcome pure genius. All they need is an explicit belief that they can fight and win, that they can overcome cleverness with unshakeable determination, tireless work, and

the desire to back each other, to cover each other's mistakes, and ultimately to triumph through sheer strength of communal purpose. [Bertrand & Robinson, 1985: 129]

Paradoxically, by the mid-1980s many had come to question whether such an approach was sufficient to win, or whether it did not also need the efforts of fierce individualists who were able to transform the nature of the game—of a Ben Lexcen, with his winged keel.

The Fourth Blueprint

What was not obvious to those immersed in the Third Blueprint was the pervasiveness of a set of assumptions that had a very important effect on managerial choice. These assumptions came to be challenged in the late 1980s.

A challenge to previous assumptions

On reflection, the systems model was characterised by six essential assumptions:

- interdependence;
- openness;
- unity;
- rationality;
- objectivity; and
- the importance of teamwork and cohesive groups.

By the end of the 1980s it was becoming clear that these assumptions were part of a mindset that was counter-productive under conditions of discontinuity. It was not *systems theory* that was problematic: it was the development of *the open-systems model*, with its inherently reactive, unitary assumptions. We will continue to use systems language and paradigms throughout this book. But the advent of the postcorporate world, with all of its social and economic features as described in Chapter 1, called for the revision of the model currently in use. We had first recognised this challenge towards conventional systems mindsets in our Frontiers study in 1984 (Limerick et al, 1984).

Interdependence

Underlying the notion that everything is related to everything else, is an assumption that systems are tightly coupled. But most of the organisations we saw were moving towards decentralisation and chunking—towards smaller business units with high levels of autonomy. They were achieving interdependence through collaboration.

Openness

The basic assumption of the open system is that it must import from the environment in order to avoid entropy or death. But this implies that the organisation becomes a reactor against environmental influences. We found that the CEOs we interviewed were entirely *proactive*—they were more inclined to choose the environments in which they operated, or to get out and act on the environment, to transform it.

Unified systems

Systems models have long been accused of over-emphasising the unity of the environment and understating differences. Our CEOs were less naive than that. While they saw their role as largely defining what the whole is about, they accepted enormous levels of differences between the decentralised parts. They were closer to Drucker's comments on Japanese managers, who were 'facing up to a pluralist society' (Drucker, 1980). In practice they recognised the need not only for external political skills, but also for internal politicisation. The problem with the systems model is that it is inclined to define every system as a subsystem of some larger system, and to blur sensitivity to precisely such differences.

Rationality and objectivity

Systems analysis implies high levels of rationality, of the capacity to abstract and codify. Our CEOs were disillusioned with the excessive focus on such capacities in general, and with their exemplars, MBA graduates in particular. They were even more concerned with the non-rational, with the empathetic processes of motivation, with the symbolic processes of corporate culture and the non-rational problems of vision in corporate strategy—with the management of meaning. Most of them would have agreed with Weick:

> There is no shortage of attention to money. Unfortunately, the same cannot be said for meaning. That is why the concept of culture is important. [Weick, 1985: 388]

Cohesive teamwork

The Third Blueprint was dominated by a concern with teamwork, and managers devoted much of their resources to the development of teams. Our CEOs, however, did not talk much about teamwork. They were far more concerned with the development of mature, proactive individuals who had the capacity to act on and transform systems.

This set of assumptions could not survive disorganised capitalism or postmodernity. The challenge became to keep the insights of systems theory without being entrammelled in the conventional systems model.

The Emergence of the fourth blueprint

What eventually came through to us was that we were observing a new paradigm—a new internally consistent vision of organisational life, related to the specific needs of the last decades of the twentieth century. As we surveyed the literature during the 1980s and the early 1990s, the essential features of this blueprint emerged with greater clarity:

- *Discontinuity.* The Fourth Blueprint environment is characterised by high levels of social, economic and technological discontinuity.
- *Loosely coupled systems.* The organisation should be chunked into loosely coupled systems.
- *Synergies and alliances.* The organisation should be boundaryless and should establish alliances between units both within and external to the organisation in order to achieve higher level synergies.
- *Collaborative individualism.* The organisation is characterised by a culture that places a high value on autonomous, interdependent, proactive, empowered, collaborative individuals.

- *Social sustainability.* The organisation has to contribute to the social fabric from which it draws its strengths. Just as physical capital and human capital facilitate productive activity, so does social capital. As Robert B Shapiro, CEO of multinational chemicals company Monsanto, has argued in a recent interview with Joan Magretta, organisations need not only focus on competitive advantage, but also on the sustainability of their organisations and environments:

  None of us today ... is living in a sustainable way. It's not a question of good guys and bad guys ... The whole system has to change; there's a huge opportunity for reinvention. [Shapiro, 1997: 80–1]

- *Holism.* What keeps the organisation together in contexts of discontinuity is holism, a field of shared values, goals and beliefs, represented in a common vision of the organisation and in a commonly accepted mission. Holism goes further: it underlines the essential interdependence between the organisation and its social context. In later chapters we will argue that the *metastrategic* perspective associated with the Fourth Blueprint organisation and mindset incorporates values associated with a just, creative and humane society alongside its concerns for productivity and efficiency. Moreover, the application of an essentially holistic vision and mission into the workplace requires a balance of transformational and organisation-wide leadership (which we describe later as *microstrategy*.) Holism and social sustainability are deeply interrelated. Shapiro's (1997) argument for the linkage between environmental sustainability and holistic thinking applies equally well to the link between social sustainability and strategy. Hart (1997) describes it this way:

  [A]s of today few companies have incorporated sustainability into their strategic thinking. ... Focusing on sustainability requires putting business strategies to a new test. Taking the entire planet as the context in which they do business, companies must ask whether they are part of the solution or part of the problem. Only when it thinks in those terms can it begin to develop a vision of sustainability—a shaping logic that goes beyond today's internal, operational focus on greening to a more external, strategic focus on sustainable development. [Hart, 1997: 71]

- *Leadership diversity.* Fourth blueprint organisations are character-ised by a high density of diverse multiple leadership roles that together are able to sustain and transform the organisation.
- *A participant-centred paradigm.* Underlying Fourth Blueprint thinking is a paradigm of organisational management that lies beyond hierarchical managerialism and is centred on participants.

This Blueprint lies at the heart of this book, and our remaining chapters will explore it in more detail. The previous mindsets or 'blueprints' are, as we have shown, related to the key problems of their times, although their residual effects can be felt in some late 1990s contexts. But, vigorous as the debates between First, Second and Third Blueprints have been, they are all based on a paradigm that pictures the organisation as caught in a dilemma between centralisation and decentralisation. This debate is played out in practice by pendulum swings between centralisation and decentralisation—but all of these changes take place within a fundamentally tightly coupled corporate paradigm. The Fourth Blueprint solution transcends this dilemma by moving into a different dimension altogether. It confronts an apparent paradox by moving towards postcorporatism—a new mindset that calls simultaneously for both loosely coupled structures and higher levels of synergy in organisation. This apparent paradox is of central importance in the matter of organisational choice.

Loosely coupled organisations

Perhaps the most influential writers on loose coupling are Weick (1976; 1982) and, more recently, Orton and Weick (1990). They point out that the notion of a loosely coupled system does not suggest a *de*coupled system. The units in a decoupled relationship are not responsive to one another: they are distinct, separate and do not influence each other. Loose coupling, in contrast, implies 'a situation in which elements are responsive, but retain separateness and identity' (Orton & Weick, 1990: 203). As Orton and Weick elaborate:

> If there is responsiveness without distinctiveness, the system is tightly coupled. If there is distinctiveness without responsiveness, the system is decoupled. If there is both distinctiveness and responsiveness, the system is loosely coupled. [Orton & Weick, 1990: 205]

A loosely coupled system, in other words, simultaneously asserts both autonomous distinctiveness and interdependence. It is less of a state or a structure and more of a deliberate strategy, a process for dealing with complex and discontinuous environments; it is 'something organisations do, rather than ... something they have' (Orton & Weick, 1990: 218). It is a dialectical process in which the organisation simultaneously searches for both differentiated units and integration between them.

Within the Fourth Blueprint paradigm, this model is extended from loose coupling *within* organisations to loose coupling *between* organisations—to strategies in which independently owned organisational units are responsive to one another and collaborate with each other. In some loosely coupled network organisational structures the issue of ownership becomes even more blurred. Ghoshal & Bartlett (1990: 612) for example, argue that multinational corporations are better understood as 'interorganisational networks' than as single organisations. Loose coupling allows them to both respond to demands for 'local isomorphism' in each host company, and deal with efficiencies in their world-wide systems.

The mindset of the Fourth Blueprint therefore underlies loose coupling both within and between organisations. The lessons learned in the one situation tend to be applied in the other. The mechanisms that give the units autonomy and that integrate them tend to be similar. Thus, while ownership and hierarchies do not hold multinational corporations and multicompany alliances together, a host of other mechanisms do (Orton & Weick, 1990; Ghoshal & Bartlett, 1995; Borys & Jemison, 1989).

In this and the following chapter we explore some of the ways in which the basic paradigm of loose coupling is expressed in different patterns of organisation.

FROM BLUEPRINT TO ORGANISATION: AN INTEGRATIVE MODEL OF CORPORATE ORGANISATION

What emerges most clearly from the above discussion of different managerial blueprints is the thesis that each of these blueprints is most relevant to a different set of conditions. This 'contingency' principle was formalised in the Third Blueprint, which asserted that the choice of a particular system of organisation was contingent upon the conditions confronting the organisation. (As we shall see later, Fourth Blueprint thinking, in a sense, uses the same precept, but in stressing responsive agency it is much more proactive: it argues that new sets of conditions can be used to create and compose organisational systems that are far better able to handle discontinuity.)

CORPORATE ORGANISATIONAL CONFIGURATIONS

The contingency principle characteristic of organisational choice within the corporate paradigm is easier to understand if we take it in two bits:

- *Configuration*. While there is theoretically an infinite number of organisational structures and cultures, it is possible in practice to recognise a more limited number of types of organisation. In other words the strategies, structures and cultures of organisations tend to form different, recognisable configurations.
- *Contingency*. Different configurations of organisation have different performance characteristics. They are therefore suited to, and related to, different sets of conditions.

The concept of configuration means that corporate managers do not have to reinvent the wheel every time they set out to design an organisation. Organisational choice becomes a process of fine judgement about different trade-offs. It involves understanding the advantages and disadvantages of different kinds of organisation and choosing those that give the most favourable balance for a given situation.

In this section we will develop and make explicit the model that underlies organisational choice from a corporatist perspective. Figure 2.1 represents a modification and expansion of a continuum of organisational choice developed by Galbraith (1977: 179). It illustrates the range of corporate structural alternatives appropriate for different kinds of strategic situations. It links key features of environment, strategy, structure and culture into a coherent contingency model of configurational choice. It is worth exploring each of the basic configurations represented in the diagram.

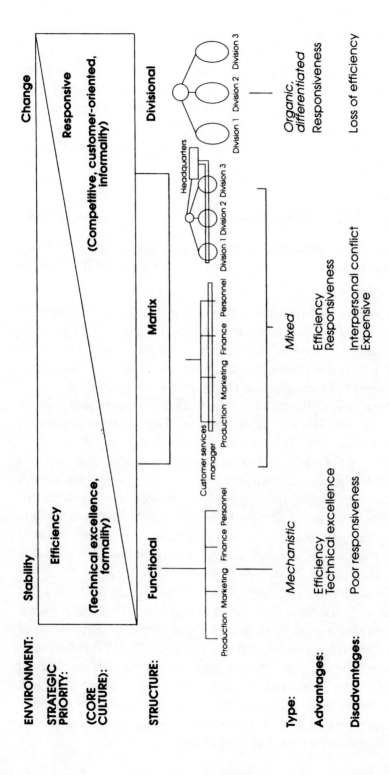

Figure 2.1 The conventional model of organisational choice

Functional Organisations

When the environment is relatively stable, the dominant strategic issue tends to be the pursuit of efficiency. Efficiency is best achieved by harnessing the advantages of specialisation—by grouping employees together by function or discipline and by carefully defining their specialised activities. These specialist groups, with their narrow orientations, have to be coordinated by a clear hierarchical structure.

The culture that emerges within this configuration has two characteristics. First, the grouping of specialists encourages a core value of technical excellence. Second, the accent on hierarchical coordination leads to, and is reinforced by, formality.

Finally, this configuration has two key performance characteristics. It produces high levels of efficiency through its technical excellence, but the high degree of specialisation and formality make it relatively unresponsive to change. It is therefore acceptable under conditions of stability, but inappropriate under conditions of change.

Divisional Organisations

As environmental conditions begin to change more rapidly, organisations tend to move from functional to divisional configurations. Under conditions of change, the dominant strategic issue is responsiveness. This can best be achieved by smaller interdisciplinary or interfunctional groups that focus on the particular needs of a given group of customers—on the special needs of different markets, products or (more commonly in the public sector) of different regions. That is, they form the basis of market, product or regional divisions. These smaller divisions can respond best if they are given reasonable autonomy through decentralisation. Their organic, flexible nature is reinforced by a culture that is very informal and that focuses on customer needs and service.

The performance characteristics of this configuration tend to be the opposite of those of mechanistic organisations. Organic systems tend to be very responsive, but they lose efficiency—they tend to duplicate resources in different divisions, and to lose their focus on technical excellence in favour of a culture that values customer service. Such cultures become highly competitive, focusing on customer needs, market share and market growth.

Matrix Organisations

No one likes to be bullied by a choice between polar opposite systems—one that gives efficiency, but loses responsiveness, and the other that gives responsiveness but loses efficiency. Sooner or later, someone was going to attempt to develop a configuration that gives the best of both. The matrix configuration, which was developed first in the aerospace industry in the 1970s, was an attempt to do just that.

There are basically two forms of matrix organisation. The first uses a functional structure as its basic mode of organisation, but superimposes on it cross-functional structures that aim to bring higher levels of responsiveness to customer groupings. Thus, the Department of Primary Industries in Queensland in the early 1990s had a disciplinary structure in which veterinarians, soil scientists, botanists and other specialists were grouped separately into their own branches. However, superimposed on that was a structure of regional managers and extension officers who pulled these specialists together to focus on specific customers. Countless large manufacturing firms, particularly during the 1960s and 1970s, used a similar matrix of 'customer' or 'brand' managers who cut across functional departments in an effort to achieve higher responsiveness.

The second form of matrix, which became the dominant organisational form of the 1970s and early 1980s, uses a basic divisional structure but superimposes a headquarters functional structure on it in order to gain functional efficiencies. Thus the Department of Agriculture in South Australia has interdisciplinary regional divisions, but also uses headquarters-level functional consultants to pull together specialists in different regions to focus on functional excellence. Within industry, by the end of the 1970s, companies like ITT had well over 300 headquarters specialists cutting across their divisions in a matrix relationship.

Matrix structures may well produce both efficiency and responsiveness, but they carry with them two problems. First, their conflicting lines of authority and responsibility generate high levels of interpersonal conflict. Headquarters functional experts or consultants, for example, are expected to cut across the divisions and to get their divisional counterparts to strive towards functional excellence. In some organisations they are expected to develop functional 'policy' for divisions, without interfering with the operational autonomy of those divisions. Relationships between headquarters consultants and divisional personnel can become highly problematic. (In one company with which we are associated, such experts are called 'seagulls' by divisional managers, because 'they fly in, crap all over us, and fly out again!'.)

While they are expected to exercise an advisory relationship, their headquarters location gives them enormous status, and their messages are received with very mixed feelings. Indeed, they can be seen by divisional personnel to severely curtail divisional autonomy. The situation is exacerbated by the fact that divisions are often charged direct and overhead expenses for their seagulls, but have little control over them. For many organisations, the loss of autonomy—perceived or real—for divisional managers can become so severe, and threaten strategically necessary responsiveness so much, that variants of the classic matrix are sought.

One way of easing the problem is to reduce the number of seagulls who have influence over divisions. This is usually done by replacing them with one or two very high-level consultants (eagles or albatrosses, depending on your point of view!) who have a mandate that is clearly restricted to policy. As one manager said to us: 'We decided that we could no longer afford two personnel managers at $35 000 each—we could only afford one at $70 000!'. While such structures tend to ameliorate the problem of division–seagull conflict, it does not disappear. The very seniority of top-level consultants makes it very difficult for divisional managers to treat their interventions as 'advice', and divisions still feel a loss of autonomy.

The second problem of the matrix structure is more subtle, and lies at the heart of the move towards Fourth Blueprint organisations. As the divisional managers themselves become more sophisticated and learn from the seagulls, and as information systems within the organisation improve, it is by no means certain that the enlarged corporate headquarters so typical of the divisional matrix really does add value to the organisation. What do the seagulls add that the divisional managers and information systems cannot contribute? If they were not there, what systems could replace them? These questions will become the focus of the following chapter.

The Efficiency–responsiveness Pendulum

The model in Figure 2.1 is basically the paradigm of organisational choice that underlies managerial practice in both the private and public corporate organisations of today. Given this paradigm, most organisations tend to opt for matrix structures. They see themselves as being caught in an irreconcilable conflict between efficiency and responsiveness.

On the one hand, they must be technically excellent and efficient if they are to remain competitive. On the other, they must meet increasingly powerful customer pressures, and must therefore be responsive to demands for quality and value in its many forms. As our three case studies at the opening of this chapter illustrate, pendulum oscillations between these two forces have been a dominant feature of organisational choice during the past decade or so. That is, as levels of change accelerate and the need for responsiveness becomes dominant, so organisations move to the right of the continuum—towards decentralisation and development as autonomous units. But as the 'costs' of these become more obvious, so they recentralise into larger units and weaken the customer axis of the matrix.

Such pendulum swings are part and parcel of reactions to the impossible dilemma of centralisation versus decentralisation, or efficiency versus socially sustainable responsiveness. Fundamentally neither action—a move to the left or the right of the continuum—will help to resolve the problems faced by the post-modern organisation. Facing the problems of the late 1990s requires a move outside the model, and this in turn requires a considerable paradigm shift in administrative thinking. This is the shift towards the Fourth Blueprint.

CHAPTER 3

POSTCORPORATE ORGANISATIONS: NETWORKS AND STRATEGIC ALLIANCES

> *Like romances, alliances are built on hopes and dreams—what might happen if certain opportunities are pursued.*
>
> [Kanter, 1994: 99]

IN CHAPTER I we saw that the 1980s and early 90s was a period of rapid, discontinuous social, economic and technological change. The Third Blueprint model of organisational choice that had become so popular in the 1970s was just not able to cope with such change. The aimless swings between centralised, decentralised and matrix structures that characterised the early 1980s were symptoms of the puzzlement and frustration felt by managers as they handled impossible dilemmas in the face of such change.

The ground was fertile for the emergence of a radically different approach to organisation based on the Fourth Blueprint paradigm of loose coupling. The global economy had produced an international marketplace in which companies were beginning to operate in ways which transcended national boundaries. According to Robert Reich (1991), the very idea of 'nation state' was becoming passé and the idea of a national economy was becoming meaningless (8). As Reich describes it, companies were beginning to operate as loosely connected networks of cooperating units:

What is traded between nations is less often finished products than specialised problem-solving (research, product design, fabrication), problem-identifying (marketing, advertising, customer consulting) and brokerage (financing, searching, contracting) services, as well as certain routine components and services, all of which are combined to create value. [Reich, 1991: 113]

Reich's view is that the new international web of companies will look dramatically different from anything currently in existence. Very few people will actually work solely for the company, the organisational design will resemble a spider web rather than a pyramid; the job of the head office will be to build partnerships and to broker the use of the company name; executives will guide ideas through the network and have little direct authority; routine functions will be contracted out; 'power' will be regarded as an attribute of value-adding capability rather than of position; and the 'threads' of the global web will be computers, fax machines, satellites, high-resolution monitors and modems.

What emerges from this analysis is a picture that does not allow for tight, corporate, bureaucratic structures, either public or private, because bureaucracy by definition is incompatible with the values which underlie the notion of 'borderless world' (Ohmae, 1990; Beare, 1995)—flexibility, autonomy, interlinking assets, horizontal communications, and so on. But, more importantly, bureaucracy does not use the abundant technological and managerial opportunities available in the 1990s for the creation of new forms of organisation that lie beyond hierarchy. We are reminded of John Naisbitt's provocative assertion in *The Global Paradox* (1994) that world markets are no longer dominated by the big multinational corporations, or by the big world economies. One is reminded also of Naisbitt's view of the reason for the change in power base that is taking place. As Naisbitt explains it, bigness is a disability in what we call the postcorporate world because it impedes quickness of response, consensus decision-making, and leverage.

Indeed, speed of action is critical in the postcorporate world. Consider the immense threat to global well-being posed by 'biological invasions'—fruit fly in northern Australia, golden snails and European gypsy moths in Eastern Asia, to name just two regional examples. Stanford University professor Peter Vitousek relates this situation to what he calls the 'concept of thinking globally but acting locally':

> What can be done to decrease the number of biological invasions and to reduce their consequences? First, we must recognise that these invasions are a problem of global significance and must be tackled globally. Biologists need to share information more effectively, so that experts can systematically track the movements of species around the world—particularly those that have invaded other regions in the past. Also, nations and regions must agree to cooperate and find effective ways to slow the spread of harmful invasions. [*The Chronicle of Higher Education*, Jan 17, 1997: B5]

The Fourth Blueprint answers the question of how to relocate an organisation in a 'spiderweb' organisational world. It builds directly and deliberately on the strategy of loosely coupled systems. The art of what to do lies not so much in creating autonomous units—that was part of the Third Blueprint and is the easy part—but in getting these autonomous units to collaborate again.

Some contemporary organisations already take very seriously the battle-cry of 'fewer *structural* relationships' within their organisation, and have been moving towards broader *networks* of activity between units within their organisations. Significantly, they have also looked for synergies through loose coupling with units *outside* their organisation. Some of them have deliberately franchised off parts of their businesses, or used subcontractors or *strategic alliances* with other organisations to gain a competitive edge. In other words, the more effective loosely coupled systems that emerged in the mid-1980s and early 1990s were not decoupled systems. They were part of a focused strategy of creating *strategic networks*. They had discovered for themselves what Ram Charan (1991: 104) calls 'the central competitive advantage of the 1990s—superior execution in a volatile environment' and, in all probability, what Inkpen (1996: 123) calls 'a window on their partners' broad capabilities'. Through this window, Inkpen says, 'alliances create the potential for firms to acquire knowledge associated with partner skills and capabilities'.

Rosabeth Moss Kanter (1994) describes it as follows:

Whatever the duration and objectives of business alliances, being a good partner has become a key corporate asset. I call it a company's *collaborative advantage*. In the global economy, a well-developed ability to create and sustain fruitful collaborations gives companies a significant competitive leg-up. [Kanter, 1994: 96]

Alliances are of similar relevance and important in the arts (Scheff & Kotler, 1996), and in service and community organisations. Educational observer Hedley Beare is of the view that, in education systems, new postcorporate organisational forms are at least partly already in place:

By the mid-1990s, then, what we once knew as the typical 'Education Department', with its hierarchy of controls, has largely gone. It has been replaced with a 'network of schools', a system of interconnecting, semi-autonomous schools and service units, each under contract, as it were, to deliver for the government an education service of a required quality. The government ensures value for money through an accountability mechanism involving mutually negotiated ' performance indicators' and regular audit or quality checks. Operationally these audits free the school to work in whatever way it chooses. The school is judged on outputs, on services delivered. Hence, 'OBE': outcomes-based education. [Beare, 1995: 14]

Implicit in Beare's statement is the complexity of postcorporate choice as it confronts managers in education. If, as Australian Federal Minister David Kemp is reported to have said, schools may eventually issue reports on the number of their graduating students who get jobs, and be judged by parents on their 'employment level' successes (*The Courier Mail*, April 8,1997: 5), major ethical questions arise for education managers. What, for example, is the responsibility of school principals in socioeconomically privileged communities to promote the exclusive well-being of their own students as opposed to the well-being of all Australian youth? Questions like this have always confronted education systems. What is different about management in the postcorporate world is that questions such as these are now the responsibility, in part, of managers individually and collectively rather than of remote, impersonal hierarchies and bureaucracies.

Such differences between postcorporate thinking and action required a change of blueprint, a new organisational form, a new culture, a new mindset—indeed, a move away from the entire paradigm implicit in corporatism and shown in Figure 2.1. It requires coming to terms with discontinuity.

Discontinuity: When Change Changed

What led to these newer forms of organisation? As we shall see, there were many factors. But at the heart of all of them was one phenomenon—*discontinuity*. The idiom that 'the only constant thing in the world today is change' turned out to be the ultimate illusion. Even change changed! Perhaps one of those who has recognised this most clearly is Igor Ansoff, the legendary 'father of strategic management'. In 1988, Ansoff argued in *The New Corporate Strategy* that what was needed was an organisational form that could cope not so much with an extraordinary degree of change, but with a different *kind* of change—one that was able to deal with *discontinuity*.

The more traditional integrated divisional organisations deal with high levels of change by encouraging the development of organic systems. But such change is incremental and familiar. Paradoxically, it involves predictable unpredictability. Discontinuity, on the other hand, involves what Ansoff calls 'novel change'.

It is useful to consider some of Ansoff's arguments in detail:

A change is *discontinuous* whenever it does not directly follow the historical logic of the firm's development. ... One test of the degree of discontinuity is the extent to which the firm makes a departure from the market needs it knows how to serve, from the technology on which the firm's products are based, or from the geographical, economic, cultural, social, or political settings in which it knows how to do business. [Ansoff, 1988: 92]

In other words, an organisation is facing discontinuous change when its past does not prepare it for the future. The problem of discontinuity is easier to see, perhaps, on an international scale. As we write, nobody has any real idea of what the former Soviet Union will look like in five years' time. Its history has not prepared it for the future. Of course, its history has brought it to that future and echoes of that history will be carried into it—but it will be metamorphasised.

In the same way, organisations in the 1980s began to confront frequent, discontinuous change in vital areas of their environments. New technologies transformed their product lines. A global village emerged with global markets. Empowered individuals and employees made unheard-of demands on their organisations. In concert, these individuals formed social movements that made unthinkable demands on organisations, and that were capable, in the end, of bringing down the Berlin Wall and of defying treaty-based national boundaries in the Balkans and Africa.

The Need for Entrepreneurship

The real problem for Western managers was that they were not doing too well in the face of these challenges. As the 1987 Nobel prize-winner, Robert Slolow, demonstrated, countries grow rich because of their ability to translate innovative ideas into physical technology, not because they have more money to invest. While US managers (and UK and Australian managers, we might add) had plenty of innovative ideas and inventions, they were not good at entrepreneurship—at translating these into a physical technology, and developing markets for them. As Slolow said of the US:

> I think in this country we're good at engineering and science, but we are not very good at transferring developments in those fields to commercial applications. [cited in Stevens, 1988]

Tony Miadich, of Oregon's Northwest Venture Capital, is one manager who saw the need for entrepreneurship clearly:

> If you look back at the seed deals that we have done they all tend to be very fundamentally new technologies; fundamental breakthrough kinds of things; secondly it is a very proprietary technology; it's either patented or a lot of know-how—very proprietary; thirdly ... there's an understanding that if it worked it would have profound economic implications. [interview with Cunnington, 1987]

The increasing rate, frequency and severity of discontinuous change in the 1980s, in the end, triggered a transformation in organisational configuration, a punctuation in the gradualism of everyday management. For, as Ansoff observes, such discontinuity 'will require revisions in the culture, power structure, systems, organizational structure and reward/incentives within the firm' (Ansoff, 1988: 92). This revision was towards entrepreneurial cultures and systems that could deal with random, episodic, discontinuous change.

There is an essential conflict between the entrepreneurial culture of the Fourth Blueprint and the competitive culture of the Third. The extent of the conflict between the two cultures can be seen in Table 3.1, which represents a précis of Ansoff's description of them (Ansoff, 1988: 170–1).

The more incremental, extra-polative, market-reactive, intra-firm, participative nature of the competitive culture can conflict vigorously with the more discontinuous, outward-looking, opportunist, vision-creating style of the entrepreneurial culture.

AN EXTENDED MODEL
OF ORGANISATIONAL CHOICE

The move towards newer, loosely coupled entrepreneurial organ-isations and networks can best be understood as a move away from the paradigm of corporate organisational choice. This can be represented as an extension of Figure 2.1. Figure 3.1 presents just such an extension, showing a range of new, postcorporate organi-sational configurations that are increasingly able to handle dis-continuous change. Two features of the new model should be emphasised. First, the move towards discontinuity does exist in a dimension different to the 'stability–change' dimension. Discontinuity is not just another degree of change—it is a different kind of change. The second point is related to the first. Any corporate organisation—functional, matrix or divisional—can learn to network or to use some of the operational tactics of the

Table 3.1   Competitive versus entrepreneurial cultures

Competitive	*Entrepreneurial*
Change	**Change**
Serial	Random
Incremental	Episodic
Continual	Discontinuous
Goal driven	**Opportunity driven**
Optimise profitability	Optimise potential
World view	**World view**
Intra-firm	Multi-industry
Intra-national	Multinational
Values	**Values**
Economic rewards	Economic rewards
Power	Personal fulfilment
Conformity	Deviance
Stability	Change
Skills	**Skills**
Participative	Charismatic
Goal setting	Vision creating
Extrapolative planning	Creative planning
	Novel problem solving

Source: Adapted from Ansoff (1988).

postcorporate organisation. But unless its fundamental mindset or paradigm has changed, it is probably best to regard it as a neo-corporate organisation, rather than postcorporate. This point will become clearer as this discussion proceeds.

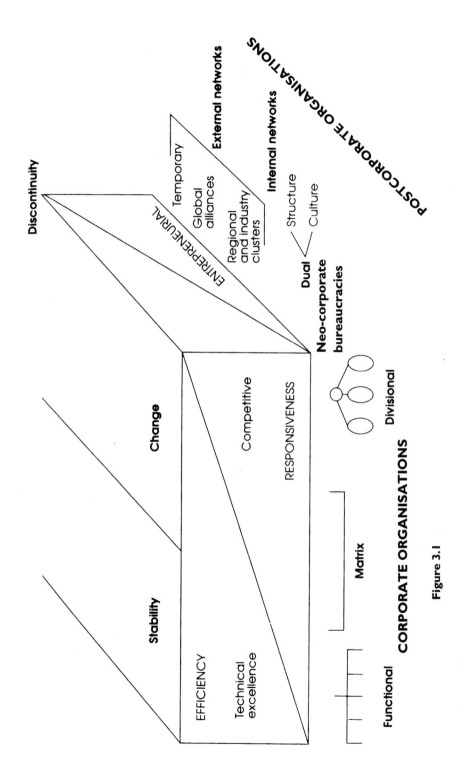

Figure 3.1

In order to understand the extent of the mindset change in Fourth Blueprint (postcorporate) organisations, it will be useful to look first at the 'purer' forms of such organisations—networks. After that we will come to consider hybrid forms of organisation such as dual organisations or neocorporate bureaucracies.

THE GIANT LEAP: NETWORK ORGANISATIONS

Ironically, the use of network organisations is not new; indeed, networks and alliances were primary characteristics of nineteenth century business organisation. The use of the formal hierarchical corporate structure is a relatively recent phenomenon:

> A long view of business history would suggest that firms with strictly defined boundaries and highly centralised operations are quite atypical. The history of modern commerce, whether told by Braudel, Polanyi, Pollard or Wallerestein, is a story of family businesses, guilds, cartels, and extended trading companies—all enterprises with loose and highly permeable boundaries. [Powell, 1990: 298]

But even in the late 1980s, as Jarillo observed, 'Networking is a fashionable topic' (Jarillo, 1988: 31), and it was receiving increasing interest in management publications. Since then, the literature on networks has just about got out of hand. As we have said in previous chapters, we do not believe in 'fads'. Networks have become fashionable because they work—they provide a superior form of organisation under conditions of discontinuity. The sheer challenges of the 1990s are leading organisations to dismantle their hierarchical structures and develop more fluid structures pulled together by information technology (Boudette, 1989). This is the giant leap towards the entrepreneurial organisation. If this leap can be made, the resultant network structures are 'lighter on their feet' than hierarchies (Powell, 1990: 303).

Network organisations come in different forms and under different labels. They include a focus on internal networking, subcontracting, strategic alliances, franchising, strategic networks, 'hub' organisations, 'solar system' organisations and the like. We like to distinguish, in the first instance, between *internal networks* and *external networks*.

Internal Networks

The key to the new network organisation is that it lies beyond hierarchy: all of the various parts learn to both handle themselves as autonomous units, and to network and collaborate with other resources within the organisation. Kanter observes such a blueprint in the US within organisations such as Procter and Gamble. She argues:

> Perhaps the flexibility with the highest potential payoff involves the ability to combine a company's various resources in collaborative efforts: joint marketing between divisions, for example, or a product package linking components from units that traditionally sold their wares separately, or the procurement staff for one business unit helping another find a supply source for a new venture. Corporations are realising that internal competition can cause hostility and must be replaced by internal collaboration to maximise the value of having all those groups under one roof. Thus, many companies are now—to parody a popular film title—'desperately seeking synergies'. [Kanter, 1989–90: 84]

Yet the change in approach is more than just pouring new wine into old bottles—more than changing the spirit and culture of the organisation. It really requires a complete transformation of the whole configuration, of the blend of strategy, structure and culture. First, Second and Third Blueprint organisations also desperately sought synergies. First Blueprint functional organisations sought them by placing units under one hierarchy. Second Blueprint organisations tried to develop interlocking group structures to get their synergies. Third Blueprint divisionalised organisations tried to get their synergies through matrix structures or through headquarters staff—ITT, at one stage in the 1970s, had over 200 such synergy-producers at its Brussels headquarters alone!

The distinguishing feature of the loosely coupled collaborative, network organisation is that *the synergies are sought and achieved by the parts themselves,* and are not superimposed on them by various structures or staff. The managers themselves have a new cognitive map: they see themselves and their units as autonomous, as having distinctive competencies, yet they focus on the broader business of the organisation and look for collaborative ventures with other parts of the organisation. They understand that they cannot do everything 'in-house'—within their own units—and learn to farm out activities to the most efficient suppliers within the organisation at large. The notion of 'organisation structure', in such a management blueprint, is hardly relevant, for it does not comprise a formal corporate organisation. We are attracted, instead, to the concept of 'social architecture' as the Fourth Blueprint counterpart of organisational structure in earlier blueprints. Ram Charan, an international consultant on implementing global strategies, describes this concept as follows:

> The foundation of a network is its social architecture, which differs in important ways from structure. Organisational structure refers to the systems of vertical power and functional authority through which the routine work of the organisation gets done. Social architecture refers to the operating mechanisms through which key managers make trade-offs and to the flow of information, power, and trust among these managers that shapes how those trade-offs get made. Social architecture concerns *what happens* when the network comes together—the intensity, substance, output, and quality of interactions—as well as the frequency and character of dialogue among members on a day-to-day basis.

> A robust social architecture does not imply absolute harmony among peers. Indeed, the single most important role of networks is to surface and resolve conflict—to identify legitimate disagreements between functions, regions, and business units and to make difficult trade-offs quickly and skilfully. A robust social architecture encourages members of the network to become mature and constructive in their approach to conflict, to direct their energies toward the substance of disagreements rather than toward personal clashes and politics, to search for creative solutions rather than to look over each other's shoulders, and to identify new challenges. [Charan, 1991: 107]

The organisation arranges itself in a way to support these views. It creates autonomous units, but it increases the volume, speed and frequency of both vertical and *horizontal* communication within the organisation to promote collaboration. The CEO focuses on the fundamental *vision* of the entire organisation and on communicating it in order to promote collaboration. And the whole package is aimed at strategies that are able to handle and even promote discontinuities. The result is an organisation with superior performance characteristics for the 1990s. Network management is, in the end, management by empowerment.

It is easy to see such internal networking within the Silicon Valley and Silicon Forest cultures, where the key organisational unit seems to be a loosely coupled engineering team. Delbecq and Weiss, after a study of Silicon Valley culture, report that:

> None of the executives talked about organisation charts, channels, or procedures as controlling mechanisms. Rather, they talked about allowing a spirited group of individuals focused on a developmental endeavour 'to have a go' at their ideas. In turn, the team feels free and obligated to stay in touch with company leadership. [Delbecq & Weiss, 1988: 35]

But it is also the larger organisation that faces most challenge in, and has the most to gain from, internal networking. It allows large organisations to become lighter on their feet so that they can compete with smaller organisations—it is part of the process of 'giants learning to dance', to use Kanter's delightful metaphor (Kanter, 1989a) or of 'being big, but acting small', in Pascale's words (Pascale, 1990).

For many large organisations, networking is part of an overall attempt to downsize (Tomasko, 1987). Yet downsizing within the Fourth Blueprint mindset is rarely just a cost-cutting exercise. It is much more complex than that—it is an integral part of creating entrepreneurial capacity. Welch, for example, reports of GE's restructuring:

> Now, how we went at this can be described from two totally different perspectives. One perspective would use words like 'downsizing', 'reducing', 'cutting'. We think that view misses the point. We see our task as a totally different one aimed at liberating, facilitating, unleashing the human energy and initiative of our people.
>
> Sure we saved. Simply by eliminating the company's top operating level, the sectors, we save $40 million. But that was just a bonus that pales in importance to the sudden release of talent and energy that poured out after all the dampers, valves, and baffles of the sectors had been removed. [in Thompson et al, 1989: 70]

While Welch expected his managers to network with each other and to use each other's strengths and competencies, he did not just leave that to chance. He created strong mechanisms for the sharing of 'best practices' across all GE divisions, such as turning his cross-divisional meetings into 'business laboratories', or engendering a spirit of collaboration through his in-company executive programs conducted at Crotonville (Kanter, 1989a; Tichy, 1989). In doing so he created what Inkpen (1996) calls 'collaborative knowledge', transforming relationships between his divisions from that of mere alliances to that of partners. He also began to develop what Mintzberg and his co-authors (1996) call the knowledge of 'how people connect' ('Is it partly psychic?' they ask).

Above all, networks are helping create organisations without *internal* walls. As modern communication technology becomes more sophisticated and ever more accessible and user-friendly, it is possible to move beyond the traditional boundaries of groups and teams and departments as basic organisational units. The organisational units of the new organisation are rapidly becoming widespread task-specific networks that go beyond the smaller structures.

Ram Charan, for example, reports on the use of extended networks of key players (sometimes smaller than 25, but never larger than 100) that focus on, and direct, various activities of organisations such as Conrail, the Royal Bank of Canada, Dun & Bradstreet, and Du Pont. Such networks of individuals selected from across the company who are often in daily contact with each other may initiate strategy formulation, or address operational issues. As Charan reports:

> [U]nlike most teams and task forces, networks do not merely solve problems that have been defined for them. Networks are dynamic; they take initiative. They become the vehicle to redirect the flows of information and decisions, the uses of power, and the sources of feedback within the hierarchy. They become a new way of doing business and a new operating mechanism for individual managers to make their presences felt. [Charan, 1991: 106]

Networks are controlled by specifying the business *output* and timeframe expected of each network, not its parameters or boundaries. Charan reports that they transform middle managers into collaborative participants in corporate change: 'By forging a strong set of relationships and values, networks reinforce managers' best instincts—and unleash emotional energy and the joy of work' (Charan, 1991: 115).

We will examine techniques for network management and empowerment in more detail shortly. For the moment, though, it is significant to note that the overall strategy of moving towards smaller units that are broadly networked internally (as well as externally, most often) has had a profound effect on the structure of Western organisations. Lash and Urry cite evidence of the move towards smaller organisations and plants in Britain, the US, Germany, France and Sweden. Many of these moves towards smaller plants are taking place within the larger organisations. Thus, by the end of the 1970s, although individual companies in the US had grown, their individual plants had not, and 'by the end of the 1970s four-fifths of net growth was occurring in plants with less than 100 employees' (Lash & Urry, 1987: 115).

But many of the largest organisations went further in the 1980s and began the process of downsizing in absolute terms as well (Tomasko, 1987). In the first five months of 1986 alone, *Fortune 500* companies shed some 2.2 million employees (Tucker, 1987). By the end of the 1980s it had become obvious that it had been an era of both 'unbundling' the larger organisations into smaller units, and a middle-management and white-collar wipeout.

For Lash and Urry, the move towards smaller units is part and parcel of 'the end of organised capitalism', and the beginning of the postmodern era of disorganised capitalism. Yet such an analysis misses the point of Fourth Blueprint thinking. The essence of the new management is not simply the decoupling of the larger corporation. It is a much more positive attempt to arrive at loose coupling—to liberate energy by moving towards smaller autonomous units, and to harness that energy by creating strategic networks. It is based on a fundamental strategic premise:

> If a firm is able to obtain an arrangement whereby it 'farms out' activities to the most efficient supplier, keeps for itself that activity in which it has a comparative advantage, and lowers transactions costs, a superior mode of organisation emerges: the strategic network. [Jarillo, 1988: 39]

This premise helps us to move conceptually from internal networks to external networks, for activities may be farmed out to any one or more of a variety of loosely coupled organisations within and outside the 'hub' or sponsoring organisation—to autonomous sub-units, subsidiaries, franchisees, subcontractors and/or independent organisations. The resultant organisation is superior precisely because it is able to orchestrate the diverse resources and distinctive competencies of different organisations to a new common purpose. There is no evidence that organisations have to learn one form of networking prior to learning another—that they have to learn internal networking before they can move on to external networks or vice versa. But the mindsets and paradigms are transferable from one form to another. Companies that start out with one form of networking soon begin to engage in the other; they become network organisations.

External Networks

The more discontinuous the environment becomes, the more impossible it is to do everything in-house. Organisations cannot structure into themselves a range of resources and competencies that can meet likely future events. Moreover, the very nature of discontinuity is that no organisation's history, and therefore its accumulated current resources, will prepare it for the future. The most efficient suppliers lie *outside* the organisation, and it must learn to collaborate with these outsiders while keeping for itself those activities that reflect its own distinctive competencies (Jarillo, 1988).

If the best centres of excellence in relevant know-how lie increasingly outside the firm (Teece & Pisano, 1987), then ways must be found of forming alliances with them. Thus is born the 'strategic alliance', or the 'strategic network'—the Fourth Blueprint organisation that will carry Western enterprises into the post-modern era and the twenty-first century.

Networks are more than just a pooling of knowledge and learned capacities. As Powell, Koput and Smith-Doerr (1996) found in a study of the biotechnology industry, they create new forms of organisational learning:

Rather than using external relations as a temporary mechanism to compensate for capabilities a firm has not yet mastered, firms use collaborations to expand all their competencies. Firms opt for sustaining the ability to learn, via interdependence, over independence by means of vertical integration. This, in turn, promotes a sense of community-level mutualism. (Barnett, 1990) [Powell et al, 1996: 143]

Similarly, Cyert and Goodman (1997) argue that an emphasis on organisational learning in university–industry alliances serves to relieve tensions in the alliances and provides benefits not just to partners but to broader communities (56). Effective networking, in other words, enhances the entire learning configuration of the partners themselves.

Forms of integration in networks

By the mid-1990s a wide range of new relationships between companies and service organisations had become evident. Kanter (1994: 98) discusses these as ranging along a continuum from weak and distant to strong and close. The very fact that they can now be conceptualised in itself extends the possibility of organisational choice beyond anything that had previously been possible.

At one extreme, according to Kanter, in *mutual service consortia*, similar companies in similar industries pool their resources to gain a benefit too expensive to acquire alone—access to an advanced technology, for example. At mid-range, in *joint ventures*, companies pursue an opportunity that needs a capability from each of them— the technology of one and the market access of the other, for example. The joint venture might operate independently, or it might link the partners' operations. The strongest and closest collaborations are *value-chain partnerships*, such as supplier–customer relationships. Companies in different industries with different but complementary skills link their capabilities to create value for ultimate users. Commitments in those relationships tend to be high, the partners tend to develop joint activities in many functions, operations often overlap, and the relationship thus creates substantial change within each partner's organisation.

Kanter recognises five levels of integration which seem to us to have application in both internal and external networks. These are:

- *Strategic integration*, which involves continuous contact among top leaders to discuss broad goals ...
- *Tactical integration*, which brings middle managers or professionals together to develop plans for specific projects or joint activities ... .
- *Operational integration*, which provides ways for people carrying out the day-to-day work to have timely access to the information, resources, or people they need to accomplish their tasks ...
- *Interpersonal integration*, which builds a necessary foundation for creating future value ...
- *Cultural integration*, which requires people involved in the relationship to have the communication skills and cultural awareness to bridge their differences.

Kanter concludes that 'Integration in all five of these dimensions—strategic, tactical, operational, interpersonal, and cultural—requires that each party be willing to let the other parties inside, which entails a risk; the risk of change' (107).

In order to see at work some of the less obvious forms of integration, such as interpersonal and cultural, it is interesting to consider an example that is drawn from a non-Western context. It involves the traditional Chinese family business firm and illustrates internal networking as a way of 'doing business' that would be unfamiliar to most.

CHINESE FAMILY NETWORKS

Murray Weidenbaum (1996) describes it in this way:

> The Chinese business enterprise family differs in fundamental ways from the usual Western business firm. The head of an expatriate Chinese company typically is a 'paterfamilias', all-powerful in both social and economic spheres. He delegates key activities and positions to members of the family. Within the family, confidence in his judgement borders on the absolute. [141]

Weidenbaum then goes on to make a point that is of compelling importance in our discussion:

> The Chinese attach great importance to developing and maintaining *guanxi* (connections or relationships), which may result in missing opportunities to use the low-cost supplier or otherwise achieve greater economy and efficiency. *Guanxi* binds people through the exchange of favors rather than by means of expressions of sympathy or friendship. The relationship, at least as viewed by Westerners, tends to be more utilitarian than emotional (Chen, 1995). The Chinese business leaders are more interested in long-standing commitments to working together than in the Western notion of a seemingly perfect contract that appears to contain no loopholes. ...
>
> People who work with or observe overseas Chinese businesses over long periods of time are convinced that their special ability at deal making and developing transnational networks gives them a substantial competitive edge. [149–50]

If one is to establish a world-class organisation, as Moss Kanter points out, it is imperative that the firm establish a worldwide network of connections. Yeung and Tung (1996: 54) comment that 'this takes on a special significance in Confucian societies' where the establishment of *guanxi*, or connections, is part of an historical consciousness—it is a powerful, culturally based form of integration.

Thus, there are some dynamics associated with successful internal networks that we are only now beginning to discover, as well as many that we have not yet begun to discover. As this example shows, much of what we learn about networking will not be drawn from our own experience. One facility for integration that the *traditional* Chinese family firm did not have at its disposal, and which the Fourth Blueprint manager (in both the East and the West) uses so comprehensively to manage beyond hierarchy, is modern information technology.

The Importance of Information Technology

The driving force that made possible the mushrooming of strategic networks over the past few years is information technology. To understand this, let us go back to the notion of 'transactions costs' introduced in our quotation from Jarillo earlier in this chapter. Jarillo, it will be remembered, argues that networks are a superior form of organisation if they 'lower transactions costs' (Jarillo, 1988: 39).

Transaction costs, a term used in economic analysis, refers to the cost of coordinating market activity through the price mechanism. In effect, transaction costs are made up of the multiple market exchanges necessary to determine what the appropriate price should be (Coase, 1937).

Logic dictates that whenever an individual entrepreneur can coordinate a market activity at less cost than the price mechanism, a new business opportunity exists. Even more importantly, an entrepreneur can use information technology to significantly reduce transaction costs in network systems. Johnston and Lawrence (1988) comment:

> Today, low-cost computing and communication seem to be tipping the competitive advantage back toward partnerships of smaller companies, each of which performs one part of the value-added chain and coordinates its activities with the rest of the chain. [Johnston & Lawrence, 1988: 94]

Johnston and Lawrence cite the case of McKesson Corporation, the $6.67 billion health care and consumer goods distributor, which became successful by moving towards value-adding partnerships with suppliers and customers. They offered independent drug-stores computerised systems that were well beyond the reach of any single store. They also used the same technique with their suppliers: a system of computer-to-computer ordering enabled McKesson to reduce its buyers from 140 to 12 and allowed suppliers to make their production more efficient. The whole strategy of tying alliances together with information technology allowed them to compete head-on with the larger drugstore chains.

But it is not only networks of smaller companies that are becoming competitive through the use of the computer chip—large companies, too, have been able to do away with layer after layer of their hierarchies because they too have found that intensive cheap communication can do the coordination job that the hierarchy used to do. As Keen (1991) notes, by using information technology, organisations can recreate organisational simplicity.

It can go further than that: information technology can be used to build a new form of community, diasporas (dispersions of people who share the same values and identity), which are far broader than the organisation or even the Chinese family. Arthur Armstrong and John Hagel III (1996) describe aspects of this as 'the real value of on-line communities'. They identify four types of 'consumer needs' that electronic communities can meet:

- *Communities of transaction* primarily facilitate the buying and selling of products and services and deliver information related to those transactions ...
- *Communities of interest* bring together participants who interact extensively with one another on specific topics. These communities involve a higher degree of interpersonal communication than do communities of transaction ...
- Many people on-line today participate in *communities of fantasy*, where they create new environments, personalities or stories ...
- Finally, groups of people may feel a need to come together in *communities of relationship* around certain life experiences that often are very intense and can lead to the formation of deep personal connection. [Armstrong & Hagel, 1996: 135–6]

Thus, opportunities will be provided in the postcorporate era for value-adding through community-building that simply were not available in the organisational settings that we are now leaving behind.

Regional, industry and global clusters

The forms of integration listed above form the basis for the emergence of different clusters of networks. These may form in regions, where all five forms of integration (strategic, tactical, operational, interpersonal and cultural) are easier, in industries where strategic and perhaps cultural integration is more obvious, or across global boundaries (usually along industry lines).

Regional clusters

One of the most significant features of the postmodern era has been the development of networks between small organisations on a regional basis. As we saw in Chapter 1, these have been interpreted as part of the 'second industrial divide' or of the move towards 'disorganised capitalism'. A number of these regional networks have attracted great interest. For example, a group of researchers has been able to document the rise of Baden–Wurttemburg as the centre of the West German textile industry. Small and medium-sized organisations, each with highly specialised skills and competencies, are tied together into a complementary system by a very effective system of networks and alliances (Piore & Sabel, 1984).

The most frequently cited example of regional networking is widely known as the 'Emilian Model' (Brusco, 1982; Sabel, 1989; Porter, 1990), after the industrial structure of the district of Emilia–Romagna, in North-Central Italy. In this district, as we noted in Chapter 1, very small and some medium-sized firms are grouped together in different zones according to product. They are each highly specialised, but collaborate with each other through a whole series of network mechanisms. Nearly all of the local political authorities in these zones were until recently controlled by the Communist Party, and provide a range of administrative, marketing, financial and consultancy services. Together these zones cover a wide range of consumer and engineering goods, and have had an enormous impact on Italy's economic growth.

The past few years have been marked by the rapid development of regional networks throughout the West, from the massive Austin–San Antonio corridor development in Texas to a small network of agricultural equipment manufacturers in the Darling Downs area of Queensland, Australia. Even in 1988, Richman was able to report on a number of flexible manufacturing networks in the US, including the East Brooklyn Metalworking Industry Network, a plastics network led by the Columbus Enterprise Development Corporation, and a metal parts and components network orchestrated by the Erie Bolt Corporation. He noted that:

Flexible manufacturing networks, whatever particular form they take, all grow out of the idea that a large number of small companies acting in partial concert with one another can achieve more than a single company of similar aggregate size. [Richman, 1988: 56–7]

Again, the role of modern sophisticated technology in allowing such network systems to be efficient and competitive should not be underestimated. As Lash and Urry argue, state of the art technology, especially in machine-tools and microelectronics, allows forms of specialisation and flexible equipment that 'weaken the impact of economies of scale' (Lash & Urry, 1987: 199). Using communication and control technology, smaller companies can both acquire knowledge of technological and market changes, and get together with others to respond to them.

Perhaps in service industries more than in business, regional networking would seem to be essential in postcorporate contexts. But difficulties have often been encountered by service providers in establishing it in meaningful and viable forms. In the instance of education, where it would be assumed to have natural applications, this is sometimes thought to be a derivative of cultural elements of the teaching profession, particularly its tradition as essentially individualistic activity (Hargreaves, 1994). But other factors come into play, including the impact historically of competitive, hierarchical bureaucracies on school-based educators' willingness to share their ideas, expertise and problems (Limerick & Crowther, 1997). Meaningful school–university collaborative research is another example of regional clustering where all of the principles of successful networking seem to apply, but have met with limited practical success.

We will examine these failures more generally later in this chapter when we look at neocorporate bureaucracies. But there are specific factors involved, too. For example, Larocque (1995) notes that, historically, collaborative research programs in education have been difficult to establish because of difficulties arising out of teachers' workplaces. She says:

The success of collaborative research depends on the extent to which university-based educators are able to enter into ... ways of talking with school-based educators. Hollingsworth (1992) describes such collaborative conversations as informal, intimate, supportive and nonevaluative. She also conveys how difficult it is for academics to become part of collaborative conversations, no matter how strong the intent. It requires us to shed our cloak of 'expert' and to struggle publicly with critical reflection on our own practice and understanding. In other words, we must become vulnerable. [Larocque, 1995: 5–6]

Thus, studies of organisational culture are conclusive: cultural factors can inhibit, as well as facilitate, networking.

Industry clusters

The distinction between regional and industry clusters is not always easy to maintain. Most clusters of organisations in any region also specialise in an industry segment (Piore & Sabel, 1984; Lash & Urry, 1987). What was not clearly understood until fairly recently is the role of these clusters in developing the competitive advantage of nations. A study by Michael Porter of the competitive situation of 10 leading nations suggests that nations become competitive, in part, by building clusters of competing and collaborating suppliers, subcontractors and the like around the home base of the leading organisations (Porter, 1990).

Most organisations import somewhere between 25 and 40 per cent of their cost from suppliers. The message is therefore straightforward: if companies are to compete globally, they must have access to competitively priced supplies and to a pool of expertise in their industry segment. These conditions are best generated by a pool of lean, efficient, vibrant subcontractors and suppliers who have been hardened in the heat of competition with each other. Such cluster development in critical industries, Porter argues, lies at the heart of the competitive advantage of nations. Where they are absent, companies find it difficult to compete globally.

Thus, the US information industry has behind it clusters such as Silicon Valley, Route 128 and the Austin–San Antonio Valley development. Japan's automobile industry provides another case in point, supported by a highly developed cluster of suppliers and subcontractors. It stands in sharp contrast with, say, the Australian automobile industry, where the number of machine-tool manufacturers has decreased from 14 to just two over the past decade or so—and where costs are accordingly very high.

Such clusters often start with the action of one or two firms that are determined to take the long-term view and to build long-term collaborative relationships with suppliers, customers or other units in the value chain. Examples abound. We are reminded of an ingenious example, that of the Oakland Ballet Company and the Oakland A's baseball team, who collaborated in 1986 to establish 'A's night'. Scheff and Kotler (1996: 58) describe this highly successful alliance this way:

> The team wanted to increase its community service and visibility during the off-season, and the ballet company hoped to expand its audience and its level of contributions.
>
> Every year between 1986 and 1994 (with one exception), several members of the baseball team appeared in one performance of the *Nutcracker* alongside the regular company dancers. …
>
> The results of this creative strategy? The event regularly sold out the house and the intensive media exposure helped boost ticket sales for other *Nutcracker* performances, too. …
>
> In 1995, A's night became All Star Night, as a variety of professional athletes from the Bay Area participated in the event.
>
> Rising costs and shrinking revenues have hurt the arts industry and created a crisis for many community-based companies. But creative action, involving external networking, can help. [Scheff & Kotler, 1996: 58]

Overall, examples of industry clusters abound, covering a broad spectrum including chemicals (Goldbaum, 1988), the automotive field (Slater identified more than 40 coalitions between Ford and an outsider by 1987; Kanter, 1989a), services (Kanter, 1989a); computers (Weimer et al, 1988b: 14), and hospital services (Olson, 1990). These are not always easy to establish and maintain, especially in neocorporate bureaucracies. Lomax and Darley (1995), for example, show that interschool competition for students makes effective alliances between schools very problematic. Nevertheless, these authors conclude that ways are being found, out of necessity!

Global clusters and alliances

Some of the most startling advances in modern organisational life have come about through the formation of cross-national alliances to compete in the global market. Benedetti, for example, led the resurgence of Olivetti with a commitment to strategic alliances that would create key markets in areas such as West Germany, the US and Japan (Higgins & Vincze, 1989: 305). He argues that:

> The traditional multinational approach is passé. Corporations with ambitions must turn to a new strategy of agreements, alliances, and mergers with other companies if they hope to survive. [cited in Higgins & Vincze, 1989: 306]

Companies such as Corning Glass (Kanter, 1989–90); General Motors, Phillips and Komatsu (Higgins & Vincze, 1989); Volvo, Saab–Skandis, Ericsson and Fairchild, Boeing, Airbus, AT&T and Toyota (Powell, 1990); Numeridex Inc and General Electric (Weimer et al, 1988a); Canon (Jarillo, 1988)—the list goes on—have in common a successful strategic commitment to alliances and networks. A major strategic alliance between those erstwhile competitors, IBM and Apple, including Motorola, has also been formed. Thus Powell notes that experimentation with various forms of networks has 'mushroomed in an unprecedented manner' (Powell, 1990: 314).

Most global alliances, of course, are extensions of local industry clusters into global relationships. The automotive industry is a case in point. Both Japan and the US have extensive local industry clusters, and both countries are simultaneously involved in widespread global alliances. Toyota produces only 20 per cent of the value of its cars, GM 70 per cent, Ford 50 per cent, and Chrysler 30 per cent (Johnston & Lawrence, 1988). All are also involved in an array of global alliances. Toyota and GM–Holden have joint, but separately badged, models in Australia. Tokyo–US relationships are just as strong—Kanter notes that as early as 1987:

> There were more than 8000 person visits by US-based Ford employees to Japan—and so much traffic between Detroit and Tokyo that many US–Tokyo flights now originate in Detroit rather than Chicago. [Kanter, 1989a: 183]

Such relationships in the automobile industry and in other industries such as the electronics industry (eg the Olivetti alliances) are directly in line with Kenichi Ohmae's 'Triad Power' strategy of establishing bases in the US, Japan and Europe and then reaching out through alliances into other markets (Ohmae, 1985).

Such developments, of course, have major national and international implications, and raise the issue of whether nation states should focus on local or global clustering. In one sense, the notion of 'Japan Inc' reflects Japan's success at developing industry clusters to support its major competitive industries. Thus the Japanese textile industry, and other sectors of the Japanese economy, are tied together by preferential trading relationships that provide a workable alternative to vertical integration (Powell, 1990). Yet the most salient aspect of Japan's performance is that it is also taking the lead in international alliances. Paradoxically, the strength of the local base gives Japan the freedom to engage in global alliances. It is not a matter of local versus global networks and alliances—it is a matter of both at the same time.

As in all matters of strategic choice, the move towards network organisations involves a series of trade-offs between strategic advantages and disadvantages. One danger, undoubtedly, is that of a move towards 'hollow corporations'—companies that orchestrate the manufacture and sale of goods, but add little value in the way of developing productive assets inside their organisations or their societies. A clear national vision and identification may provide one set of brakes on one weakness—the lack of attention to national interests. The point is open to debate, however. As Fallows argues:

> Japan gets the most out of ordinary people by *organizing* them to adapt and succeed. America, by getting out of their way so that they can adjust individually, *allows* them to succeed. America's talent for disorder allows it to get surprising results from average people by putting them in situations where old rules and limits don't apply. [Fallows, 1989: 48–9]

In other words while national openness and lack of cohesion do have problems, they are also a major point of competitive advantage. This question of collaborative individualism will be explored in further detail in Chapter 4. Significantly, even Fallows' comments may be based on patterns or stereotypes that are dating quickly; there is persuasive evidence that Japanese organisations, in order to deal with discontinuity, are also beginning to place more emphasis on individual 'self-reliance' (Mroczkowski & Hanaoka, 1989). Moreover, other less-organised societies have also produced excellent examples of clusters. Silicon Valley and Route 128 in the US, and the Swedish capacity to share research and development resources between Swedish companies, are cases in point (Powell, 1990).

The various nations of the world will undoubtedly continue to develop both local clusters and global alliances, and these in turn will become part of larger, more complex, macro-networks that act as a basis for worldwide technology transfer and that reflect the increasing globalisation of economic activity. The more sophisticated communication technology becomes, the more it will be possible for these larger, more diffuse networks to act more coherently, and the more they are likely to emerge as the dominant organisational forms of the twenty-first century.

Temporary networks

We should not end this consideration of different kinds of strategic networks without also considering the emerging symbol of the postmodern period, the *temporary network*. The ultimate discontinuity in organisational life is the one-off event that demands a unique, one-off organisation. Examples that come to mind are Bob Geldof's Band Aid, or the World Expositions (Expos) held in Vancouver and Brisbane during the 1980s, and in Barcelona in 1992. Organisations set up to deal with such events have all the hallmarks of networks: they consist of a 'hub' that identifies the overall vision and mission of the organisation; they consist of autonomous parts, brought together into collaborative action by the proactive efforts of both the hub and the parts themselves.

The advantages of the network structure for temporary events are obvious—it can orchestrate the skills and competencies of a whole range of people throughout the world to meet the need of a one-off event such as an Expo or a severe crisis such as the Ethiopian famine. At the end of the event, they can be disbanded without undue dislocation to the participants. They share many of the values of network organisations, spring from the same broad cultural roots, and present some similarities in their 'management'.

HYBRID ORGANISATIONS

Most managers today have become aware of the narratives and stories of Fourth Blueprint organisational managers such as Semler of Semco, and Welch of GE. But many, particularly within large corporate bureaucracies, have found it difficult to develop the mindset of these exemplars, or, more often, to push their organisations into a quantum shift of blueprint. The result is the widespread emergence of organisations that lie at the cusp of change, or that use Fourth Blueprint organisational tactics within Third Blueprint corporations.

Dual Cultures

Some firms attempt to work within the one overall formal structure, but to develop two collateral cultures within it—two cultures that exist as overlays on each other, and that allow participants to move from one 'world' to the other, obeying different rules and values as they make the transition.

This, for example, was the basic strategy adopted by 3M in the early 1980s (Peters & Waterman, 1982). Any manager, normally a law-abiding citizen of one of 3M's competitive divisions, was also able to change worlds and become an entrepreneur, to 'bootleg' time and resources for riskier new ventures and to champion these through the organisation using decidedly non-participative, entrepreneurial strategies and tactics. Engineers, for example, were able to spend up to 15 per cent of their working time on their own individual ideas and projects (Thompson et al, 1989: 251). 3M put up some structures, such as project groups, to support the entrepreneurial culture, but on the whole this entrepreneurial system existed within the normal corporate bureaucracy.

Art Fry, the entrepreneur who championed Post-it Notes through the normal 3M structures noted that there are both advantages and disadvantages to such a system. On the one hand:

Bureaucracy represents accumulated know-how, which will really test you before a product is released. … First you need a product champion to get that core vision going. Then, you need the facilities that 3M has and a willingness to pull the concept together. [*Journal of Business Strategy*, 1988: 22]

On the other hand, there is the problem of communicating the idea to others in the organisation, and getting their support for the idea:

Many times, a big part of the problem is in communicating things about the idea and keeping the same vision within the whole team. If the product idea had been the sort of thing I was pursuing on my own as an entrepreneur on the outside, there wouldn't be this problem. But here, you are in an organisation. [*Journal of Business Strategy*, 1988: 21]

The latter form of difficulty often gets in the way of maintaining a vital entrepreneurial subculture. This has led a number of organisations to adopt a second form of the dual organisation—the dual structure.

Dual Structures

One way to keep both corporate and postcorporate systems alive in the same firm is to place them under different organisational structures. This was Ansoff's preferred solution to the problem. He suggested that keeping entrepreneurship apart from the rest of the organisation by placing it in a 'new venture' substructure might provide an answer. Olson makes essentially the same point: 'To minimise resistance to change, firms often separate new venture activities from their more routine tasks (ie, those associated with existing products)' (Olson, 1990: 44). To do this, he reports that they use a venture team, or 'a small group of people who operate as a semiautonomous unit to create and develop a new idea' (Olson, 1990: 43).

A large number of organisations have followed this route. Companies like 3M and Security Pacific Corporation are among those that have used venture teams successfully. ICI (Australia) for some years placed its new venture business units under a separate 'group' executive. BHP, too, tends to keep its new venture units apart from its normal divisions. Banc One, one of the most profitable bank holding companies in the US, has been experimenting with a 'greenhouse' that nurtures new ventures (Kanter, 1989–90: 82).

The intention of the dual structure is, quite simply, to help the coexistence of both cultures by keeping them apart. New venture divisions or units foster entrepreneurial structures and cultures and develop new business areas and products. Once these have become established, they are set up as separate competitive-culture divisions, or transferred across to already established divisions. At least, that is the theory of it. In practice, over time, the dominant corporate mindset just cannot be kept apart from the newer postcorporate culture. Traditional managers look at their post-corporate counterparts in fellow divisions (with whom they are competing for resources) and just 'know' that they are bad managers with inappropriate values (such as risk-taking). Eventually, in most of the dual structures we encountered, the dominant corporate system eventually overwhelmed the post-corporate entrepreneurial system. In ICI Australia, for example, the new venture group was disbanded after a few years, and its assets returned to the conventional divisions.

Neocorporate Bureaucracies

Three decades ago, looking at the impact of bureaucracy on people, Chris Argyris (1962) argued that the strategies being adopted by the administrators of his time were leading to human and organisational decay. The situation today in many bureaucracies is even worse. They should carry a warning on all their job application forms:

Warning: working for bureaucracies is a health hazard.

This has become particularly clear to us during a series of interviews carried out by David Limerick with managers in large bureaucracies in the 55–60 age group. Fairly early on in our interviews we became aware that many of the participants were

telling very similar stories about their experiences in large bureaucracies. Most of them started off with very positive experiences in
the large corporations of the 1960s and 1970s. They were often
members of small professional primary groups from which they
received a great deal of satisfaction as they carried out their
professional mission. But over the years two things happened.
First, they moved into middle or senior management ranks, in
which they were much more exposed. Second, the organisations in
which they were working were changing dramatically, and were
becoming arenas in which they were experiencing a great deal of
pain. As we looked across these stories we received a good picture
of the dysfunctional nature of what we came to see as 'neocorporate bureaucracies'.

Clumsy though it is, the phrase neocorporate bureaucracy has
been chosen with care. These are not postcorporate organisations.
They are a new form of corporatism, still embedded in the major
paradigm of the hierarchical corporate organisation, but with an
attempt to apply some of the precepts of the Fourth Blueprint.
The effect has been equivalent to grafting a gazelle's leg onto
an elephant—an ungainly being which neither sustains nor is
sustained by its environment. Yet even here, we were taken by the
extent to which people were able to recover from pain and craft
their lives with such an unpromising context.

These forms of organisation tend to occur particularly (although
not always) within government departments, which are dominated by an overwhelming concern with accountability in a world
in which their operations are becoming increasingly transparent to
those in the environment. Moreover, their various constituencies
are becoming more powerful. Under such conditions managers
become risk-averse and hold on to the form of control they know
best—hierarchy. Yet they are simultaneously under pressure to
decentralise in order to cope with increasing rates of change, and
in order to reduce the costs of their swollen central bureaucracies.

What happens when top management attempts to hold on to
hierarchy as its major coordinative strategy, but also attempts
to apply postcorporate concepts such as devolution and decentralisation? There are a number of outcomes, each with unpleasant
consequences for those within them.

Delayering

Most government organisations have gone through the process of 'delayering'—of cutting out layers of middle management at both corporate and divisional levels. Unfortunately, they have kept intact their hierarchical systems of coordination! The result is a situation in which fewer and fewer people do more and more work, as professional knowledge workers in the middle of the hierarchy find themselves carrying out all the activities of the hierarchical control process above and below them. This process of *work-intensification* has become an overriding pervasive feature of neocorporate bureaucracy and those within them are experiencing increasingly high levels of stress accompanied by feelings of alienation from the organisation. The situation has become so severe that many of our participants report that their organisations have been experiencing difficulty in recruiting applicants for their senior positions. Said one, a principal of a medium sized school:

> Why should I [apply for the principal's position of a large school]? There's not much salary difference in it. Why should I put up with all that crap?

Pseudo-devolution

If decision making has been 'decentralised', but those at the top feel exposed and wish to keep control of the outcomes, one way of handling this is to constrain the decision making process. This can be done at two levels. The first is to adopt a 'strategic control' approach. Effectively, the corporate centre says to those in the operating divisions: 'You are in charge of your own strategic decision making. But to ensure that you do it properly and professionally you must use the following processes'. The result is the proliferation of a host of systems and procedures covering appointments, planning, reporting, training and the like. The second level is at the operational level. The systems and procedures can be made so detailed through the spelling-out of decision making criteria that little discretion is left. This is normally accompanied by a detailed reporting system that ensures that the 'appropriate' decisions have been made. Finally, it is enforced and sanctioned through a system of performance indices and performance management.

This system is made all the more pervasive and unbreachable by dressing it up in the language of postcorporatism. The systems are defended by asserting that they ensure equity, make decentralisation possible, are aimed at program delivery and customer satisfaction, ensure merit-based decisions, and allow autonomy within the bounds of accountability.

Who within or without the organisation could possibly disagree with such purposes?

The reality, of course, is that these values and objectives are not attained. People within the organisation become so inward-looking and so preoccupied with procedures and reports that they give little attention to adding value for clients and customers. Moreover, attempts to make routines of decision making create what the CEO of Scotrail called 'bureaucracies in the mind'. This results in *bureaucratia*—the nonsensical acts of bureaucratic systems. A participant, an employee in a large organisation, described a recent selection committee on which she had sat as follows:

> We knew we were making the wrong decisions, but we were following the criteria. We even became confused about the CVs. We have to take account of the quality of the written CV—but recently an instruction has come around saying that it is OK to get your CV done professionally. But we still have to take it into account! So for some we were evaluating how well they write. For others, we were looking as how well they manage subcontractors.

One of the outcomes of pseudo-devolution, of course, is that participants experience ever decreasing job satisfaction. Rice and Schneider (1994), for example, found low satisfaction amongst many teachers in US schools, despite a decade of 'empowerment'. They found more positive outcomes of empowerment only when the entire system tended to adopt the postcorporate model of site-based management.

Another outcome of routinising decisions is *decision-avoidance*: it allows people at both higher and lower levels of the bureaucracy to avoid making decisions, and therefore to avoid carrying the can for them. It is easier to follow criteria than to take the responsibility for making a decision. This applies to resource allocation decisions as well as selection and promotion decisions. For example, one of the strategies for resource allocation within government departments is competitive bidding for bundles of resources. This allows the bureaucrat to set up a committee, set criteria, call for bids and avoid having to make and defend a strategic decision on the allocation of resources.

Ironically, such decision routinisation, while it is often put up as a protection for merit and equity, more often tends to act against them. The rich get richer and the poor get poorer. Women and other disadvantaged groups who have not been able to build up their capital in order to meet decision criteria suffer badly relative to those who have. Even sympathetic parties are not able to step outside the criteria and, for example, make decisions on the potential of the applicant. Moreover, women tend to suffer disproportionately from the effects of work intensification, because they tend to bank up at middle-management and professional levels where the effects of work-intensification are worst. This in turn creates a downward spiralling effect, because they become so busy that they do not have time to build up their CVs.

Politicisation and outering

The overall result of these sets of dynamics within the neocorporate bureaucracy is the creation of a highly political system and culture. Those participants who have a well developed sense of professional identity find little opportunity for composing their professional lives within the bureaucracy. They tend to withdraw from coordinative positions (a strategy we will call 'outering') and leave the field to those who enjoy exercising the control processes of the system. Paradoxically, the system becomes inward looking, absorbed with the politics of setting up control systems and criteria, and impervious to the changes taking place in the environment, other than in the political environment.

We suspect that neocorporate bureaucracies will be with us for a long time. The political conditions that have given rise to them are so endemic, and the postcorporate narrative that is used to justify their processes is so persuasive in the postmodern world, that they will be difficult to dismantle. It is possible that their level of incongruence and ineffectiveness is so pervasive that governments will find it increasingly difficult to remain in the business of delivering services and that they will outsource the latter, keeping for themselves a primarily policy role. Nevertheless, there is considerable evidence in our interviews that many individuals are beginning to find ways of using such bureaucracies in the construction of their lives. We will return to this in the following chapter. In the meantime, it will have become clear that Fourth Blueprint, network management techniques cannot comfortably be partially lifted and applied within a different paradigm. The management of networks requires an internally consistent set of processes and capabilities.

THE MANAGEMENT OF NETWORKS

Network organisations are not an easy panacea for the ills of the modern environment. They are extremely tricky to manage for they present a host of what Powell calls 'inherent complications'. 'As a result of these inherent complications, most potential partners approach the idea of participating in a network with trepidation' (Powell, 1990: 305). They do so with good reason. Without careful design and management, the manifold advantages of networks are difficult to realise.

To conclude this chapter, we will be focusing on the challenges offered by networks and on the essential elements of effective network management.

Pitfalls and Problems of Strategic Networks

While the modern industrial world is alive with examples of successful alliances, it is also littered with unsuccessful ones. Two separate studies by McKinsey & Company and Coopers & Lybrand suggest that some 70 per cent of formal strategic alliances fail or fall short of expectations (Kanter, 1989b). A brief look at some of the potential problems in alliances helps in understanding the challenges facing managers of networks.

Goal Ambiguity and Network Boundaries

There is no common hierarchy in networks to hold the organisation together. Instead, they rely on each partner to direct his or her own efforts towards the common purpose. When that purpose is ill-defined or ambiguous, the network tends to fall apart or become ineffective, because, as Borys and Jemison (1989) argue, 'collaboration among sovereign organisations means that different purposes must be reconciled and moulded into a common purpose'(237).

Sovereignty

The fact that networks consist of sovereign independent units is in itself a threat to the stability of the network (Borys & Jemison, 1989; Kanter, 1989b). For some or all of these partners, the survival of the network may be relatively unimportant for the survival of their own organisation. This may, in turn, lead to problems of what Kanter calls 'undermanagement' (inadequate design and resourcing) and 'hedging' on resource allocation (Kanter, 1989b).

Asymmetry

Problems tend to arise in networks when the arrangement favours one partner more than the others—for example, when there is a one-way flow of technology transfer (Kanter, 1989b), or when one partner pulls cash out of the alliance while the others put it in. In other words, there can be both input and output asymmetries which threaten alliances. Trust, as we shall see, is the key element in the success of networks. But it springs from both shared values and a carefully negotiated mutuality in the relationship.

Creation of Potential Competitors

One of the persistent nightmares in the minds of those who enter external networks is that the transfer of technology and know-how will create a potential competitor. Of course, non-networks are not immune to the same problem: any employee or manager can potentially withdraw and set up in competition. But networks of powerful partners do exacerbate the problem.

Focus on the Short Term

The vast majority of studies of networks demonstrate very clearly that they work best when they are set up as long-term relationships. A short-term focus carries with it a number of problems. First, it is difficult to establish trust in such a relationship (Jarillo & Ricart, 1987). Second, it can lead to problems of undermanagement, with inadequate resourcing of the alliance (Kanter, 1989b). Third, it can lead to evaluation of outcomes on short-term financial results rather than on long-term strategic objectives (Modic, 1988). Finally, it can threaten the very coordinative base of networks: the long-term development of clear, shared norms, beliefs and values (Borys & Jemison, 1989).

Communication and Control

Networks, as we have seen, demand intensive, fast, sophisticated communication between networked operations. The need for both vertical and horizontal communication can place enormous strain on information systems and can require considerable investment in setting them up in the first place. Without such communication and control, 'with operations so scattered the company could wind up sacrificing quality control, its ability to respond quickly to changing customer need, and its role in product innovation' (Andrews, 1989: 38).

Different Cultures

One of the prime reasons for entering into alliances with others is often to make use of their different capacities built into different cultures. Yet these differences are in themselves difficult to manage. Alliegro, of Norton Abrasives R&D, argues that:

> Companies think differently, and culturally you have to start shifting gears to accommodate the differences. It's [also] like a marriage in that you have to work at it to make it succeed. [cited in Modic, 1988: 49]

Together, these sets of potential opportunities and problems call for managerial approaches, techniques and competencies which are very different from those needed in conventional hierarchies.

The Essential Elements of Effective Network Management

Strategic networks have emerged as a major force so recently that it is perhaps not surprising that there has been very little systematic research on how to manage them effectively. There have, however, been a large number of reports from the firing line—from those who have been deeply involved in networks. What is significant about these reports is that there is such a high level of consensus among them that it is possible to build up a picture of the essential elements of effective network management. This picture covers the preparation required, the techniques used, and the competencies demanded from their managers. If you are about to contemplate setting up internal and/or external networks, there are nine management areas on which you need to focus:

- liberate your managers;
- develop your boundary roles;
- develop your communication systems;
- get the mindset right;
- set up the alliance carefully;
- define the focus;
- manage the soft issues;
- manage the hard processes too; and
- manage the network control systems.

Liberate your managers

The essence of a network is that the unit managers themselves take responsibility for linking together with others—they do not rely on hierarchy, or on corporate 'seagulls' to take the initiative for them. So, flatten the hierarchy and trim the corporate headquarters. Replace the seagulls with one or two eagles at most.

Develop your boundary roles

Boundary roles were formerly carried out either by top executives or by low status 'gatekeepers' like purchasers. Now you need to encourage a sense of responsibility in all participants to manage boundary relationships. You should also convert the low status gatekeeping roles into focal strategic roles, because they manage strategic alliances.

Develop your communication systems

The 'soft' communication systems that consist of relationships and contacts between the participants are vitally important in network organisations and need to be carefully nurtured and designed (Bovee & Thill, 1995). What is different about networks is the importance you must give to *horizontal* communication systems: without exception those networks that have succeeded are those that have put their resources into high-tech communication systems. These systems are needed for a number of critical functions, such as the transmission of values and opportunities, the integration of the system, devolution and control.

Get the mindset right

To develop the new mindset that reflects both understanding of, and belief in, networking, it is necessary to deal with two components: a new *cognitive framework* and a new *set of values*.

A new *cognitive framework*: this requires participants to mentally 'break up the firm into smaller units of analysis' and to think about 'which activities are integrated and which should be farmed out' (Jarillo, 1988: 35). One way of doing this, suggests Jarillo, is to use Porter's concept of the value chain:

> The concept of the value chain is very useful in this effort to break up the firm. Distinguishing different activities within the firm that are, to some extent, independent although interrelated, is important because it reflects reality much better than thinking of the firm as a one-dimensional production function or a 'typically integrated manu-facturing firm'. [Jarillo, 1988: 35]

Once managers are thinking in these terms, it is a small step to thinking about farming out activities to others *outside* the organi-sation as well. Lovelock and Yip (1996) for example, show that value chain thinking underpins network, global strategies. Even then, the notion of 'value chain' has to be interpreted holistically. Similarly, Normann and Ramirez (1993) show that IKEA does not just add value—it *reinvents* it. Moreover, it focuses on the whole value constellation, bringing the customer into the system of action:

> The goal is not to create value for customers but to mobilise customers to create their own value from the company's various offerings. [Norman & Ramirez, 1993: 69]

A new set of values: the key value in running networks is trust. As Jarillo argues, high levels of trust help reduce transaction costs:

> [L]ack of trust is the quintessential cause of transactions costs. ... Being able to generate trust, therefore, is the fundamental entrepreneurial skill to lower those costs and make the existence of the network economically feasible. [Jarillo, 1988: 36]

Survey after survey has shown that American managers, unlike their Japanese competitors, do not trust anyone—especially their partners!

Set up the alliance carefully

There are two main issues to watch out for in setting up alliances: choosing partners and defining the objectives of the alliance.

Choosing partners. The one message on managing alliances that has come from the trenches more stridently than any other is: choose your partners carefully. The compatibility of structures, processes and procedures, as well as their styles, has to be taken into account.

Symmetry of contribution. Perhaps the most fundamental rule in choosing partners is to choose strong partners. You do not get synergies out of combining weaknesses. Altogether, the process of choosing partners is so central to the effectiveness of networks that the consistent message coming from the trenches is: take your time in choosing partners: it should involve a long period of courtship, not unlike a marriage (Goldbaum, 1988; Weimer et al, 1988a).

Define the focus

The careful definition of the focus of an alliance is important for two reasons. First, one of the issues that tends to bedevil alliances once they are operating has to do with conflicts over scope—over what falls within the purview of the alliance and what does not

(Kanter, 1989b). It is not important whether the scope is broad or narrow—just define it! A second reason for defining the focus is more subtle. Alliances tend to be expressed in long-term relationships that are complex and difficult to comprehend. Defining the purpose of the alliance acts as a 'legitimating mechanism' for the partners (Borys & Jemison, 1989)—as a way of justifying the relationship to all the constituencies of the participants, and helping to provide a legitimate basis for the choices and actions towards each other.

Manage the soft issues

Trust, as we have seen, is critical to effective networking (eg Ogilvy, 1995; Kumar, 1996). The very intangible issues of trust and reciprocity that are so problematic in choosing partners in the first place require constant reinforcement and management over the life of the alliance. Johnston and Lawrence (1988) suggest that there is a basic set of ground rules you can use that 'generates trustworthy transactions'. There are three fundamental requirements in managing trust relationships. They are the need to:

- *focus on equity and fair-sharing*: gains and risks should be equally shared;
- *focus on long-term relationships*: most successful alliances are built around a focus on long-term relationships, because they stimulate reciprocity and reduce transaction costs; and
- *focus on shared leadership*: alliances rely so heavily on voluntary collaboration that they require the vision-creating and co-ordinative impact of leadership at *all* levels in the organisation

Manage the hard processes too

Trust lies at the heart of alliances. But it is only relatively recently that we have come to realise that the English word 'trust' is too limited to really convey the essential relationship within alliances. English usage usually implies an unconditional relationship. But the trust relationship within alliances has a hard, pragmatic edge: it is more reciprocal, and is based on a mutual set of understandings about the expected behaviours of each partner. Zaleznik suggests that the closest we come to this notion within the traditions of English scholarship is the concept of 'amicitia', drawn from the field of politics and political relations. He writes:

> Unlike the bond of trust, 'amicitia' is not open-ended or unconditional. Implicit in 'amicitia' are the conditions that people accept obligations and are committed to their fulfilment, but never to the degree that one person in the relationship will expect the other to endure harm and neglect self-interest. Obligations are mutual and therefore one member does not ask for conduct that will create an imbalance. [Zaleznik, 1989: 230]

Developing this form of trust requires careful negotiating, based on skills in issue-based negotiation. In contracts that facilitate amicitia, the operational word is 'cooperative'; the contract must express the basic conditions of equity and fair-sharing. But to arrive at such a contract is no mean feat. It sometimes means that you have to change the negotiating kill-or-be-killed habits of a lifetime. It means a commitment to fair-sharing and fair process (Kim & Mauborgne, 1997).

Manage the network control systems

Money has to be put into extensive communication systems if successful networks are to be developed—the use of modern communication technology is essential for the management of meaning. But it is even more essential for the development of a new network control technology.

This is so critical that it is worth spending a little time on it.

A New Management Technology

Networks, as we have seen, demand intensive, fast, sophisticated communication between networked operations. If networked units arrayed along a value chain are to be more efficient than hierarchies, a number of conditions must be met:

- products or services from one unit in the network arrive just in time for the next part of the network (just-in time—JIT—technology);
- the quality of the goods or services flowing from one unit to the next is appropriate (total quality management—TQM);

- each unit must have the right to audit the quality management processes of the previous unit (TQM);
- each unit must see the next unit in the value chain as its customer, and try to meet its needs (TQM);
- each unit must know what it is relatively bad at, and who is the best candidate for receiving that subcontract (benchmarking); and
- people within organisations have to be able to use their expertise flexibly within a number of different networks and value chains (broadbanding and multiskilling).

In retrospect, Japanese *kanban* technology had little to do with the integrated corporation, and attempts to graft it on to such hierarchies were bound to meet with limited success. It was fundamentally a technology pioneered by Japanese organisations to deal with the problem of integrating networks.

The very implementation of *kanban* technology, in its fullest form, is likely to trigger changes within the conventional systems towards networking. As the responsibilities of each unit are stressed, so those within them are likely to demand empowerment and autonomy. As their interdependence is stressed, so they are likely to pursue the development of trust relationships. As these are stretched within the everyday processes of relating to others, so they will begin to look for clearer, contractual relationships with others in the network. Almost every major 'fad' that has emerged over the past few years is fundamentally part of a new paradigm that sets out to use networks efficiently.

It is worth looking at the Toyota management model as an illustration of this holistic approach to internal and external networking.

THE TOYOTA SYSTEM

For the two decades prior to the oil crisis of 1973, Japan's productivity had grown at the rate of 10 per cent per annum. The Arab oil embargo changed this, and for the first time many previously successful Japanese companies found themselves in the red. Facing unprecedented cost-push inflation, and unable to reduce the labour force to accord with the fall in demand, the performance of Japanese companies began to fall off more rapidly than some of their Western counterparts. One company, however, stood out from the rest: Toyota. Instead of falling into the red, it continued to show a huge profit.

> Its secret was a philosophy and method of production that had been developed by a machinery department manager who became Vice President of Toyota in 1975, Mr Taiichi Ohno. This philosophy, which has often been misunderstood in the West, was evolved from a laborious process of trial and error in the factories of Toyota and, as commented upon by Taiichi Ohno: 'it was difficult for the people of outside companies to understand our system; still less was it possible for the foreign people to understand it'. [Ohno, 1983: i]

What then is the Toyota production system? It was born out of a need to develop a system for manufacturing automobiles of many different kinds, in small volumes, utilising a common process. In the West, automobile manufacture was based upon an assumption that high efficiencies were only possible through the repetitive manufacture of standardised products.

Economic production models are based upon the assumption that the total cost of production is made up of two components: a holding cost and a set-up cost. For a fixed holding charge, the economic production quantity is determined completely by the value of the set-up cost. In general, this set-up cost is measured by the dollar value of the time required to prepare the equipment or work station to do the job and to dismantle it after the job is finished (Tersine, 1980: 138).

One key purpose of the Toyota production system is to minimise set-up costs. This adds flexibility to the production system, because the smaller the set-up cost, the smaller the quantity that must be produced on each run for that run to be economic. Schonberger reports that in 1981 it took an hour to set up 800 tonne presses used in forming auto bonnets and fenders. After five years of intensive work, the time was down to 12 minutes. In comparison, a US competitor took five hours to accomplish the same operation.

The second element in the Toyota production system is the structural redesign of work areas. Traditionally, work flow had been designed on a functional basis in which departments were organised according to manufacturing technologies. Further, the inventories held of work-in-progress often transformed a factory into little more than a warehouse for storage of inventory that was in transit from place to place.

Structural redesign at Toyota took place in two forms: first, a macro change from a functional to a product-based departmental superstructure; and second, a redesign of machinery layout to enable the alteration of the number of workers in accord with changes in demand.

Closely associated with this last idea is the concept of the multifunction or multiskilled worker. In the West, the application of the principles of the First Blueprint had resulted in each worker playing an atomistic role in the production process. In contrast, the Toyota system requires that each worker be trained to be skilful at any type of job and any type of process in their work area. Toyota uses job rotation with each worker regularly rotating through each job to achieve this end.

The third feature of the Toyota system is 'autonomation', the purpose of which is never to allow defective units from a preceding process to flow into and disrupt a subsequent process. In the West the emphasis on role specialisation resulted in the creation of quality control inspectors who inspected a statistically selected sample of a production run; this methodology was largely replaced in Japanese companies in the 1960s by the autonomous control of defects within the production process itself via the 'self-inspection of all units'. Hence, those most directly affected by defective parts are given the responsibility for detecting and preventing the defects.

The fourth feature of the Toyota system is designed to produce the required type of unit in the required volume at the required time. Commonly called JIT or *kanban*, once again there is a clear break with previous Western practice. Western practice was based on the idea that an earlier stage in the production process should push its output upon subsequent stages. As a result, it became difficult to adjust the production process to changes in schedule and demand. Thus substantial stocks of inventory were kept at the output of all stages of the process. By contrast, each stage of the Toyota system 'pulls' inputs as and when it needs them from the previous stage.

In the methodology of production associated with Henry Ford and the First Blueprint, productivity improvements could only come about through working harder. Under the Toyota method, increased productivity is achieved through the action of small groups of workers called 'quality circles'. Suggestions for improvement are developed by means of small group meetings of those directly involved in the production process.

The total effect of the changes at Toyota was to de-emphasise the hierarchical coordination of the manufacturing process and replace it with a multitude of horizontal integrating mechanisms (tactical, operational, interpersonal and cultural), to place autonomous control of the various parts of the process within the individuals and groups concerned, and to devise a system that replaced the implacable momentum of large-batch production with finely controlled, low-cost flexible production capable of meeting different niches. The Toyota system, in other words, was an essential part of transforming the organisation into an internal network, with the attendant capacity for external networking. It was a way of managing networks.

Our final comments on managing networks would be: *do not underestimate them, and do not go into them unprepared.* To handle their inherent complications and keep their transaction costs down, sophisticated management technology must be used. The equivalent of Toyota technology needs to be used to handle both internal and external networks. Without such systems, attempts to network could well be disastrous. With them, a superior mode of organisation can emerge—one ideally suited to an age of discontinuity—networks. But networks make very different demands on people within organisations: they require a different mindset, different values, a different culture and different competencies. We have called this mindset 'collaborative individualism', and it is to this topic that we now turn.

CHAPTER 4

COLLABORATIVE INDIVIDUALISM AND THE END OF THE CORPORATE CITIZEN

> *What, you ask, has gotten into the brains of these kids? Nothing less than a new attitude towards life and work—a quirky individualism that is characteristic of the baby-busters. ... These are the Employees Who Can Say No.*
>
> [Deutschman, 1990: 22–3]

WE ARE OBSERVING a battle for power in modern organisations that has enormous implications for management. It has nothing to do with the battle between unions and management—that is just a minor skirmish left over from past wars. The real battle is the one taking place between the individual and the organisation itself.

This is the era which signals the end of the obedient 'good citizen'. It is an era of the empowerment of the individual. It is also an era, paradoxically, in which we have recognised most clearly the interdependence between individuals. It is the age of *collaborative individualism*.

Collaborative individualism is a world view held by a growing number of people in Western society. In some organisations it is a management ideology—a view held by the dominant coalition in the organisation. In others it is a complete culture, a shared world of meaning, with its own patterns of values and characteristic systems of action. Collaborative individualism is the dominant culture of network organisations: it stresses the need for individuals to work together with others towards a common vision and mission. But it also stresses their emancipation, their freedom to reject hierarchical organisation and bureaucratic rules.

The significance of such change can be seen in the following example. For over a decade now we have been giving our first-year classes a simple questionnaire. It is so simple, in fact, that it has only one question. It goes this way:

> Think of the relationship you have with your organization (if you are not in an organization now, think of the relationship you would like to have when you join one). Now consider the following two alternatives, and distribute five points between them, according to the extent that you think they reflect that relationship.

> *Alternative 1*: You have joined the organisation, hopefully for life. It will develop your career by recognising your brilliance and putting you onto a fast career track, offering you constant support. In return you will be loyal, fight its competitive battles, devote your energies to it, and be a good citizen of the organisation.

> *Alternative 2*: You are in charge of your own career. You feel free to contract in or out of the organisation depending on two things:
> —the contribution it is able to make to your asset-base (including your physical/ financing assets, competencies, capacities, opportunities etc), and
> —whether you agree with its values.

When we first started asking this question in the mid 1980s our first year class numbered some 3–400 students: about 50 per cent of them were mature-age—that is, many were in their late 20s or even significantly older. In those days about 80 per cent or more would give most points to Alternative 1. Now, 10 years later, with the same age range in the class, 70 per cent or more would favour Alternative 2.

The change of expectations has been fast and dramatic. Why should that be so? *What has happened in the past decade to bring about such a shift in relationships between people and organisations?* This chapter explores the emancipation of the individual, the shape of the world view we have called collaborative individualism, and its conflict with the older cultures of the previous blueprints. It examines meanings of individualism and collaboration as they are emerging in Western society, and looks at the characteristics and competencies of the collaborative individual in Fourth Blueprint organisations.

THE EMANCIPATION OF THE INDIVIDUAL

The central value of collaborative individualism is a form of autonomy for the individual which was not a part of industrialised work settings associated with earlier blueprints. The individualism that we associate with earlier blueprints was driven by Enlighten-ment beliefs in rationality and scientific technology as ways of controlling and improving the human condition. One result, as we have shown in Chapter 1, was a factory system that separated family and work. Another was a system of mass production that destroyed social relatedness. Another was the rise of forms of nation state that imposed human improvement through ever-increasing regulation, control and intervention (Dale, 1989; Habermas, 1976; Hargreaves, 1994). But with the approach and emergence of the Fourth Blueprint, that has begun to change. As early as 1984, in our Frontiers study, the word 'autonomy' was used by CEOs more often than any other to describe the core values of their organisations. In the years since, it has come to lie at the core of a world view that stresses the freedom of the individual from *groups, organisations* and *institutions*.

Before proceeding to our analysis, it is worth drawing attention to the wide range of meanings associated with *individualism*. Our concern is primarily, though not exclusively, with what Stephen Lukes (1973) calls 'personal independence and self-realisation' rather than, for example, with 'anarchy and social atomism'. Levinson (1996) provides another perspective on individualism, relating it to what he calls 'a new age of self-reliance'. He says:

> [T]he forces changing the world in which we work and live have also changed the relationship between the employer and the employee. As we read in the paper every day, most companies no longer expect to have long-term relationships with their employees. In turn workers—

even executives—make sure that they are not too dependent on any one job or employer. They no longer look to the employer to support them. They now look to themselves.

A psychological and practical result of these changes is that we are now living in a new age of self reliance. On a personal level, we must get feedback, advice, and moral support from family and friends. On a professional level, we each need to develop fallback positions. By *fallback*, I mean an alternative course of action if the current job fails us. In today's world, we need to worry less about the next rung up the ladder and more about the variety of opportunities available to us should the ladder disappear and we find ourselves thrown back on our own resources. [Levinson, 1996: 162–3]

But these perspectives provide only half the picture. Collaborative individualism stresses not only self reliance, but interdependence and collaboration. It is emancipatory, but it is the focus on both collaboration and individualism that is the hallmark of the new world view.

Freedom from Groups

Managers in the West were so exposed to the rhetoric of teamwork over the past few decades that they came to take teamwork as the most important index of good management. However, with the emergence of the Fourth Blueprint came a very different vision of ideal relationships between people in organisations. They were to be populated by empowered, autonomous individuals who worked together with others, often in groups, but who were not bound by loyalty to those groups as an end in itself. They were bound by a common mission and collaborated, as autonomous individuals, towards its achievement.

Collaborative individualism reflects, in part, a set of values about relationships that strategic managers would like to see in their organisations. The Frontiers, Silicon Valley and Silicon Forest interviews with Australian and US managers in entrepreneurial organisations, reported earlier, were saturated with the language of collaborative individualism. Managerial literature from the UK, and to some extent Japan, also reflects a growing awareness of this newly developing set of values. It is a world view held not only by managers, however; it is also held by others in the organisation. As we shall see, the autonomous 'Self, Incorporated' view of the 'yuppie', and the world view of the 'gold collar' worker (Kelley, 1985), essentially express the same values.

It is important to understand that collaborative individualism is a post-teamwork, not an anti-teamwork, phenomenon. In the Frontiers study, Australian CEOs rarely referred to teamwork, not because it was unimportant, but because it was vitally important (Limerick et al, 1984). It was so important that it was a 'prior assumed' for effective organisations. During the 1960s and 1970s it was their dominant problematic issue, and they devoted significant amounts of their resources to the development of teamwork in both permanent and matrix teams.

The language of organisational development was the language of teamwork. But that language changed in the 1980s. It did not go back to the destructive individualist corporate buccaneer of the 1960s: it expressed a new concern with a new set of problems that lay at the other side of teamwork. The word 'autonomy' began to dominate managerial discourse, followed closely by words and phrases such as 'proactivity', 'initiative', 'accountability', 'creativity' and so on. Nevertheless, teams continue to promise much to organisations and they continue to be a popular, if un-satisfactory, response to organisational malaise:

> In the first instance, it is important to understand the reasons for this appeal to avoid inappropriate expectations and likely disappointment. Teams are seductive because they promise inclusion, comfort and belonging. Defined as task-oriented, and united around a common goal, teams promise to remove from organisational life intractable conflict and divisiveness. Reinforced by pictorial images and case anecdotes of jolly workers sharing the load, these tales of teamness portray groups which have overcome, one is asked to believe, frustration, boredom, jealousy, resentment, and prejudice. [Sinclair, 1995: 58]

The balance between individualism and collaboration, and the distance of that system from the 1970s notion of teamwork, is difficult to capture. Several metaphors tend to be used to express very similar images. For example, Bailey, of the ANZ Bank, argued: 'I do not want a team of football players: I want a team of cricketers!'. North American readers may want to substitute the term 'baseball players' for cricketers—the meaning is the same. He did not want employees who feel that if they missed the tackle someone else in the team would make it. He wanted someone who would confront that 100 km an hour ball on their own. Yet that person had to be collaborative. The person who normally batted flamboyantly, for example, had to be willing to dig in when things got tough for the team. Similarly, the head of a government utility expressed very much the same balance of individualism and collaboration, but more simply: 'I want a team of individuals'.

Viewed from the perspective of the Third Blueprint, the idea is difficult to grasp: from that point of view, collaborative individualism can be seen to be just a normal part of teamwork. Collaborative individualism in the Fourth Blueprint asserts that the *individual* is the basic building block of the organisation. Organisations—network organisations—are no longer seen as being made up of interlocking teams and committees to which individuals are assigned in order to achieve organisational goals. They are made up of mature, autonomous, proactive individuals who collaborate to achieve personal and organisational goals and who, through this collaboration, create what we call the organisation.

Freedom from the Organisation

The organisation provides a learning place for the development of shared values and beliefs among its participants. These values and assumptions become part of the world views of their participants. A paradigm shift in organisations therefore brings with it a new world view, a new set of expectations about the way people should relate to each other, and a new set of values and aspirations. This shift was captured admirably by Peter Drucker in a recent interview with T George Harris (1993). Drucker provided the following graphic example:

> Take a hospital. ... One company I got to know in Southern California has a cleaning woman who came in as an illiterate Latino immigrant.

She is brilliant. She figured out how to split a bed sheet so that the bed of a very sick patient, no matter how heavy, could be changed. Using her method, you have to move the patient only about six inches, and she cut the bed-making time from 12 minutes to 2. Now she is in charge of the cleaning operations, but she is not an employee of the hospital. The hospital can't give her one single order. It can only say, 'We don't like this; we'll work it out'.

The point is, managers still talk about the people who 'report' to them, but the word should be struck from management vocabulary. Information is replacing authority. [Drucker, 1993: 116]

The shift from the Third to the Fourth Blueprint brought with it such a change in world views, even amongst those employed within organisations. Table 4.1 summarises broad features of the world views of those who gained their formative experiences in Third and Fourth Blueprint organisations.

The Third Blueprint: Corporate Citizenship

The organisations of the 1960s and 1970s had stable structures with defined, stable roles, and with predictable career paths. For individuals in such a system, self-identity and role become fused— the individual *is* what he or she *does*. As Emerson wrote, 'Do your job and I shall know you' (cited in Sullivan, 1990: 17). Identity (which is usually defined as that which remains the same while participating in change) was provided by the continuity of role. This was reinforced by a psychological contract of membership, of lifelong employment. For people in such a system a long-service award is not trivial—it represents the successful completion of reciprocal rights and obligations—the fulfilment, over time, of citizenship of the organisation.

Those in the integrated organisation come to value those things that support this self-definition. They value a group of behaviours that can broadly be termed 'citizenship' behaviour: altruism, conscientiousness, loyalty, teamwork, good relationships with others, and a general willingness to contribute to the system (Bateman & Strasser, 1984). In sum, they develop what Bateman and Organ (1983) refer to as the 'good soldier syndrome' (Bateman & Organ, 1983; Organ 1988).

Table 4.1 Differences in world views

Corporate citizenship pre-1980 (Third Blueprint)	Collaborative individualism post-1980 (Fourth Blueprint)
Identity	
Role as continuity	Self as continuity
Psychological contract	
Lifelong employment	Issue-related contract
Values	
Loyalty	Integrity
Service	Maturity
Field integration	Field independence
Processes	
Commitment	Negotiation
Career the responsibility of the organisation	Career the responsibility of self
Relating to the system	Traversing many systems
Membership of middle-range organisations	Collaborating with others on issues

As we have shown previously (Chapter 2) the essence of the integrated organisations of the Third Blueprint is an unshakeable nexus between the individual and the structure. People within them find that changes in organisational structure are often personally devastating because they require a redefinition of self. Part of the psychological contract is for employees to give high levels of commitment to the organisation in return for security, mentorship, growth and development. The responsibility for the development of the individual's career lies in the hands of the organisation and its human resource planning systems. In a very real sense, employees 'belong' to the organisation—they and their careers are owned by it!

The Fourth Blueprint: Collaborative Individualism

Individuals within loosely coupled network organisations simply cannot use structure and role as a definition of identity. They find themselves moving in and out of a whole series of systems of action, many of them temporary, which demand different role definitions. The structures in which they are engaged are temporary affairs, treated by participants as tools, as temporary expedients to achieve collaborative action. Structures can be changed to meet discontinuous events, and provide impossibly flimsy templates for definitions of identity.

Under such conditions, individuals turn to self-definition as an axis of continuity. They define their identities in terms of the unique set of vectors that they regard as self. For such individuals, the ability to tolerate the uncertainties of engaging in multiple, temporary systems of action demands a mature understanding of self. Those in network or collaborative organisations therefore become very concerned with self-mapping, getting to know and understand self, and getting to develop a mature self-acceptance.

This focus on self is not to be confused with selfishness, even though the latter is part of the commonly held stereotype of those who went through their formative organisational experiences in the late 1970s and 1980s—the young urban professionals or 'yuppies'. Those who have experienced the organisations of the 1980s, including yuppies, value collaboration, for they have come to terms with the need to network in order to deal with discontinuity.

However, the relationship they develop with others is not one of commitment to the *organisation*—it is one of commitment to the *issue*, to the mission and vision of the collaborative enterprise. It is the yuppie, for example, who supported Geldof's Band Aid and Live Aid in their mission to relieve starvation in Ethiopia, and who has rejuvenated the green movement.

In effect, the individuals in the network organisation go through a process of what Tucker calls 'mentally incorporating' themselves. Each individual becomes 'You, Inc.' (Tucker, 1987), networking and collaborating with others towards common missions. The individual accepts responsibility for self, for their own career development across many systems of action, and for the achievement of the organisational mission, and in return expects sufficient autonomy and empowerment to unfold activity. Deutschman quotes Bell South's Roy Howard as saying: 'the younger workers coming in now aren't as prone to mold their lives to fit our environment' (Deutschman, 1990: 23). They form an alliance with the organisation—they do not become owned by it. According to Drucker (1994), situations such as these point to a post-capitalist variation of Marx's notion of workers owning the means of production. He says:

> [I]n the knowledge society the employees—that is, knowledge workers—own the tools of production. Marx's great insight was that the factory worker does not and cannot own the tools of production, and therefore is 'alienated'. There was no way, Marx pointed out, for the worker to own the steam engine and to be able to take it with him when moving from one job to another. The capitalist had to own the steam engine and to control it. Increasingly, the true investment in the knowledge society is not in machines and tools but in the knowledge of the knowledge worker. Without that knowledge the machines, no matter how advanced and sophisticated, are unproductive. [Drucker, 1994: 100]

This rejection of being imprisoned by the organisation is expressed in its fully fledged form by a movement towards establishing real contracts with the organisation, or by becoming a consultant. Manter (1989) notes the propensity of the newer generation to prefer the freedom of consultancy. She quotes the case of Stuart Bauman, formerly a human resources vice-president in a large company, who 'in his mid-30s, began to see colleagues in their 40s and 50s who seemed "stuck and miserable"'. Said Bauman: 'I realized as I watched those people in their misery that I needed now while there was still time, to learn how to make career moves'. Bauman became a consultant with Towers Perrin (Manter, 1989: 66). Such people, says Manter, want freedom to set their own hours, to exercise their own values, and to make as much money as their talents will allow. The same drive, presumably, is affecting MBA graduates. Kotter reports that in 1991 only 23 percent of Harvard's graduating class of MBAs joined big business, as opposed to 36 percent in 1974. By the year 2004, 75 percent or more of the class will be working in small businesses (*Harvard Business School Bulletin*, June 1995).

This world view is a far cry from the compliance of the corporate citizen. It has much in common with the attitudes of what Kelley calls the 'gold collar' worker:

> These new workers are the gold collar workers, and they hold the key to the future. … Perhaps the most significant difference (between them and white collar and blue collar workers) pertains to the nature of their work and the freedom and flexibility with which they conduct it. They engage in complex problem solving, not bureaucratic drudgery or mechanical routine. They are imaginative and original, not docile and obedient. Their work is challenging, not repetitious, and occurs in an uncertain environment in which results are rarely predictable or quantifiable. Many gold collar workers don't know what they will do next, when they will do it, or sometimes even where. [Kelley, 1985: 8]

Collaborative individuals are emancipated by discontinuity, empowered by knowledge, and driven by values. They collaborate with others because they agree with their values and the joint mission, and not because of their commitment to the organisation. This is the 'inside-out' credo expressed by Covey, Chairman of the Covey Leadership Center:

> The inside-out approach says that private victories precede public victories, and making and keeping promises to ourselves precedes making and keeping promises to others. Inside-out is a continuing process of renewal, an upward spiral of growth that leads to progressively higher forms of responsible independence and effective interdependence. [Covey, 1990: 4]

To keep promises to ourselves while in an organisation requires that our values and those of the organisation are congruent. So the collaborative individual searches for clarity in the mission and vision of the enterprise. They work from the basis of mature self-acceptance, integrity of purpose, and a commitment to the issues. Within that value congruence, the psychological contract with the organisation is negotiative, not one of commitment—indeed, the average tenure for the knowledge worker, or the 'gold collar' worker, is less than four years (Kelley, 1985). They want, argues Drucker, autonomy and mobility (Drucker, 1989b).

As we shall see, it is not just knowledge workers who develop the values of collaborative individualism. Strategic alliances in general 'may be fragile, disrupting work force loyalty and stability' (*Personnel Administrator*, 1987). Moves towards award restructuring, multiskilling and other practices needed to handle discontinuity demand of other workers that they too cut the bond between themselves and the structure. This leads to a de-emphasis on job security which, as Doyle argues, 'will be increasingly regarded as anachronistic by employees throughout the next decade' (Doyle, 1990: 37). This, in turn, leads to a new view of the world as individuals negotiate with, and contract into, organisations with compatible values.

Commitment *v* Negotiation

The world of the good corporate citizen is one of reciprocal rights and obligations between the individual and the organisation. These come from commitment—an identification with the organisation. When the young worker joined the organisation in the 1960s it was with every expectation that he or she would develop a lifelong career within it. The organisation, in turn, was committed to nurturing and mentoring the career of the individual.

The relationship between the collaborative individual and the network organisation, in contrast, is negotiative and contractual. The individual moves between systems and organisations, developing an asset-base of skills and abilities and using these to contract into each organisation. They *are* value driven, and are keenly committed to the values and mission of the organisation. But they are decidedly not committed to the organisation as an end in itself or to blind loyalty to its commands. The organisation becomes not the end, but the means—the means to fulfilling the individual's own objectives and the agreed mission.

The severance of the bond between the individual and the organisation can be experienced as extremely painful by many in the organisation, for it is precisely the new negotiative contract that the good citizens find so distasteful. As their organisation moves from Third to Fourth Blueprint, they find the very things they stand for—loyalty and commitment—despised, and the things they hate—the pursuit of selfish ends—rewarded.

But if the pain for the good corporate citizen caused by being in a Fourth Blueprint organisation is great, the pain of being in a neocorporate bureaucracy is even greater. For example, the restructuring of education systems in Australia in the late 1980s and early 1990s left a well-recorded trail of personal devastation among some senior managers. Researchers from the University of New South Wales (Bergin & Solman, 1992) have shown how career educational administrators whose positions were eliminated or reconstituted by organisational restructuring frequently felt a sense of betrayal and experienced destructive, personal stress. Another researcher (Whyte, 1992) has shown that, faced with such circumstances, managers often adopt a stance of 'accommodation'. That is, they demonstrate surface commitment to the proposal for organisational change but privately work to undermine and sabotage it. It goes without saying that neither people nor organisation win in such situations.

Collaborative individuals do not find the neocorporate bureaucracy (NCB) any easier—for the opposite reason. It is not that the NCB will not fulfil corporate citizenship obligations, it is that they do not allow the construction or pursuit of the individual's professional identity. Faced with the overwhelming suffocation of work intensification, pseudo-devolution, inappropriate performance indicators—who can measure the performance of a professional when it takes, say, 10 years to get accurate feedback? —and the bureaucratia of management, many go through the process of *outering*. They disengage from the management in-group altogether, define themselves as part of the outgroup and focus exclusively on their professional activities. From there it is not a big step to outering altogether, to setting up their own small business and contracting with bureaucracies.

We do not see outering as a personally destructive, abandoned act; on the contrary, it is more often a constructive act of positioning oneself so that one can compose a satisfying professional identity. But the consequences for NCBs are profound—they have to learn to manage beyond commitment and loyalty, and manage what

Deutschman calls the 'Yiffie'—young, individualistic, freedom-minded, and few (they represent the bursting of the boomer bubble). In the end, this means full-scale conversion to Fourth Blueprint management.

Freedom from Institutions

The good citizenship view of the 1970s and early 1980s was echoed in the social relationships of Third Blueprint participants. These social relationships were structured in terms of membership of middle-range organisations and institutions such as unions, professional associations, Rotary, political parties or churches. The essential contract was commitment to the organisation itself in return for continuity of membership with its intrinsic and extrinsic rewards.

Group membership skills were important to effectiveness in such an arena, and individuals and organisations alike devoted much of their time and other resources to the development of team-oriented interpersonal competencies. Overall, the good corporate citizen of the tightly coupled organisation became the good citizen of the integrated society, belonging to, and bound by obligations to, its various institutions and teams within them.

The social and political relationships of the collaborative individual stand in sharp contrast. These individuals do not seek commitment to middle-range organisations for a definition of self or for direction on values and beliefs. Membership of organisations such as unions and political parties has been dwindling over the past few years (Lash & Urry, 1987) in favour of broader, collaborative issue-oriented systems such as the green movement, one-off charismatic or television churches, law reform movements and like systems, or in favour of more local processes such as plant-level negotiations in which the individual can have greater impact. Collaborative individuals do not 'join' such enterprises in the sense of membership, with its reciprocal rights and obligations—they collaborate and network with such movements on an issue-by-issue basis.

This is an enormous challenge to middle-range institutions, which are fighting for survival. In Australia, a senior union official, Kelty, gave warning to his unions of the need to 'transform the psyche of the nation'. Unions and other middle-range institutions cannot continue to rely on historical membership obligations for functioning; they have to clarify and redefine their mission in modern terms and offer real services to their clients. We agree with the overall thrust of the argument advanced by Lash and Urry (1987)—we are not seeing the end of unionism, or of large political parties and churches for that matter. But we are observing the beginning of a period of turmoil and restructuring as they attempt to come to grips with the postmodern era.

The social upheaval associated with empowered individuals has been a time of trial for those who cling to Third Blueprint world views. The basic nature of the psychological contract between people and organisations has changed. Individuals can no longer rely on the comfort of lifelong employment. In the first half of 1986 alone, the *Fortune 500* companies in the US shed 2.2 million jobs (Tucker, 1987). In Australia the restructuring of the public sector has seen individuals having to reapply, not always successfully, for their own jobs. As the nexus between the individual and the permanent job has been shattered, so have the identities of those within them, who have been left with an anxious reappraisal of their own skills and assets. This, in turn, has involved a search for a new, independent identity.

The situation is made even worse by the progressive collapse of corporatism—of the larger institutions of class, political party and religious organisation that also gave meaning and identity to the individual. In postmodern language this leads to a further 'decentring' (Lash & Urry, 1987) of identity, a 'liminality' (Martin, 1981) or threshold-like quality of the personality. People simply do not know who they are or what they could become. As their class and political identities evaporate, they lie perpetually on the threshold of an unknown identity.

There is a pessimistic, melancholic note in much of the post-modernist literature on the atomisation of both society and the individual. But on the positive side, the trauma of decentring may be balanced by the discovery of an emancipated identity, defined not by the external agencies of social and institutional membership, but by self.

Perhaps the most subtle and profound changes have occurred at national and international levels where we have moved to the age of the *diaspora*—the dispersion of people who share values and missions. As Toynbee, in a remarkably prophetic passage, argued just before he died:

> The present-day possibility of participating simultaneously in a number of different organisations promotes individual liberty. Allegiances to world-wide diasporas, which cut across allegiances to local organisations, are both a safeguard for individual liberty and milestones towards the social unification of mankind on a global scale. [Toynbee & Ikeda, 1989: 142]

Country after country in eastern Europe in 1989 found itself liberated from the institutionalised domination of their communist parties by the momentum of diasporas—of networks of individuals collaborating towards a common vision. But this social change also has a negative face. As people locate themselves in diasporas and define themselves in terms of them, the nation-state identities created by post-war treaties are seen to be foisted upon them. This lies at the heart of the 'new tribalism', which ignores nation-state boundaries and which has torn apart the Balkans and much of Africa. Solutions that ignore the diasporas are likely to be short-term and unstable. Thus collaborative individualism is no social panacea: its weakness (disorder, a search for identity, and a lack of protection for the disempowered (discussed later)), lie in the shadows of its strengths (emancipation, empowerment, self-reliance and voluntary collaboration).

THE DEVELOPMENT OF COLLABORATIVE INDIVIDUALISM

The development of collaborative individualism has its roots in two key factors: *continuity* and the continuation of a tradition, and *discontinuity* and the impact of modern information technology.

Continuity: The Continuation of a Tradition

It is impossible to understand the emergence of collaborative individualism in the West without seeing it as an extension of deep-seated historically held values. The Christian–Judaic heritage (particularly the reformist Christian tradition) has always been individualistic. The West's historical consciousness is saturated with images of the individual soul standing alone before God for judgement. As St Peter reminds humanity in Kipling's *Tomlinson*,

[T]he race is run by one and one,
and never by two and two. [Kipling, 1958: 360]

Henley, that other apostle of nineteenth-century rationalism, asserts in the same vein:

I am the master of my fate

I am the captain of my soul. [Henley (1907), *Invictus*]

Such images are particularly a part of Anglo-American colonial traditions, with their archetypal heroes, the colonial pioneers, striding out into the wilds of the unknown continents, alone and unafraid. To be sure, while these images survived strongly in the US, they were diluted in Australia by an anti-establishment emphasis on mateship, with its origins, perhaps, in the scarcity of women and the need for the early settlers to survive in the face of the machinations of the New South Wales Rum Corps. In the management area, these individualistic values were strengthened and translated into managerial ideology by humanist psychologists such as Maslow and McGregor, with their emphasis on the proactive individual and self-actualisation.

The move towards teamwork and groupwork during the 1950s and 1960s is thus more surprising than the re-emergence of individualism in the 1980s. Perhaps it is best understood in terms of the dominance of the Second and Third Blueprints during that period, with their focus on social causation and integrated systems. Perhaps the uneasy combination of individualistic values and authoritarian organisations that dominated the First Blueprint had to give way to a period in which we learned the art of integration and collaboration—and that, in turn, provided a more suitable background for the re-emergence of individualism.

Whatever the historical argument, there has been a strong stream of individualistic images emerging in the past few years, which represents a departure from our immediate past of team-work and mateship. What we are observing is the strengthening of one stream of values in Western society, a subtle change of emphasis in myriad values. It is significant to note, for example, that a survey of the heroes of British youth in the mid-1980s placed Geldof and Thatcher in the top three! And those who participated in, and gave drive to, the emancipation of eastern European countries echo the same mix of a diaspora of youth giving massive support to autonomous, independent older leaders like Gorbachev and Walesa.

It is customary to think of Western individualism as existing in sharp contrast to the Japanese group achievement ethic and Japanese corporate paternalism. Yet there is considerable evidence that the Japanese system is also changing in response to the pressures of the late 1980s and early 1990s. Mroczkowski and Hanaoka, for example, report that the Japanese employment relationship is being redesigned:

> Japanese employees realized that they could not place all their reliance on their companies and that they would have to start relying on themselves. Today, the latest catchword amongst personnel specialists in Japan is 'employee self-reliance'. It is not only that the attitudes and expectations of employees—especially younger employees— are changing, but the companies themselves are creating programs designed to promote new attitudes of self-reliance. [Mroczkowski & Hanaoka, 1989: 50]

They have, in effect, modified the lifetime employment system in favour of greater mobility between organisations, and a more independent set of attitudes. This is not to argue that Japanese organisations are becoming 'like the West', but it does suggest that Japanese employees and organisations are beginning to confront similar problems to those in the West.

Discontinuity: The Arrival of Modern Information Technology

The final catalyst that enabled a more atomistic structure of isolated individuals to become a proactive system of collaborative individuals was information technology. The groundwork had been laid in the empowerment of the individual through improved educational and living standards. Improved information technology allowed those individuals to share the same vision and to coordinate their action despite loose structural coupling. It allowed a movement from physical commuting to tele-commuting—people were able to come together without being together in space. It allowed the use of coupling devices such as just-in-time technology, which orchestrated the efficient collaboration of dispersed units.

But modern communication technology did more than facilitate networking. It turned out to be an instrument of further empower-ment for both the broader body of individuals and their leaders. It allowed two simultaneous changes in social power relationships. First, it brought information to a multitude of individuals in society and, since knowledge is power, it brought power to the people. Second, it facilitated the simultaneous *centralisation* of information; it allowed CEOs and prime ministers alike to access immediate feedback on events and sentiments in their loosely coupled systems.

Paradoxically, while information technology has given power to the people, it has also given power to the transformers. Clinton and Howard are today, as were Reagan, Hawke and Thatcher in their heydays, able to manage by instant plebiscite (by reading the polls) and to virtually ignore their middle-range party institutions—as long as they stayed within the limits of popular opinion. There were obvious stylistic differences between them—the economic Howard, charismatic Clinton, empathetic Hawke, institutional Reagan, and the cold but implacably committed Thatcher—but the overall patterns of their activities were remarkably similar.

Individuals and leaders in business organisations found them-selves with similar opportunities. Managers and workers at the coalface were able to obtain more information about the mission and activities of their organisation and of the broader networks of which it was a part, and this empowerment enabled them to take autonomous action. CEOs were able to use information technology to communicate their aspirations and values to dispersed employees without the tight control provided by enormous corporate head-quarters. The CEO of a merged large multinational, for instance, was able to contemplate the development of a new corporate culture through his own personal example. 'I am just going to get out there and show them', he said. And, with the aid of information technology, that is exactly what he did (Limerick et al, 1984).

The issue of information technology will arise again in later chapters where we will look at corporate culture, and the tricky problem of placing checks and balances on the power of transformational leaders. For the moment, it is sufficient to note that the development of sophisticated techniques of communication enabled the world view of collaborative individualism to become translated into a feasible social system. This translation has not been experienced as positive by all. Indeed, as observed earlier, the move to a new system, based on different values, with different patterns of interaction, will be experienced as abhorrent by many, and chaotic and destructive by many nation-states.

CHARACTERISTICS AND COMPETENCIES OF THE COLLABORATIVE INDIVIDUAL

The world view of collaborative individualism worked through into network organisations makes special demands on those within them. Central to the world view is an image of the nature of the collaborative individual. This image is partly prescriptive and partly descriptive, for it describes the values and competencies individuals should have—and in many cases have come to develop. Overall, the central vision of the collaborative individual is reasonably coherent. The shorthand descriptions above have included adjectives such as 'autonomous', 'proactive', 'collaborative' and 'mature'. But the concept is so important to the processes of network organisations that it is worth further exploration.

Looking across our studies and the emergent literature on managerial and organisation development (eg Morris, 1987; Hargreaves, 1994), it is possible to identify a number of key characteristics, competencies and skills of collaborative individuals. They are:

- autonomous;
- proactive;
- empathetic;
- intuitive and creative;

- transforming;
- politically skilled;
- networking;
- mature; and
- lifestreaming.

Each of these fields of characteristics needs to be developed in greater detail.

Autonomous

The concept of autonomy implies both a *voluntary* relationship with the organisation, and a set of characteristics that are needed to operate that relationship successfully. Thus the concept of delegation is subtly being transformed in current management usage into the concept of devolution. To delegate in managerial terms means to pass on to others the right to make decisions on *your* behalf. To devolve is to pass on to others the right to make decisions on *their own* behalf. Stated differently, autonomy in a collaborative relationship presupposes that the relationship draws its strength from its own perceived value, not from coercion or administrative need. Of course, to make your own decisions on your own behalf requires a certain set of personal qualities. Thus 'autonomy' describes neither personality nor role: it describes what Bales more accurately called 'personality-role space'—the person-in-process (Bales, 1970).

Proactive

Autonomy and proactivity go hand in hand. The autonomous individual must accept responsibility for acting collaboratively with others in the interests of the organisation as a whole. They have to initiate synergies with others in networks; they have to be able to cope, to fix their own problems and those of their groups: 'the need is for … the will to manage … and so we are saying to people—you do not have to be reactive, you must go out and plan and act on the business' (Limerick et al, 1984).

Autonomous, proactive individuals do not adapt easily to the middle ranks of Third Blueprint organisations. They are more easily described thus: 'You will find them in the corners, making a nuisance of themselves, pushing at the limits'. But truly mature collaborative relationships enable individuals to present themselves more assertively and confidently than is possible in either the Third Blueprint team situation or in the social atomisation of bleak postmodernisim.

Proactive individuals are prized in network organisations, where they are recognised as 'self-driven', 'doers', 'ambitious' people with a 'bias for action' (Limerick & Cunnington, 1987; Peters & Waterman, 1982). Such proactivity, more often than not, is combined with a healthy pragmatism—with what Australian managers call 'a smell for the dollar', 'common business sense' and 'a good knowledge of what the business is about' (Limerick & Cunnington, 1987).

Proactivity does not imply a random atomistic readiness to go into action: it implies the steady attention to and pursuit of an ideal, and the readiness to act on things in that pursuit. Without an ideal, as William James (1905) pointed out many decades ago, there is no will. As the following chapters will address, the management of network organisations rests heavily on the identification of the mission and vision of the organisation. The development of proactivity relies in part on techniques for enabling managers to envisage the desired goal.

Empathetic

Managers are no longer required to be the rational analysts of a decade ago. The development of vision and mission and the communication of such symbolic processes demands that they be *managers of meaning*. The glue that holds the network organisation together is a common corporate culture, a shared world of meanings that allows independent, autonomous action to be focused and collaborative. The management of this common world of meanings calls on empathetic capacities among managers that were largely irrelevant in the Third Blueprint. At its best, the creation of collaborative individualism provides a means by which people who might otherwise be discarded or left to fend for themselves can be assisted through periods of frustration, distress and need. It also provides a means of strengthening resolve so that the manager's responsibility in addressing personal issues changes from one of dependency-generating paternalism (what Fromm and Maccoby, 1970, call 'symbiotic relatedness') to one of mutual preservation of integrity (which Fromm and Maccoby call 'love').

The focus on the development of empathy and love in managers has brought with it new areas of interest and lively debate in the management literature. The 1980s saw a re-awakening of interest in the use of the Jungian personality typology, represented in the burgeoning use of the Myers–Briggs personality inventory, and the Hogan and Champagne Personal Styles inventory among managers.

The use of such instruments has had two potentially very important spin-offs. First, the Western stereotype of the rational thinking-sensing manager has come under challenge as just that—a Western stereotype, and a malestream stereotype at that. It has become clear that other societies, such as those based on Zen Buddhism, give as much or even more weight and legitimacy to the affective functions of intuition and feeling, and that management in such countries (eg Japan) has benefited from such capacities (Pascale, 1978). Moreover, the debate has highlighted the extent to which these functions are associated with gender stereotyping in the West. Males are seen to be thinking-sensing, without much feeling or intuition. In fact, the latter qualities are frowned upon in males: as Neville Wran, a past premier of New South Wales (born in the workers' suburb of Balmain) put it in a moment of stress, 'Balmain boys don't cry!'.

Related in some ways to the use of the Jungian typology is the current interest in brain laterality and personality functioning. This area of study has become one of the most controversial in psychology, and is no less so in managerial psychology (see, for example, Gazzaniger, 1983; Levy, 1983). For many years, the thesis of a linear, logical left hemisphere of the brain and an empathetic right hemisphere was impossible to test satisfactorily, because the only feasible way of observing brain functioning was through the Aero-Encephalogram (AEG)—which, with a five per cent mortality rate, was not a preferred experimental procedure! Modern techniques, including CAT scans and biochemical procedures, have enabled more sophisticated research.

With this research, however, the picture has become even less clear and more controversial. This has not stopped a number of authors in the field of management and training from writing unconcernedly about 'right-brain' abilities. Peters and Waterman, for example, argue that excellent organisations place great store on, and are very sensitive to, the creative, intuitive, and empathetic right-brain processes of their members (Peters & Waterman, 1982). The relationship between brain laterality and personality is so complex that no simple generalisations can be made or accepted with equanimity. There is nothing inherently unacceptable in using phrases such as 'right-brain' activity as a sort of metaphorical shorthand for intuitive, holistic, empathetic processes (indeed, words such as those in the Jungian typology are so cumbersome that we, too, have often been driven to use the shorthand form!), as long as this does not imply a simplistic acceptance of the laterality thesis.

So the reader should be warned: we are prepared to be academically naughty for the sake of brevity, and may slip into left-brain, right-brain language. In the interests of caution, however, we prefer to use the longer field of phrases, such as feeling, empathy and intuition.

Intuitive and Creative

Associated with an emphasis on empathy in collaborative individualism is a focus on non-linear, intuitive and creative intellectual capacities. An increasing number of managers and academics alike have attacked the West's business and management schools for their exclusive emphasis on linear rational analysis (Limerick et al, 1984). Such an approach was part of the Third Blueprint.

The management of discontinuity, however, has placed a greater emphasis on the need for non-linear, entrepreneurial, intuitive, creative abilities. Managers in the Frontiers study were unequivocal: they felt that managers should be 'creative', 'imaginative', 'innovative', 'able to think laterally' and 'able to ask "what if?" questions'.

The development of such abilities requires that management schools move away from their current educational paradigms towards an increased focus on process learning (Limerick et al,

1984). It goes without saying that individuals who are intuitive and creative may also be seen as spontaneous and unpredictable in their working relationships. They will form relationships that evolve from their own needs and interests and they will perplex Second and Third Blueprint managers by generating project outcomes that run against the grain of hierarchical dictates. In other words, some managers in Fourth Blueprint contexts may find themselves confronted with what they may interpret as problems of control, when in reality they are experiencing postcorporate creativity.

Transforming

Part of the dynamics of the Fourth Blueprint has been an overwhelming interest in what, following the work of Burns (1978), has come to be called 'transformational leadership'. Transformational leaders are conventionally visionary, inspirational figures possessing certain ideals and goals. They are charismatic and can inspire intense emotion. To do this, they must empathise with and hold accurate perceptions of others.

Organisational transformations are usually sanctioned at the top. Some writers argue that that is where transformational leadership exists, and that below that level the need for transformational leadership diminishes and the need for 'managers' increases. Leaders create goals, while managers help implement them. Those in Fourth Blueprint organisations would be less than comfortable with the whole direction of the current debate. They would be particularly ill at ease with a forced artificial distinction between leaders and managers. As Zaleznik notes: 'This concept of leadership changes the idea that "it is lonely at the top" to the idea that the position "at the top" involves shared purposes, mutual trust and implicit support' (Zaleznik, 1990: 13).

A model of shared leadership, or multiple leadership roles (eg Limerick, 1970, 1976) is far more congruent with collaborative individualism. While transformational programs are initiated at the top, many of those who implement them require similar transformational skills. And even after transformation into Fourth Blueprint organisations, the network organisation faces such a chronic state of flux and discontinuity that it makes constant demands on transformational capacities—on 'leadership'—among a majority of its managers and, indeed, among participants. Authentic Fourth Blueprint organisations construe processes of transformation more broadly than is implied in much of the leadership literature. Contemporary leadership approaches have not for the most part thrown off the shackles of 'legitimate power' that were part and parcel of the origins of 'authority' as Weber and others construed it. The result is a continuing fascination with control of 'leaders' over 'followers' that is not only irrelevant, but damaging, in postcorporate organisations. We agree with Gronn (1995) that:

> The conception of leader–follower relations underpinning the full range model of leadership, as its advocates now prefer to call it, is grossly theoretically undernourished. A strong air of human perfectability infects the exposition of TF leadership, and the terminology about elevating people to previously unheard of levels of potential, altered levels of awareness, autonomy, mission and vision, and even the very idea of transformed individuals and organisations, carries with it the hallmarks of a religious crusade and being born again. [Gronn, 1995: 25]

What is required of participants in Fourth Blueprint organisations is that they have the flexibility to use both managerial and leadership skills, and the judgement to separate their positional authority from leadership as an attribute of the total organisation. We will return to this issue of shared leadership in Chapter 6.

Politically Skilled

The capacity to transform a large number of people into a collaborative network and to keep it in touch with the rest of the environment makes enormous demands on political skills. When change is incremental, relatively stable relationships can be maintained between the organisation and its environment. These require few novel transactions between them. Discontinuity, however, requires that organisations continually move into new fields, disturb current states of equilibrium, and push at the boundaries of the possible. To do so safely and successfully requires effective political processes between the organisation and its environment.

The internal dynamics of loosely coupled systems also demand effective political processes within the organisation. The changing nature of alliances and networks within and between organisations requires that their members have 'a capacity to see the big picture', can 'understand the political climate' and are able to 'deal with the political environment' (Limerick et al, 1984) of both the organisation and its environment. Moreover, in highly discontinuous situations, individuals may develop a desire, even a yearning, for security, safety, tranquillity and solitude. Collaboration can degenerate into conformity and complacency (Hargreaves, 1994), creating challenges for the manager that are unique to the post-corporate era.

Managers had become largely politicised by the mid-1980s. In the Frontiers study, for example, they nominated 'government decision-making' as one of the most dominant threats to their organisations. They could not simply treat these as constraints and react to them. Part of the ethos of the proactive individual is that they act on the environment, and so managers set out to act on the governmental environment. One Australian CEO notes, in retrospect, that 'our biggest breakthrough was in developing techniques for dealing with government'.

The success of Iaccoca in dealing with the interface between Chrysler and the US government underlines the same point. The collaborative individual today has to be able to 'see the big picture', 'have a helicopter view', 'understand the political climate' and 'deal with the political environment' (Limerick et al, 1984).

There are three aspects to this set of political skills. First, each individual needs to develop a macro view of the organisation—a holistic appreciation of its relationships with its environment. Second, participants need to be sensitive to and understanding of the internal political processes of the organisation, to be part and parcel of what the Japanese call its *nemawashi* so that they can network with others, and form long-term relationships of trust. And third, they need to be skilled in political transactions—in recognising and forming coalitions, in the use of power and sometimes force, and in processes of negotiation and compromise.

At first glance such skills seem a far cry from the picture of the open, harmony oriented manager of the 1960s and 1970s, striving to create a larger arena of shared information between all. Some have been led to suggest that modern organisations may, and sometimes should, focus on a 'power' approach to organisation development (Dunphy & Stace, 1988). The truth is that the old-fashioned harmony virtues remain important, for without them there can be no trust, but also that managers in networks require political skills. The final chapters of this book raise a whole host of questions about power relationships in network organisations. Neither managers within them nor organisational analysts can afford to ignore such issues. John Akers, IBM's CEO, comments:

> You have to be politically capable. You have to be able to sell your ideas, to get people on the team. Those who can't get things done, who can't get people to work on their problems, don't rise as high as people who can. [cited in Waterman, 1987: 205]

Networking

Loosely coupled systems are so characterised by multiple systems of action that individuals within them need a capacity to network between their elements. They are held together by common cultures, shared worlds of meanings and values. The management of these cultures often requires empathetic interpersonal contact, backed up by acute political sensitivity. Therefore an integral part of the development of shared corporate cultures is the presence of individuals who can, as Pettigrew, after an English study, puts it, 'walk the talk' (Pettigrew, 1986).

Peters and Waterman noted a similar concept in their excellent organisations in the US; they were characterised by 'MBWA'—Management By Walking About. Australian participants in network organisations are just as dedicated to the need for networking. In the Frontiers study we came across one divisional manager who refused to have an office. His secretary had an office, and was able to page him where necessary, but he did not. He was constantly 'walking about'.

There are two elements to these networking skills. The first is the capacity to see the broader picture—networking is not a random process; it is a purposeful process driven by an overarching vision of the whole and an understanding of its various parts. The second is an empathetic sensitivity to the values of each of the subcultures, a capacity to deal with the symbolic management.

Mature

The task of networking throughout very different autonomous systems makes enormous demands on the maturity of the individual, who is no longer able to cling to a specific role within a coherent structure for a sense of identity. Participants in Third Blueprint organisations know who they are because they know *where* they are. Participants in Fourth Blueprint organisations do not have such continuity. Moreover, concepts of time and space, which were integral to both organisational identity and organisational cohesiveness and control in earlier blueprints, assume different meanings in postcorporate contexts. Hargreaves (1994a) describes it thus in the work of teachers:

> Scheduled meetings and planning sessions may form part of collaborative cultures but they do not dominate the arrangements for working together. In collaborative cultures, much of the way teachers work together is in almost unnoticed, brief yet frequent informal encounters. ... Collaborative cultures are, in this sense, not clearly or closely regulated. [Hargreaves, 1994a: 20–1]

Fourth Blueprint managers regulate themselves: they require a degree of maturity in accepting and facilitating workplace cultures that for many will be a real challenge. Indeed, the manager's own identity and self-concept may come under threat as this challenge is explored.

The problem of identity may be somewhat less precarious in Japanese management systems. A stable social structure defines identity for its members, and allows them to traverse a range of work roles without insecurity. But the atomistic, individualist, nuclear family structure of Western society offers no equivalent comfort. The result is that participants in network organisations in the West have to develop a mature self-concept. They have to know who they are, regardless of where they are. This calls for a considerable degree of self-insight and self-acceptance. They have to understand and accept their own identity values and relate these to the core values of the organisation as a whole, for this is what provides a continuity of relationship with the organisation.

Such a sense of identity, if it is to survive discontinuity, must be flexible and robust enough to grow and evolve. The concept of the 'career-resilient workforce' developed by Waterman and others addresses this point:

> By a career-resilient workforce, we mean a group of employees who not only are dedicated to the idea of continuous learning but also stand ready to re-invent themselves to keep pace with change; who take responsibility for their own career management; and, last but not least, who are committed to the company's success. ... And it means moving on when a win–win relationship is no longer possible. [Waterman et al, 1994: 88]

Fourth Blueprint organisations, therefore, focus on organisational development strategies that allow their managers to map and understand themselves and their strengths and weaknesses, and to continue to learn by self-evaluation (Limerick & Cunnington, 1987). Even with such facilitation, the demands of networking through multiple systems of action and of handling their political interfaces can be highly stressful. Thus, concomitant with an emphasis on self-mapping, is a widespread and still growing use of stress-management programs in such organisations.

Lifestreaming

At the heart of collaborative individualism is a very different understanding of the ways in which people are living out their lives. As Burgess-Limerick (1995) found in her study of women owner-managers of small businesses, people today are concerned with composing their own lives—with what she calls 'lifestreaming'. They do not see self as a static structure; but rather as a lifestream, to be developed and composed on a day-to-day, year-to-year basis. For example, they bring work and home together into a set of relationships which are continuously evolving and which define who they are. Organisations that do not give support in the process of developing their lifestreams will lose them and cannot be sustainable in the long term. This, as Deutschman (1990) pointed out, is the generation that can say 'No!'.

The flat organisational structures found in Fourth Blueprint organisations are fundamentally important to the lifestream compatibility of the organisation, for they give the individuals within them the capacity to participate in moulding the organisation and its systems to their own circumstances. In doing so, these organisations are able to attract and keep the individuals they need. In later chapters we will show how organisations can be managed to make them lifestream-compatible.

The delayering and flattening of the organisational structure does not in itself lead to lifestream compatibility, as the emergence of the neocorporate bureaucracy has demonstrated. The fundamental configuration of the organisation has to be changed to one which manages beyond hierarchy. Much of the stress that is leading to burnout in so many workers today can be attributed to naive delayering. If you simply remove layers of people without simultaneously removing the hierarchical system, those who are left have to manage the hierarchy in addition to their usual roles. Such work intensification will lead, and is leading, to human decay. What is required is a transformation of the entire system to a horizontal, empowered system which can be adapted by the participants to be compatible with their lifestreams. This basic principle underpins many of the other characteristics of socially sustainable high performance organisations that are described below.

What is also required is a collaborative individual who is self-reliant, and whose lifestream focus gives them a fallback position when their relationships with the organisation become intolerable. Levinson, in updating his *Harvard Business Review* classic on burnout, makes this point well:

> [W]e are living in a new age of self-reliance. On a personal level, we must get feedback, advice, and moral support from family and friends. On a professional level, we each need to develop a fallback position. By *fallback*, I mean an alternative course of action if the current job fails us. [Levinson, 1996: 162]

If Burgess-Limerick is right, they will have a number of fallback positions—they will be continually crafting new possibilities from the material of their lifestreams.

THE GENDER ISSUE

Current management literature is characterised by a vigorous debate on similarities and differences in the managerial styles and competencies of men and women. Much of this debate is structured within the context of Third Blueprint complex hierarchical organisations. Indeed, this framework is so limiting that Ozga and Walker (1995), for one example, accuse management literature of 'gender blindness' despite, or perhaps because of that debate:

> The vast, repetitive and intellectually arid literature on leadership recycles idealised masculine virtues of decisiveness, incisiveness and strength ... . In the conventional literature and thinking, then, there is little acknowledgement of gender. [Ozga & Walker, 1995: 36]

The advent of Fourth Blueprint organisations has not made that debate any easier—in fact, it has added considerably to its complexity.

The debate is indeed a complex one. There is a strong stream of evidence and opinion that suggests that the notion that there are real differences between the managerial and leadership behaviours of the two genders is a 'myth' (Statham, 1987; Rizzo & Mendez, 1988). If this were so, both genders would be equally challenged by the movement towards collaborative individualism. But, as Shakeshaft (1987) points out, much of this research is androcentric. It views women from a male point of view, within a male context, using male theoretical structures. Shakeshaft and others suggest that there are real differences between men and women in their managerial attitudes, styles and behaviour (Shakeshaft, 1987; Chusmir, 1985; Eisenstein, 1985; Marshall, 1987; Bass & Avolio, 1994; Brigid Limerick & Lingard, 1995). Shakeshaft, for example, argues that women in educational administration:

- [A]re more likely than male administrators to use an informal style with teachers and others;
- communicate differently from male administrators as they use more expressions of uncertainty, hypercorrect grammar, and give more justification for statements;
- listen more, while men interrupt more often;

- are more democratic and participatory, while men make final decisions and take action without involving others;
- use power tactics such as coalition, cooption and personality;
- are more likely to withdraw from conflict or use collaborative strategies, whereas males use authoritative responses. [Shakeshaft, 1987, cited in Ehrich & Limerick, 1989]

Such a blend of consensual and relational skills and orientations seasoned by a readiness to use political power tactics is what collaborative individualism is all about. This is perhaps what Rogers has in mind when she suggests that the male mechanistic world of control and objectivity would be replaced by a female world view. She suggests that the three new leadership concepts of transformative leadership, vision and empowerment all embrace the values of the female ethos (Rogers, 1988). Loden (1985), focusing on women's creativity, concern for people, interpersonal skills and intuitive management, voices similar sentiments:

In some respects, it seems that women managers may be better prepared to cope with the challenges of the future than many traditional leaders who succeeded in the past. [cited in Ehrich & Limerick, 1989: 4]

Therefore, says Peters, 'Gone are the days of women succeeding by learning to play men's games. Instead the time has come for men on the move to learn to play women's games' (Peters, 1990: 142).

The picture, however, is not quite as easy to interpret as that. First, Third Blueprint male-oriented power structures still pervade industry. For example, Blackmore (1987, 1995) argues that the traditional masculinist model of leadership stresses power, individualism and hierarchy. Eriksen (1985), too, notes that independence is typically thought of as a masculine characteristic. Therefore discrimination against women still persists: 'It is distressing but true that male resistance to women's advancement persists as the single most difficult challenge of the late twentieth century' (Raynolds, 1987: 268). For this reason, women have been turning away from formal organisations in droves, and creating their own small businesses. It is projected that they will own

50 per cent of all small businesses in the US by the turn of the century (Raynolds, 1987).

But even if hierarchies disappear in favour of networks, flat structures and collaborative individualism, there will inevitably still be pockets of discrimination and even mass discrimination. The problems of women and minority groups will not disappear. While collaborative individualism de-emphasises the importance of the hierarchy, it raises a different power problem. It is a system that depends on the empowerment of the individual, for without such empowerment individuals cannot participate autonomously and proactively in the system. In a society that is characterised by systematic discrimination on a gender basis, individualism can be extremely problematic, for it may leave women (and other minority power groups) exposed.

Collaborative individualism does not assert hierarchical power, but equally it does not solve the problem of power-balancing, either. Staples makes this point brilliantly:

> Individual empowerment is not now, and never will be, the salvation of powerless groups. To attain power equality, power relations between 'have', 'have-a-littles', and 'have-nots' must be transformed. This requires a change in the structure of power. [Staples, 1990: 37]

This issue of power balancing might seem a far cry from the concerns of the manager. But managers are deeply involved in problems such as equity, equal employment opportunity, union relationships, freedom of information, anti-discrimination, diversity management and the like on a day-to-day basis. Collaborative individualism will affect these issues, and management needs to prepare itself for these effects. The problem is therefore examined more fully in the final chapters.

Even this discussion of gender, so far, misses the point that is central to Fourth Blueprint thinking. If the organisations are to be gender-compatible, rather than gender-blind, they will have to be compatible with women's ways of being. We will discuss this point in the final two chapters of this book. In the meantime, it is worth closing this brief discussion with the words of Ozga and Walker:

> Feminist management requires an explicit commitment to forms of organisation that reflect and value women's strengths. That organ-

isational form is not hierarchical, but ensures participation; more than that, it produces a situation in which there is constant and critical engagement with the possibility that things could be otherwise. [Ozga & Walker, 1995, 39]

DEVELOPING THE COLLABORATIVE INDIVIDUAL

Discontinuous change can be an alienating experience for the good corporate citizen, for it takes away the predictable structures and processes that have become part and parcel of their self-definition. Western society cannot, from an ethical, social or economic point of view, exclude or drive an entire cohort from the workforce. A move towards Fourth Blueprint organisations entails the problem of helping many come to terms with a new world view and developing the skills to be effective in a different organisational milieu. It is tempting to solve this problem by focusing on the corporate citizen and 'changing' him or her. That would miss the point entirely, for it is the organisational *system* as a whole and the human resource management system within it that must change.

A program that successfully moves all its participants to share a new structure, a new vision and a new culture is essentially a quantum, transformational, strategic change program (cf Dunphy & Stace, 1988; Kilmann et al, 1985; Doz & Prahalad, 1988). Such change processes are discussed in Chapter 7. It is worth focusing for the moment on changes to human resource management processes, which are more directly aimed at developing some of the key competencies of collaborative individualism.

Transfer Responsibility for Career Path Planning

A fundamental step is to pass responsibility for career planning back to the individual. This involves the removal of secrecy in career path planning, asserting the legitimacy of career paths that straddle the organisation and other possible employers, focusing on the career assets of the individual as an end in itself, and relating organisational opportunities to the plans of the individual. This is close to what Schein calls the 'internal career' (Schein, 1990).

The likely outcome of such activity is to assist the individual to construct not a linear role-related career path, but what Driver (1985) calls a 'spiralling' career path, which consists of a combination of vertical and lateral career moves. Indeed, it is likely to have an even more profound impact on individuals. It will enable them to move away from the conventional hierarchical industrial model of 'career' as the addition of more responsibilities within a system, to a more holistic model of career as a path in the individual's life (Connell, 1985: 157), or to what Brigid Limerick has described (1995: 69) as 'accommodated careers'.

There is some evidence that it may be particularly important for women managers to engage in clear career planning in order to provide enough momentum to break through discriminatory systems (Hodgson, 1985). Overall, it is the act of taking respons-ibility for one's own development in terms of one's own identity that helps break the bond between the individual and the structure, and that enables the individual to move into more network relationships.

Develop Contracts with Employees through Objectives Negotiation

Related to the concept of transferring responsibility for career management to the individual is the technique of forming shorter term career contracts (not to be confused with employment contracts) with the individual. Rather than engaging in manage-ment by objectives (setting organisational objectives for the individual), human resource managers can overtly compare the objectives of the individual with those of the organisation and negotiate a contract of activities and mutual objectives that satisfy both. It is useful to set time horizons and sunset clauses on each contract and to negotiate times for the re-evaluation and renegotiation of each contract.

It is significant that the three relocation agencies in our Canadian study of redundant managers reported that those who were most successful in handling their redundancies were those who were accustomed, in their life span, to contracting their activities out to others. They were more autonomous, and more ready to form partnerships with others.

Help Employees to Map their Assets

As Tucker argues, one of the first steps in dealing with discontinuity ('when the rules of the game change') is to:

> Start by incorporating yourself mentally. Incorporating yourself mentally requires you to begin thinking of yourself as 'You, Inc.', a company with one employee: you. [Tucker, 1987: 58]

Tucker's article was so relevant to the self-mapping, self-evaluating process that it was used widely by Canadian agencies to help unemployed 50-year-olds to adjust to the new world view. But that is too late. What is required is assistance to all employees in mapping, evaluating and developing their career assets.

The process is mutually advantageous to the organisation because it gives human resource management a better overview of the current and potential resources available within the organisation, and facilitates clearer placement expectations on the part of both the individual and the organisation.

Help Employees to Map their Intuitive and Empathetic Capacities

The use of scales such as the Myers–Briggs scale in training and counselling programs does help to legitimate right-brain capacities. More important, however, is a more systematic and consistent use of action learning as a primary training and development strategy. It promotes creativity and experimentation. More than that, it promotes the very paradigm of collaborative individualism. It places the onus for proactive intervention squarely on the shoulders of the individual, but at the same time places each individual in a collaborative learning arena. Finally, its focus on process skills helps the individual to get feedback on self-in-process and to develop empathetic capacities.

Help Employees to Develop Marketing and Negotiating Skills

The first thing that corporate citizens have to do in starting again after redundancy or in confronting a change towards more discontinuous systems is to learn to 'market' themselves. In terms of their previous role stability and loyalty, they tend to find the entire process difficult and distasteful, for they feel that the organisation has reneged on its reciprocal commitments to them.

For those who find themselves in the hands of outplacement firms, exposure to self-marketing skills comes too late. The development of marketing skills requires self-mapping, the development of an awareness of the broader labour market within and without the firm, training in career strategy formulation, and training in the presentation of self. An essential part of marketing is networking, and it may be particularly important for women to expand their networking activities (Brigid Limerick et al, 1994).

Finally, marketing skills and negotiating skills go hand in hand, for the individual needs to market to find appropriate contracts, and negotiate to arrive at equitable contracts. Therefore part of the ongoing program of management development must include a focus on both sets of skills.

It may be necessary to come to terms with the fact that, as people become more confident of their own abilities and their capacity to exploit them, the organisation may have to help the individual to move outside the organisation. Delbecq and Weiss report that much of the culture of Silicon Valley springs from this recognition:

> To be sure, as much as possible, the executives would like people to find opportunities for entrepreneurship inside their company. But a certain percentage of time they realise it is not possible and they see part of their obligation to assist the continuous spin-off process that has created a unique and prolific genealogy in Silicon Valley. [Delbecq & Weiss, 1988: 37]

Open up the Information System

Instead of keeping the implications of organisational changes and expansion to themselves and making unilateral placement decisions, organisations need to learn to open up information on the job market within the organisation. Individuals who are managing their own careers can then plan to take advantage of opportunities that arise. Such information should cover the range of the business units in larger organisations, and might even be extended to information on other organisations with which the firm is establishing long-term alliances. Japanese organisations are already promoting intercompany human resources leasing and transfer through regional company groupings called *igyoshu koryu* (Mroczkowski & Hanaoka, 1989). To back these up:

> Companies like Toshiba and Yamaha use extensive career counselling to help employees develop new skills and attitudes that would enable them to survive in a horizontal labour market. [Mroczkowski & Hanaoka, 1989: 51]

Manage by Empowerment

At the heart of all of these ways of developing collaborative individualism is the philosophy of empowerment. As Mills (cited in Pickett, 1992: 10) argues: 'Clusters [networks] make possible the full empowerment of people'. Conger's definition of empowerment is a good one:

> We can think of empowerment as the act of strengthening an individual's beliefs in his or her sense of effectiveness. In essence, then, empowerment is simply a set of external actions: it is a process of changing the internal beliefs of people. [Conger, 1989: 18]

Self-mapping, career-path transfer, contract formation and the like are some of the external actions that help the individual achieve a sense of effectiveness. But what gives them force and guides participant behaviour is a commitment to the importance of individual autonomy and the power to exercise it on behalf of the organisation. Some participants and organisations have embraced this view. Doyle, GE's senior vice-president of external and industrial relations, has done exactly that:

> People-power will be a source of corporate opportunity to the extent that it compels us to liberate employees to do only the important work

by eliminating the unimportant work. We have begun to recognize that at GE, where we are encouraging our diverse business cultures to be guided by what we call 'speed, simplicity and self-confidence'. [Doyle, 1990: 38]

Yet many managers, says Tom Brown of *Industry Week*, are 'fearful of empowerment'. Will it not flatten managerial ranks, rob managers of power and throw the organisation into decision-making turmoil? Such reactions can be associated with feelings of threat and resentment (Manz et al, 1990). These views and feelings, of course, are lodged in that old enemy, the zero-sum model of power: if you get some, I have less.

Just as networks and alliances are built on strengths, not weaknesses, so the philosophy of empowerment is one of accumulative power—it implies more power to all. Collaborative individualism would be impossible without it. Notes Brown:

> It's not an easy process ... Empowerment can be a process of 'plugging in' the entire organisation to the goal of getting—or staying—ahead. Properly managed, it can be electrifying. [Brown, 1990: 12]

Improperly managed, empowerment programs can actually be harmful (Matthes, 1992; Rice & Schneider, 1994). Used within the neocorporate bureaucracy, they can be plainly manipulative. Empowerment requires not only the full use of Fourth Blueprint management technology—it requires that it be exercised within the very different participant-centred paradigm of the Fourth Blueprint. This paradigm is explored more fully in our final chapter.

Confront Contrived Collegiality

Collaborative individualism as we have described it can pose challenges that some managers may prefer not to acknowledge. It generates confidence and assertiveness, but this may be perceived as a challenge to the status quo. It encourages self-reliance but this may be construed as rejection of team work and of traditional leader–follower relationships.

These challenges are often misconstrued, particularly in neo-corporate bureaucracies. There are important lessons to be learned, for example, from the educational literature, where it has been shown that senior managers frequently have trouble 'letting go' their authority when confronted with postcorporate reforms (Mulford, 1996). Compelling evidence exists that reforms that have masqueraded under the cloak of 'devolved decision-making' and 'teacher empowerment', but which have retained real authority in the hands of administrators, have had negative effects on teachers' morale, status and image (Rice & Schneider, 1994; Australian Teaching Council, 1995). The clear lesson to be learned is that collaborative individualism can be easily transposed into pernicious forms of contrived collegiality. If this happens, the implications for workplace productivity in its numerous forms are very serious. Again, the critical aspect of managing through collaborative individualism is the participant-centred paradigm in which it is lodged.

Allow for 'Outering'

We have made the point on several occasions that collaborative individualism is different from forms of individualism and of collaborativeness that characterised earlier organisational blueprints. If forced, it loses authenticity and generates cynicism. Voluntarism is part of its essence. The question that then arises is 'What if individuals, or, indeed, groups, opt out?'.

Such problems are difficult to manage in Third Blueprint organisations and neocorporate bureaucracies which do not recognise them to be legitimate. But in Fourth Blueprint organisations, everybody is 'out' and 'in' simultaneously. They are taking part in a constructive act of self-positioning or lifestreaming as well as collaboration. Each individual's construction of reality is as important or as valid as anybody else's, and these constructions have to be overtly negotiated in Fourth Blueprint organisations. Such negotiation need not end up in homogenised world views. A Fourth Blueprint organisation has the maturity to accept its rebels, its revolutionaries and perhaps even its anarchists. A Fourth Blueprint participant is aware that in conventional organisations only a small percentage of an organisation's conventions are ever challenged, with the result that only a small percentage of the organisation's creative potential is ever harnessed (Hamel, 1996).

A CONTINUING BATTLE

Discontinuous change, network organisations and collaborative individualism are tightly interwoven. The degree of discontinuity is increasing in the environment, and no organisation will remain untouched by it. We are therefore witnessing the progressive demise of organisation man and woman—of the good organisational citizen, or the good soldier. In this era of a battle for power between the individual and institutions, collaborative individuals are slowly winning. They won outside the Berlin Wall and the Moscow White House and they are slowly winning inside the everyday organisations of the West. The victory is not assured and there may be many setbacks such as the tragedies of Croatia and central Africa, as people search for alternative bases of self-definition.

But there is much that is positive in what has been won. We are seeing the end of the 'good corporate citizen', but not the end of citizenship. Citizenship, of organisations or of society, has been redefined in terms of a clear recognition and negotiation of reciprocal rights and obligations between the individual and the institution.

But this new dispensation does bring with it new and unpredicted challenges. It is certainly problematic for the good soldiers of our current organisations. But it is also problematic for the new collaborative individuals. Both groups are in uncharted waters and both will contribute to our emergent organisational systems over the next few decades. That is the nature of discontinuity.

CHAPTER 5

METASTRATEGY: BEYOND STRATEGIC MANAGEMENT

> *Real strategic change requires inventing new categories, not rearranging old ones.*
>
> [Mintzberg, 1994: 109]

Managerial work can be viewed as managing myth, symbols and labels ... because managers traffic so often in images, the appropriate role for the manager may be evangelist, rather than accountant. [Weick, 1979: 237]

THE IDEA OF the modern manager as an evangelist is somewhat shocking to managers raised in the rationalism of the Third Blueprint. As it happens, Weick is probably overstating the case in order to make a point. The point does need to be made, though, for it is critical to the management of loosely coupled systems—of networks. The strategic management of such organisations is largely the management of mindsets; it has to do with constant attention to establishing and communicating the very meaning of the system.

Indeed, for most organisations that face discontinuity, or for loosely coupled network organisations, the management of the identity of the organisation becomes the key strategic problem. What is needed is a model of strategic management that *integrates* the processes of vision and identity management with the more customary processes of strategic design and implementation.

Traditional models of strategic management come nowhere near to doing this. They have two problems. First, they lack a self-transcendent capacity. They do not lead the organisation to re-examine its very identity assumptions. Because they assume continuous change, they do not help the manager to get above current definitions of the organisation, and to transform those if necessary.

Second, they underestimate the strategic importance of the management of meaning. We need to explore both of these points. In this chapter, we will explore a self-transcendent model of strategic management. In the next, we will look at the processes of day-to-day, microstrategic management. But first, it might be helpful to look briefly at traditional models of strategic management.

MODELS OF STRATEGIC MANAGEMENT

Table 5.1 presents a summary of stages in the development of strategic management. It suggests that as we moved from First to Third Blueprint thinking, our models of strategic management began to change. Each new stage attempted to add to the contributions of the previous stage and to overcome some of its problematic features.

Business Policy

Organisations within the First Blueprint had functional structures, and there was therefore a need for a general management perspective that could coordinate the various specialities. For some 30 years prior to 1933, the Business Policy course at Harvard had provided such a perspective. In 1933 this program was expanded to include the study of 'top management' or 'the top management point of view'.

The Harvard approach did ask top managers to focus on both internally integrating the firm, and integrating it with its environment (Summer, 1980: 76–7). But it had two problems. First, it still thought of this task as developing *functional* policies for each functional area, and so it did not really address the structure of the organisation as a whole. Second, it was basically *reactive*. Using a 'general survey' (Gilmore, 1973: 33–4), it would scan the functional areas, then scan the environment, and then adjust the areas to meet the environment. Thus it was ideally suited to slowly changing environments. Third, because it focused on functional structures, it also focused on the single organisation: it had little to say about networks.

Table 5.1 Approaches to strategic management

Approach	Contribution	Positive	Problematic
Business policy (First Blueprint)	Top management perspective	Top management role	Functional Reactive
Long- range planning (Second Blueprint)	Proactive perspective	Top management role Proactive	Functional
Strategic planning (Third Blueprint)	Focus on the whole	Top management role Proactive Holistic	Separation of planning and implementation
Strategic management (Third Blueprint)	Integration of planning and implementation	Top management role Proactive Integrated planning and implementation	Incrementalist Rationalist
Meta-strategic management (Fourth Blueprint)	Self-transcendent, transforming capacity Focus on meaning Multi-organisational	Top management role Proactive Holistic Integrated planning and implementation Handles both incremental and transformational change	Creates problems of power distribution

Long-range Planning

The Business Policy approach could not cope with the more complex and rapidly changing conditions of the 1950s. It became evident that a new approach was needed. As an intermediate step, the process of sporadically sizing up the environment was replaced by the development of a 'long-range plan'. In this new approach, the sizing up of the situation became translated into a reappraisal of the suitability of present policies.

The practice of long-range planning was significant in that reactive management could become more proactive. However, the new method was still largely based upon the analysis of *functional* problems. As long as a firm's diversification remained confined to related businesses the method had some hope of coping, but once diversification took place into products and markets that were different from the core business, it became virtually impossible to base a firm's strategy on functional analysis. What was needed was an approach that would deal with the organisation *as a whole* and relate it to its environment.

Strategic Planning

Thus was born the logic of strategic planning. The new method centred upon relating an organisation's strengths and weaknesses to the opportunities and threats present in its environment ('SWOT' analysis). It recognised that better policies at only the functional level could not provide the desired direction for overall corporate activity. In general the new approach was grounded in the open systems logic of the Third Blueprint—the organisation is open to the environment and must adapt to it. Thus Andrews of Harvard University wrote:

> General management skills center intellectually upon relating the firm to its environment and administratively upon coordinating departmental specialities and points of view. [cited in Learned et al, 1969: 9]

Katz puts it even more explicitly. The purpose of strategic planning is 'to develop a personally useful, explicit way of thinking about the business enterprise as a total system in a total environment' (Katz, 1970: 8). Such a 'holistic' organisation–

environment approach begins with a general overall view of the organisation in its environment. It then works through an iterative (cyclical) process of developing a strategy that will match strengths with opportunities while minimising weaknesses and threats.

This approach was a considerable advance on the previous more reactive approaches. Yet it still had a number of limitations that became more exposed as the environment grew more turbulent. The first problem had to do with the anticipation of future trends. In the pursuit of an impossible dream, many firms attempted to use sophisticated computer-based planning models only to find that such sophistication was no antidote for environmental discontinuities. Kami comments: 'The planning lessons to learn from such rapid social changes are not how to foresee or predict better, but how to react faster' (Kami, 1979: 149).

A second problem was that the strategic planning model, which treated the firm as one large monolithic entity, was unable to deal with the problem of how to allocate scarce resources to each of its parts. The solution was to view the firm 'as composed of many largely independent units whose strategic directions are independently achieved' (Hax & Majluf, 1984: 127)—hardly an approach likely to yield the competitive advantages of synergies!

A third problem was that it offered no guidance as to how to make the strategic processes work in a given organisation. The logic of the strategic planning process could select the 'best' method of competition in terms of products and markets, but it had nothing to contribute to the question of implementation—of the design and management of structures and systems that would translate the plan into action. The design of such action systems should ideally be part of the strategic process. Without it, many plans are likely to be lost in the CEO's left-hand drawer.

Finally, if it had little advice on how to allocate resources between business units, it had even less to say about how to relate to other organisations. It still treated the business of the organisation as that which lay within the organisation.

The cumulative effect of these problems is that the strategic planning process can often stifle creativity and become an instrument of control (Wall & Wall, 1995).

Strategic Management

The strategic management paradigm, fathered by Igor Ansoff, brought strategic planning and strategic implementation together. It consisted of a coherent, continuing set of managerial processes that formulated and implemented both incremental responses and new strategies aimed at handling discontinuity. Hofer et al, for example, define strategic management as:

> [T]he process that deals with fundamental organisational renewal and growth, with the development of the strategies, structures and systems necessary to achieve such renewal and growth, and with the organisational systems needed to effectively manage the strategy formulation and implementation processes. [Hofer et al, 1980: 7][1]

Such a development marked a point of transformation to Fourth Blueprint thinking, in its focus on processes of renewal in the face of discontinuity. Yet in the early 1980s it was frequently lodged within the competitive, as opposed to entrepreneurial, cultures and structures of Third Blueprint organisations (see Figure 3.1). For example, in the same year that Hofer and his colleagues penned their brave words, Quinn published a book on his own research into 'how real companies actually arrive at their strategic changes and how this fits into accepted formal planning and management concepts' (Quinn, 1980: 2). His results favoured the thesis of incrementalism:

> The most effective strategies of major enterprises tend to emerge step by step from an iterative process in which the organisation probes the future experiments and learns from a series of partial (incremental) commitments rather than through global formulations of total strategies. Good managers are aware of this process, and they consciously intervene in it. They use it to improve the information available for decisions and to build the psychological identification essential to successful strategies. The process is both logical and incremental. Such logical incrementalism is not 'muddling' as most

---

[1] Reproduced with permission from Hofer, C. W., Murray, E. A. Jnr, Charan, R. and Pitts, R. A. (1980). *Strategic Management: A Casebook in Business Policy and Planning.* Minnesota: West Publishing Company.

people understand that word. Properly managed, it is a conscious, purposeful, proactive executive practice. [Quinn, 1980: 58]

Strategic management was fundamentally incremental in both planning and implementation. It had little hope of capturing the problems of managing discontinuity. It also had little hope of handling the problems of networks, for the very concept of the strategic network—as we have seen—requires a massive, non-incremental paradigm shift. Finally, it focused so much on matters of core business and restructuring that it ignored the deeper levels of the social sustainability of the organisation-in-context (Dalton et al, 1996).

Towards Metastrategic Management

The main problem of the strategic management movement was that it was based on conditions of the 1970s. At that time it was undoubtedly appropriate. But incrementalism, logical or otherwise, in the face of discontinuity is downright dangerous!

Up to this point the unwary reader might have taken us to imply that discontinuity is the permanent and only environmental condition of the late 1990s. Yet a careful analysis of our models shows that this is not a position that can be taken seriously. Figure 3.1 suggests that the dominant problem in organisations is that they have to handle both gradual, familiar change *and* discontinuity. Writing on this subject recently, Mintzberg offered the following distinction between strategic planning and strategic thinking and the relevance of each in times when change is multi-dimensional. (It is a distinction that supports the difference between the strategic management of earlier blueprints and what we propose in this chapter as Fourth Blueprint metastrategy.) Mintzberg says:

While certainly not dead, strategic planning has long since fallen from its pedestal. But even now, few people fully understand the reason: *strategic planning* is not *strategic thinking*. Indeed, strategic planning often spoils strategic thinking, causing managers to confuse real vision with the manipulation of numbers. And this confusion lies at the heart of the issue: the most successful strategies are visions, not plans.

Strategic planning, as it has been practised, has really been *strategic programming,* the articulation and elaboration of strategies, or visions, that already exist.

Strategic thinking, in contrast, is about *synthesis.* It involves intuition and creativity. The outcome of strategic thinking is an integrated perspective of the enterprise, a not-too-precisely articulated vision of direction. [Mintzberg, 1994: 107–8]

Loosely coupled systems are able to handle both kinds of problem—but they are still different problems. In order to make this point clearer, it is time to turn to a concept developed by Stephen Jay Gould, 'punctuated equilibrium'.

A Punctuated Equilibrium Model of Change

Gould writes:

Speaking most generally, our usual concept of time and history, abetted by traditional gradualism, views change as continuous and intrinsic, and structure as a temporary incarnation of the moment. The alternative view, the basic vision underlying catastrophism if you will, sees stable structure and organisation as the usual state of things, and change as a rare and disruptive event provoking rapid shifts from one configuration to another. [Gould, 1989: 64]

The model of punctuated equilibrium was originally developed by Eldredge and Gould to explain the evolution of animal species. It sees change as a rare discontinuous event interspersed with relatively long periods of structural stability. However, the idea behind punctuated equilibrium has been 'discovered' independently by a number of other researchers in different areas, including, for example, the work of Kuhn (1962) on paradigm changes in science and Koestler (1975) on path-breaking dis-coveries. Both suggested a recurrent pattern of activities that moved from equilibrium to crisis and back again.

The application of the model of punctuated equilibrium to individual organisations would suggest that the lifecycle of an organisation would be comprised of brief periods of discontinuous rapid change followed by periods of relative stability. Today discontinuities are occurring at a faster and more furious rate, yet at the same time, between discontinuities, the organisation has to get on with the daily business of competition.

The model of punctuated equilibrium has three major implications for strategic management. An adequate strategic process today must meet these requirements:

- It must *straddle* continuity and discontinuity. Although it is not possible in advance to predict when such changes will occur, we do know that when they do happen they will threaten the very survival of the organisation, unless it changes its configuration. The change from one configuration to another will involve a quantum jump—a discontinuity in the organisation's very identity. Unfortunately, traditional strategic management models do not deal with such issues. The concept of 'meta-strategic' management gets much closer to such quantum leaps.
- It must be constantly reappraising the very identity and mission of the organisation as new discontinuities arise. What is needed is a *self-transcendent* capacity. The late Erick Jantsch has written of the capacity for self-transformation and evolution in systems terms as follows:

But it is not sufficient to characterise these systems as open, adaptive, nonequilibrium, or learning systems; they are all that and more; they are *self transcendent*, which means that they are capable of representing themselves and therefore also of transforming themselves. [Jantsch & Waddington, 1976: 9]

Mintzberg argues that strategic thinking has the capacity to create what he calls a 'not-too-precisely articulated vision of direction', or new 'categories of meaning' which facilitate both adaptation to a changing environment and the involvement of employees from across the organisation in the planning process. But it is more than that: to deal effectively with a discontinuity, the organisation may have to critique and transform its very identity and self-concept, which strategic management takes for granted or changes incrementally. This means that, during periods of discontinuity, the strategic manager must pay a great deal of attention to problems of identity—strategic management and the management of meaning become one.

- Since they frequently face discontinuity, and their own past does not prepare them for their future, strategic managers will have to learn to use the resources of others—to learn to use strategic networks. This means that they will have to transcend their own organisation's identity, and define it as part of a broader, *second-order identity*—that of the strategic network. The definition of the network's identity is doubly important, for that is what basically keeps the network together.

What is needed, then, is an approach to strategic management that continually addresses the problem of identity, and that therefore focuses on the management of meaning.

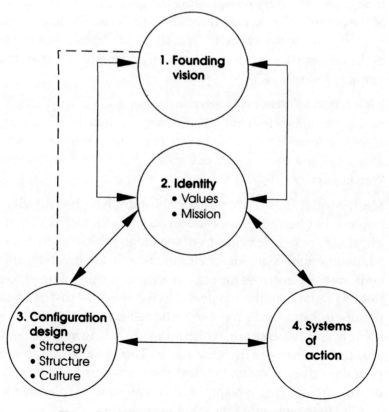

Figure 5.1   The metastrategic management cycle

THE FOUR ELEMENTS OF
METASTRATEGIC MANAGEMENT

Metastrategic management fulfils this need by starting with the concept of a metastrategic cycle that links together vision, identity, configuration and organisational action. This cycle is depicted in Figure 5.1.

The metastrategic management cycle has four basic elements within it:

- founding vision;
- identity;
- configuration design; and
- systems of action.

A *metastrategic design* brings together all of these elements—vision, identity, configuration and systems of action—into a coherent whole. We will first trace the cycle in its entirety before returning to a more detailed consideration of how to manage the various phases of metastrategic management.

Founding Vision

Schein (1983) has commented on the impact of the founder on the culture of the organisation. This impact has largely to do with the founder's vision for the organisation as a whole. Bennis and Nanus argue that such vision is vitally important:

> To choose a direction, a leader must first have developed a mental image of a possible and desirable future state of the organization. This image, which we call a vision, may be as vague as a dream or as precise as a goal or mission statement. The critical point is that a vision articulates a view of a realistic, credible, attractive future for the organization, a condition that is better in some important ways than what now exists. [Bennis & Nanus, 1985: 89]

We found such a vision behind the activities of most of the founders in our Frontiers and Silicon Forest studies. As we noted in 1984: 'All of our organisations have a dream, a Utopia which they find persuasive and which directs their activities' (Limerick et al, 1984: 8).

For a founder, such a vision seems to be a precursor to many of the decisions they will take. From our discussions with entrepreneurs in the Silicon Forest, attempting to go it alone after being a part of a large corporate monolith, it is evident they had a very clear idea of what type of business they desired to build. This idea was related to both the values and the ends or purpose of the organisation. In other words, they knew what the desired identity must be like in terms of the values and purposes it must represent rather than the products and markets it must secure. Indeed, they often explored many different product–market–technology combinations before selecting one that had sufficient promise to justify the building of an organisation, and during this period their vision remained unaltered.

Identity

The vision of the founder becomes established in the minds of those at the strategic apex of the organisation as a shared overall image of the identity of the organisation. This identity image consists of a number of elements, including:

- its overarching values; and
- a continuing vision of the potential of the organisation as it moves through the environment and through time—a vision of its mission.

The notion of 'identity' is a difficult, subtle one. The word 'identity' comes from the Latin *idem* meaning 'precisely that' or 'the same'. It refers to *that which remains unchanged, although participating in change*. In many ways it is analogous to the concept of self at the personal level. While it is relatively enduring and continuing, this identity image is capable of change in the long term; like the identity image of the individual, it may go through periods of growth and transition. It is also capable of rapid, traumatic, transformation in moments of crisis.

Identity has no reality outside of the meanings attributed to the organisation and shared by its members. It is, in effect, a socially constructed 'reality'. It is a holistic, inarticulate image that often defies logic, represented subtly in the symbols, language, myths, labels, allegories and metaphors of the organisation. But for all its vagueness, it gives legitimacy and continuity to action. Millett (1994), in a grounded study of traumatic changes in three Australian tertiary education institutions, found that the central core social process of the organisation undergoing such change is one of redefining identity. Identity, personal or organisational, is always problematic for the Fourth Blueprint participant. Yet the more effective organisations plough ahead into uncharted territories, constantly confronting the need to redefine identity. As Welch is reported to have commented: 'In the nineties, the heroes, the winners, will be entire companies that have developed cultures that instead of fearing the pace of change, relish it' (in Tushman & O'Reilly, 1996: 20)

Effective strategic managers do attempt to make the identity image more concrete and accessible, often by writing it down in the credo, philosophy or mission statement of the organisation. For example, Dayton–Hudson's philosophy,

> [R]eflects or explicitly states the basic beliefs, values, aspirations and philosophical priorities that the strategic decision makers are committed to emphasize in their management of the firm. [Pearce, 1982: 19]

Basically, though, as Pearce observes, 'discussions of self-concept do not appear per se in company mission statements' (Pearce, 1982: 21). They are reflected in the statements, but not encompassed by them.

Configuration Design

The identity of an organisation, then, is a holistic image, often vague and implicit, of the continuing nature of the organisation as it moves through social space and time. Those at the strategic apex of the organisation, or at the hub of a network, who hold this image must translate it into something more practical, into an integrated, operational model—a design that brings together a desired *strategy, structure* and *culture* of the organisation into a coherent whole.

Like identity image, the *configuration design* of the organisation may exist at different levels of explicitness and conscious articulation in different organisations. As organisations come to face discontinuity, it becomes crucial that top management makes it more explicit, for it provides continuing direction for the temporary, loosely coupled systems that are characteristic of network organisations. The clearer the overall configuration design is, the more it allows autonomy. It enables members to constantly experiment with the operational objectives, with structures and control processes, with strategic and operational values, and with the rituals, symbols and routines in which values are embedded.

In particular, the more the organisation moves towards internal networks, the more important it is to make the configuration design explicit, for it describes the common system in which the units, despite their autonomy, seek synergy and it provides the basis for most of the kinds of integration that replace hierarchy (see Chapter 3).

Systems of Action

The configuration design of an organisation provides a template for the development of the ongoing *systems of action* that together form the organisation. The entire metastrategic design that links configuration and identity can only become actuality when various practical systems are developed to meet the needs of different product–market segments specified in the design. Desired structures are translated into real structures. Control designs are turned into real control systems. Formal and informal communication systems are set up, together with routines and rituals that express the organisation's values, or that make action predictable, or that create a problem-solving capacity.

It is more accurate to think of these systems as being composed of *actions*, rather than people. People come together to create these systems of action. They negotiate them, and give them substance. Any single individual may move between many such systems, particularly in network organisations.

While people create these systems of action, they may eventually come to have a momentum of their own. They become routinised, and over time these routines may be slowly modified. Imperceptibly, these modified systems of action may lead to a slow change in the very identity image of the organisation, which is shared by those within it. The cycle becomes closed: it moves from identity to configuration to systems of action to identity.

So the process of movement from vision to identity to configuration to systems of action is an 'ideal' one. In periods of stability, the actuality of the ongoing systems of action feeds back to influence the identity image of the organisation held by its members, often including those at the strategic apex. What the organisation *does* develops a momentum of its own, and becomes what the organisation *is*. This was seen to be a major problem by many of the CEOs in the Frontiers study. Each felt that they had little control over the shape of the organisation: it no longer reflected its foundation identity, and it could not easily be changed to a new identity. All within it were prisoners of its own implacable systems of action.

Systems within Systems

As in all models of social action that draw on the systems paradigm, it is possible to think of systems within systems. In the next chapter we will show that at any stage of the metastrategic cycle, or in any part of the cycle, participants may be using a very similar process to the metastrategic cycle. Thus, for example, the managers and participants in a school as a whole may have gone through the cycle for the school. Within it, though, the music department, say, may have gone through a similar cycle for its department. They may have asked: 'What is the changing identity of the music department (eg does it embrace all students)? What is its vision (eg to bring out the music in all)? What configuration will best achieve this (eg we must become boundaryless and use the resources of all in our community)? What systems of action will achieve this (eg shall we get parents to teach in the school)?'. Of course, they will be anxious to ensure that the (microstrategic) cycle they create is congruent with the metastrategic design of the school as a whole.

Just as there are subsystems within the metastrategic cycle, so the cycle is often part of larger metastrategic cycles. Thus within a network, an organisation will have its own cycle, but it will also be part of a larger *second-order* metastrategic cycle for the network as a whole in which the participants will have come to an understanding of the identity, vision, configuration and systems of action for the network.

The issue of systems within systems should not be regarded as problematic or confusing by the reader—indeed, it should give leverage in the task of changing levels of analysis. What is of concern within all systems is the extent to which the parts are compatible and mutually reinforcing: it helps to use the same system of analysis for the parts. It is readily apparent that continuous attention to the whole cycle is crucially important in managing loosely coupled systems. The systems of action that are brought together do not share a common hierarchy and it is difficult for them to take on a momentum of their own. The partners and the participants need a continual reaffirmation of their common identity and values, and of the shape and mission of their organisation.

MANAGING THE PHASES OF METASTRATEGIC MANAGEMENT

In conceptualising metastrategy as process, it is possible and helpful to think of cycles or phases of management, including:

- *Phase 1: founding*—a period of discontinuity;
- *Phase 2: consolidation*—a period of relative equilibrium; and
- *Phase 3: renewal*—a period of discontinuity and reconfiguration.

From renewal, the organisation would proceed to consolidation, and then again to renewal as discontinuities develop—and so the cycle of punctuated equilibrium proceeds.

Each phase makes its own unique demands on the management of organisations. For example, managing identity in a period of equilibrium is very different from managing identity in times of crisis. We will therefore look at metastrategic management in each of these phases. In each phase we will first look at managing the modern loosely coupled organisation that looks for internal networks, and then look at the more specific problems of external networks.

Phase 1:   Founding—a Period of Discontinuity

The founder of an organisation or a network has the critical responsibility for establishing the entire metastrategic cycle, and for ensuring congruence between the values and mission of the organisation, its strategy, structure and culture, and its ongoing systems of action. The cycle begins with an act of vision.

An act of vision

All organisations come into existence as an act of vision. Some person or group of persons develop(s) a mental image of how people and resources can be combined to satisfy some form of human need. It may be as vague as a dream or as precise as a business plan, but this vision must exist and it must be sufficiently compelling to act as a focus for sustained human effort. As Ulrich and Wiersema note:

> A vision, or strategic intent, looks to the future and establishes a sense of direction to an organisation. It goes beyond gaining 'fit' through assessment of strengths, weaknesses, opportunities and threats and emphasizes the long-term intent of the firm ... It offers a road map of the future, generates enthusiasm, focuses attention, and instils confidence. [Ulrich & Wiersema, 1989: 118]

This vision acts as the nucleus about which may form the metastrategic design that goes from identity, through configuration, to action. It represents a future desirable state of the organisation—desirable in the minds of the founder and those at the strategic apex of the organisation. It will often incorporate an image of a desirable mission, values and even a hoped-for configuration of strategy, structure and culture. It is not necessary that this image should exist in detailed form at the time of founding, when it is often vague and imprecise, but it must give sufficient direction to be turned into an identity image. It must provide, as Morris points out:

- [A] future direction;
- an overall framework for an organisation's mission and goals; and
- an energising force for employee communication, participation and commitment. [Morris, 1987: 54]

The problem with any discussion of vision in today's managerial climate is that it is a concept that is so overworked and so under-defined that it becomes mushy. Collins and Porras (1996) make this point well and provide a helpful response of their own:

> We recommend a conceptual framework to define vision, add clarity and rigor to the vague and fuzzy concepts swirling around that trendy term. A well-conceived vision consists of two major components: *core ideology* and *envisioned future*. Core ideology, the yin in our scheme, defines what we stand for and why we exist. Yin is unchanging, and complements yang, the environmental future. [65–6]

That is, it has to articulate both the values and the desired future of the organisation.

A key feature of the founding period is the immanence of the corporate vision in organisational life. This is exemplified in Figure 5.1 by the existence of unbroken feedback paths between the founding vision, the configuration design and impressed identity. These feedback paths ensure that the configuration design remains responsive to both the corporate vision and the implementation of that vision in organisational form.

Vision in networks

The prime responsibility of the hub of any network is to develop the vision of the network as a whole. The partners who come together share the same initial problems of Bruggere and Hahn (1987) in the following section. But their difficulties are magnified, for not only must they develop a vision that surpasses those of their individual organisations, they must communicate it to a wide range of very different groups in their organisations. Part and parcel of their task is the development of the new mindset referred to in Chapter 3—they have to develop a vision of their own organisation as part of a second-order, broader, value-adding chain, of what Rayport and Sviokla (1995) refer to as 'the virtual value chain'.

Defining the organisation's identity

The process of converting vision into identity was highlighted during our study of the formation of high technology spin-off companies in the Silicon Forest. Two examples will illustrate the range of approaches.

> When we had just nine people, we sat around and we talked about what kind of company we wanted it to be and we made lists of the kinds of descriptors of the company; we had words, like we wanted to be ... let's say a customer oriented company, a technological leader, a hardworking company, a market driven company, an ethical company—we would talk about that at our staff meeting that we had; and as a result there was a lot of agreement as to values and the way we wanted to approach things and had reasons for each one of the things that we wanted the company to be. Because we talked about it, everyone had the same view of what we wanted to be and everyone communicated that same kind of flavour to people that they would hire in turn. [interview with Tom Bruggere, Mentor Graphics, 1987]

At the opposite end of the spectrum is the experience of Al Hahn of Support Technologies:

> Culture came into my mind 18 months before we started the company; we used to talk about it; to be very candid what I found when we started the company was that culture was an easy thing to talk about and a hard thing to accomplish. I was honestly surprised at what was happening because we began hiring people that came from diverse cultures, different values and it was hard to assimilate them and it was hard to figure out what to do about culture other than talk about it. [interview with Al Hahn, Support Technologies, 1987]

They had to work at communicating their image to those below. As they did so, they were developing what Pearce (1982) calls the organisation's 'self-concept': 'This idea—that the firm must know itself—is the essence of the company self-concept' (Pearce, 1982: 21).

As our Silicon Forest founders progressed, they were gradually learning to translate their vision into an ongoing image of the identity of the organisation, an image shared by others in the organisation. In the same way, managers who set out to change the identity of an organisation have to learn the same things. For example, Nuno D'Aquino, Chief Operating Officer of Carlton and United Breweries, in the process of transforming his organisation, focused his participants on a new identity and image of CUB—that of 'a lead organisation'. D'Aquino and his colleagues have indeed taken a leading role in pioneering the move towards Fourth Blueprint organisations within Australia. They are creative, self-defining and re-defining—and very effective as a cohesive but boundaryless organisation.

An agreed identity also provides coherence and continuity in times of equilibrium. It frames the minor and major decisions of the organisation as they proceed through the processes of logical incrementalism, giving each step purpose and thrust. It is more than an image of the operations of the firm and it is more than just defining the business that the organisation is in. Identity has to do with the *meaning* of the organisation in the minds of its members. It consists of two major elements:

- values; and
- mission.

We will consider each of these in turn.

Values

Most writers on corporate culture treat 'values' as an homogeneous class of variables, and make fairly rudimentary distinctions between different kinds of values. The exception is Lundberg (1985), who distinguishes between four levels of meaning: 'artefacts', 'perspectives', 'values', and 'basic assumptions'. We prefer to make another distinction between different kinds of values—transcendental, strategic, and operational. These are attached to different levels of organisational experience.

- *Transcendental values* are those that transcend all action: they hold true, whatever the field and whatever the particulars of the situation—they are held to be universally true, and are ends in themselves. The true meaning of transcendental is 'beyond the sphere of knowledge that is attainable by experience'. Therefore, *transcendental values* are closely associated with the organisation's metastrategy and identity. They include values such as 'respect for the individual', 'honesty' or 'caring', which are not bound by experience (in contrast with operational or strategic values, which are), and which are beyond the reach of the ordinary, everyday experience. In general they tend to be values that are ends in themselves, related to the higher nature of humanity. In a sense they define 'what *kind* of people we would like to be'. The example of transcendental values in Australian Catholic Schools illustrates this point well.

TRANSCENDENTAL VALUES IN AUSTRALIAN CATHOLIC SCHOOLS

As an example, prominent educator Hedley Beare (1995) tells us that three of the values built into the operation of Catholic, as opposed to state, schools in Australia are subsidiarity, pluriformity, and complementarity. *Subsidiarity* requires that, in designing a system, you start at the parochial or local level, not from the 'centre' or the 'top'. *Pluriformity* is a logical sequence. It denotes diversity or a plurality of forms. If a parish or a community believes that a certain configuration of schooling best suits its needs, conformity will not be imposed from without. *Complementarity* means that each part of the enterprise will dovetail, will complement, help and encourage the other parts, and will not impede them or get in the way of their functioning. Beare concludes:

> When these kinds of principles become the guidelines for the operation of the system, there develops a structure of organisation which is refreshingly different from the centralised formats so long taken for granted in the government systems. The organisation charts of the Catholic systems—if they are drawn at all—do not at all resemble those familiar boxes and lines of control which prevail in the public service. And why should they? Indeed, why should government schools need to conform with such a consistent stereotype? [8]

- *Strategic values* are those closely related to the strategic logic of the organisation, such as a commitment to market share, growth, or the value of technical excellence. It is recognised that they do not transcend all behaviour—they define that which is good for the particular firm in which the holders are located and that they are important for a certain strategic direction. They define not what kind of people we *are*, but what we *do*.

* *Operational values* are those intimately related to the day-to-day operations of the different parts of the organisation. They define *how* things are done. For example, they are often concerned with meeting production deadlines, safety on the job, reporting of expenses, etc. Sometimes they appear to be more nit-picking. For example, IBM Australia systems engineers are expected to wear *white* shirts, not striped or coloured. Those who work at Disney World are referred to as 'cast' members, not employees.

Thus, a founder who is establishing the identity of an organisation is usually trying to establish the transcendental values of the organisation—those that will remain the same, even though events require a change in the organisation's strategy or structure. The next step after that involves developing a configuration, and choosing strategic values. The final step, establishing systems of action, usually involves choosing operational values. (As we disclose in Chapter 6, workplace management in the Fourth Blueprint mirrors the principles of metastrategy. In so doing, it extends the underlying values of the metastrategic process to directly emphasise social sustainability, lifestream compatibility, communal belonging, power, sensitivity, and concern for diversity).

Mission

Mission, in a sense, is the ongoing established vision of the organisation, and the two ideas are often inseparable. But mission is perhaps more directed than vision—it has more to do with the purpose of the organisation. Purpose and meaning too are related: purpose gives meaning to both individuals and organisations. As Waterman commented:

> The need for meaning runs so deep in people that organizations must supply it if they are to renew. Many don't. The best they can come up with is 'more profit, continued growth.' Serve the shareholder, and the rest will take care of itself. That is a dangerous perspective. For most of us, 'the shareholder' is an abstraction—that fickle and faceless money manager who buys shares on rumours of good news and sells

on hints of adversity. If this view gives meaning, it does so for only a few. Pursuit of profit is hardly a cause that inspires loyalty or makes life meaningful for most people, unless company survival is at issue, and even then it may not be enough. Meaning should be bound up in the work we do. If we cannot find meaning in work, we spend our eight hours every weekday in quiet desperation. If we can find meaning in work, we can keep ourselves recharged, and the organizations we work for stand a chance of staying renewed themselves. [Waterman, 1987: 277]

Harman and Jacobs (1985) point to the same link between purpose and identity, which they call the 'psychic centre' of the organisation:

As in the individual, the effectiveness of the corporate personality depends upon the extent to which energies are released by some powerful centralized motive or goal, harnessed by the organization, clearly focused in the given direction ... The more developed and integrated the corporate personality is, then the higher are the values and goals it aspires to, the more powerful the energies it releases and harnesses.

The highest levels of corporate intensity are achieved when a company accepts the greatest challenge of them all—the pursuit of an ideal, the striving towards a high value, the quest for excellence.

Who determines the guiding values of a company? At the heart of the corporate personality is a deeper psychic centre, consisting of the company's most cherished beliefs, values and true mission, which give life-long direction to the activities of the corporation. [Harman & Jacobs, 1985: 66–7][2]

The identity—the psychic centre—of the organisation, then, consists of the transcendental values and the mission of the organisation. The founder starts with a vision, translates this into an identity, and then is able to go on to establish a configuration of strategy, structure and culture to express this identity.

---

[2] Reproduced with permission of the publisher, from *The Vital Difference: Unleashing the Powers of Sustained Corporate Success*, by Frederick G. Harman and Garry Jacobs © 1985 AMACOM, a division of the American Management Association. All rights reserved.

Network identity

Perhaps the most difficult and important task of network managers is to define the identity of the network. The difficulty of finding values that transcend those of different corporations and often of different cultures is precisely the reason why managers spend so much time choosing partners, and often go through prolonged periods of courtship. The values that are most important and that lie at the core of the network are the transcendental values of trust, reciprocity, fair-sharing and the like. The task of defining the mission of the organisation is just as difficult, for it must transcend the mission of the partners and yet also be compatible with them.

Thus network managers have to focus on defining the scope of the network and on the various symmetries and compatibilities of the goals of the network and those of the participants.

Creating a configuration design

At the stage of configuration design, the founder becomes involved in the determination of a specific design or configuration that reflects its chosen identity. The more conscious and deliberate this process is, the more direction it gives to the ongoing organisation. The more metastrategy is intuitively perceived rather than consciously articulated, the more the organisation will engage in a costly process of trial and error in pursuit of a 'sensed' configuration.

It is also more likely that managers will attempt to change one variable without considering the others. For example, Telecom Australia, during the 1980s, attempted a massive cultural change program without simultaneously changing the structure in which it was embedded. The program had little real impact until they eventually began to embark on structural change.

There is, therefore, a need for organisations to consciously articulate configuration in the same way that organisations today consciously formulate strategy. This will involve a deliberate attempt to design a mutually supportive pattern of strategy, structure and culture that expresses the identity of the organisation and that meets the needs of the environment.

As we saw in Chapters 2 and 3, a limited number of generic types of configuration exist. Implicit in every viable configuration is a 'logic' that shows how each element in the design is related to every other element. When this logic is consciously perceived, each element in the design reinforces every other element in a synergistic manner, and the ultimate metastrategic design achieves 'more than the sum of its parts'. When such a logic is not present, the energies of the organisation will not be focused in a coherent manner. In the worst case, negative synergy comes into play—the combined effect is less than the sum of the individual effects acting alone!

This logic and the operational configuration design as part of the overall metastrategic design tend to emerge in the months that follow the act of founding, and they require intensive communication. This was obvious, for example, in our Silicon Forest interviews. Thus, although the three founders of Support Technologies had agreed upon the twin values of having fun and serving the customer as guidelines for themselves, they did not attempt to pass these values or their implications systematically on to members of the organisation who subsequently joined: 'Our first priority was survival, to train these people and get the product out.' They assumed because each of the founders had developed an almost intuitive understanding of the way the others worked, this would automatically spread to other members of the organisation. However, because the organisation was small, there were no job descriptions and people were necessarily moved around a lot:

> [W]e had people at the bottom feeling the least secure; they kept getting shifted round; do this today, do that today and it doesn't take many paranoid neurons to say 'they're singling me out; I'm getting screwed by this; I used to manage this and this and this and now they've got me doing this...'.

Eventually a consultant was brought in to sort out this and a number of other problems. As a first step, the founders sat down and wrote four pages on 'the vision and values and so forth'. A representative group was then put together to define 'cultural expectations and behavioural expectations for the company' in the light of the company's visions, objectives and priorities.

Choosing a fit between strategy, structure and culture

We have traced the linkages between strategy and structure in earlier parts of this book. Figure 3.1 presented a fair summary of that discussion, and we will not labour those points again. It is necessary at this moment to look more closely at the third point of that triangle: the choice of culture.

The notion of a 'choice' of culture would be rejected outright by a number of analysts, who would ask whether a culture can be 'chosen' or 'managed' at all. Such a question is a vexing one. There are some who see a culture as a 'root metaphor' for an organisation (Smircich, 1983). That is, for them the organisation is a culture, and the notion of choosing culture doesn't make much sense. Others, like ourselves, tend to see culture as one variable within an organisation. Like other variables, such as structure and strategy, it can to a greater or lesser degree be consciously shaped or managed by those within the organisation.

For us, corporate culture is a set of beliefs, assumptions and values shared by a majority of those within an organisation. It is expressed in rituals, ceremonies, images and artefacts, and supported by various organisational structures and systems. It is, in short, a shared field of meaning. We make no easy assumption that all participants in an organisation share that field of meaning. Some have values that are sharply in opposition to the majority (a counterculture), and others share transcendental values but differ on strategic or operational values (a subculture, or an orthogonal culture, as it is sometimes called).

We also do not assume that the founder of an organisation has unilateral control over a culture. On the contrary, a host of individuals and interest groups are normally trying to shape the culture according to their own vision or interests. But we do assert that founders form a very powerful, if not the dominant, influence on corporate culture.

Schein, for one, in a paper that is becoming a classic in the short-lived field of the study of corporate culture, points to this enormous influence of the founder of an organisation in shaping its core culture (Schein, 1983). The point has not escaped those in the field either. Burke, the CEO of Johnson & Johnson, for example, acknowledges the key role of the founder in establishing the company's central values more than 50 years ago—values that are still reflected today in its credo (Burke, 1984). Similarly Finn, the CEO of IBM Australia, was able to trace for us the impact of Watson on the core values of IBM. It was, simply, phenomenal.

In exercising this role of shaping culture, the founder faces a series of dilemmas and trade-offs. What kinds of values is the founder to impress on the organisation as its core values (core values are those at the heart of the organisation—those shared by the majority, which define and direct their behaviour)? In particular, the choice of transcendental, strategic or operational values as core values has very different outcomes for the organisation.

Transcendental values as core values

The founder may choose to build a culture around only the transcendental identity values of the organisation. This ensures considerable strategic flexibility. Since they are values that are beyond experience, they can remain relatively enduring, regardless of the slowly changing circumstances of the organis-ation. They are able to play an enduring overarching role in a number of ways:

- They can be held to be applicable to all business units in the organisation, and often to new businesses as they are acquired and developed.
- They may be used at all levels of the organisation (strategic, tactical, operational).
- They may apply with equal effect within any functional area (eg marketing, production, personnel, finance).

IBM, for example, under the leadership of Tom Watson, developed a list of nine values that were to be the driving core values of the organisation. However, as Brian Finn, CEO of the Australian subsidiary, notes, three of these (respect for the individual, service to the customer, and the pursuit of excellence) are the real survivors of that original list: 'They always exist, strongly, all over the world'. Of these three, service to the customer can be seen as more of a strategic value, and more dispensable: 'In fact, I believe that you need only focus on respect for the individual and the pursuit of excellence'. Similarly, Nuno D'Aquino's emphasis on CUB's future as a 'lead organisation' allows enormous flexibility in adapting to different strategic contingencies.

However, while the use of transcendental values to define identity allows considerable flexibility, it does have difficulties attached to it. Core cultures that are based on transcendental values only are often weak cultures (cultures that do not greatly affect action), exactly because they transcend action. They are often difficult to translate into action and it is often difficult to define and communicate such values. For example, what does 'caring' mean when handling customers and creditors?

The trade-off in using transcendental values as core, driving values is therefore tricky. On the one hand, they allow the organisation to be more flexible. On the other, the organisation will have to spend a lot of its time and resources communicating and translating the values if they are to result in a strong culture.

Most organisations that are after a strong culture therefore support transcendental values with strategic and operational values. For example, IBM does support its transcendental values with strategic values such as customer service. These, together with a string of operational values, form its core culture.

Strategic values as core values

While transcendental values define core culture in some organisations, this is by no means so in all organisations. In some, strategic values are driven into the organisation by the founder. Thus an organisation may use a value such as 'technical excellence' as its core value, as an overarching directive for all its units for all time. Or it might focus on growth, or on customer service, or on any value that is central to its strategic posture.

There are advantages and disadvantages to such a choice. On the one hand, it is likely to provide a fairly strong culture with clear implications for action. As long as the organisation stays in the one business where technical excellence is important, or as long as the business environment does not become so turbulent that a more competitive culture is needed, the culture will be appropriate. But if those circumstances change, a strategic culture can be downright dangerous.

For example, over a span of many years, ICI Australia developed a strong engineering culture based on a shared commitment to technical excellence. It *became* an engineering firm. As the company came to face strong competition and an unpredictable market, however, this culture, this definition of identity, became a liability, for it often prevented the company from responding fast enough to customer needs. The company had to change its strategic values from technical excellence to customer service. But since technical excellence was a core value, the company in effect faced a problem of transformation.

Examples of such problems abound. The ANZ Bank, a major player in Australia and New Zealand, saw as one of its major strengths the fact that it had a '150-year-old banking culture', dedicated to the conservative handling of customer funds. When the banking industry was deregulated in the 1980s, however, the bank's major weakness *became* that 150-year-old banking culture (Limerick et al, 1984).

Operational values as core values

Operational values are even more problematic as core values. They can have a direct, strong influence on behaviour, but are so operation-bound that they can be exceptionally rigid and impervious to change. For example, Disney's core values of decency and family entertainment have survived the decades. But its operational values, which focused on the nuclear American suburban family, were also part of its core culture. By the end of the 1980s Disney was coming under great pressure from the Mutant Ninja Turtles, who reflected a different kind of social structure altogether!

At a more trivial level, IBM's penchant for white shirts backfired. They came to reflect not respectability but old-fashionedness. Most founders attempt to avoid using operational values as core values: while they can be extremely powerful in directing behaviour, they may have to be changed too often as circumstances change.

Strategic networks: second-order configuration designs

For those in strategic networks, it is necessary to work with two sets of configuration—a first-order design that brings together strategy, structure and culture for their own organisation, and a second-order design for the broader network in which it is involved. As Thorelli observes: 'For some strategic management purposes it may be helpful to look upon the entire network as a single organisation' (Thorelli, 1986: 47). One Australian public utility, for example, has developed two mission statements—one for the utility itself, and one for a broader strategic network of which it is the hub.

The hub organisation clearly has a major role in formulating second-order configurations. But this is tempered by the input of the other partners: it may be more accurate to think of the role of the hub organisation as providing original input and then of facilitating an arena in which the partners can formulate the configuration. In a sense, most organisations are involved in formulating a larger collective strategy:

> A true understanding of organizational strategy formulation and implementation requires that we move beyond the focal organisation to an appreciation of the network of relationships in which any single organisation is embedded ... Implementation of a collective strategy takes place through a network of linkages—both direct and indirect—to other organisations. [Fombrun & Astley, 1983: 48]

But in a network organisation, this collective strategy becomes the property of the entire network, not just of the single organisation.

In choosing a second-order configuration design for a network, the matter of shaping an appropriate core culture is particularly difficult. Managers in loosely coupled network organisations rely heavily on shared norms, beliefs and values to keep those organisations together and to make them effective. They simply do not have other integrative devices such as hierarchies and matrix facilitators. But strategic networks tend to span many different societal and organisational cultures, and there is little prospect of finding an exact match between partners.

Most network systems, as we have seen, therefore adopt transcendental values as core values. Most important of these are those values that support long-term relationships, such as care for others, trust, supportiveness and risk-sharing. Also important, as we have seen, are values that stress proactivity, risk taking, inter-organisational and transnational perspectives, and other sentiments that help each partner to see itself as an autonomous, entrepreneurial part of a larger system.

These are the values, therefore, about which a network culture is shaped. A culture built around transcendental values allows the various parties in networks to find common ground within the network while allowing each autonomous unit to retain its own distinctive culture. In selecting partners, this issue of transcendental compatibility becomes critical, and founders of networks are well advised to pay a great deal of attention to it.

Forming systems of action

The founder of an organisation has one final task to perform—and this is just as critical as the others. They must convert the configuration design into action—into myriad systems of action that get the whole job done. The process must reflect an integration of design and implementation. Whipp et al, for example, looked at nine British firms and found that: 'A fundamental attribute visible in the more successful firms in our study is the coherence between strategic and operational issues' (Whipp et al, 1989: 96). But the process must also reflect an extraordinary degree of flexibility at the implementation stage. The image that comes to mind is that of 'stump-jumping'. Lawrence and Bunk, who saw the aptness of applying the term to management issues, make the following arguments concerning its meaning:

> [S]tump-jumping, the vision to conceive and the perseverance to reach the goal no matter what the complications is a too-often overlooked way of Australian life … the essence of stump-jumping is the ability to remain uncowed by set-backs and to find, by hard work, courage and native 'nous', a way of turning adversity to advantage.
>
> So, if there is no clear path, how do we find our way? Well, we're not sure that we know, and even if we had the formula it might work for us and not for anyone else. It's a trial and error process of playing the game and learning what works for ourselves as individuals. [Lawrence & Bunk, 1985: 10–11, 413]

(*Note*: the term 'stump-jumping' is based on the action of an Australian innovation, the stump-jump plough. The idea is that each blade of the plough is allowed to operate independently through a series of springs and balances; this allows the plough to jump stumps and continue ploughing at the same time. It is a fitting image for loosely coupled network organisations operating on a basis of collaborative individualism.)

Systems of action in networks

Without thinking metastrategically, founders of networks are likely to underestimate the impact of network design on their own organisations. The systems of action that define networks are very complex. They rely heavily on the compatibility of the decision-making and problem-solving styles of the various participants, and often demand the creation of new horizontal systems of information and control in both the participant organisations and the network.

As we saw in Chapter 3, managers of networks have to be prepared for the networks to impact significantly on their own internal systems of action. This means that it is critically important for them to be aware of the entire metastrategic cycle of both the network and their own organisation as they build their networks. They have to be able to conceptualise the impact of the external alliance on the identity of their organisation, and to continually move between identity and systems of action. As they confront the problems of converting their vision into coherent systems of action, they have to be stump-jumpers *par excellence*.

Phase 2: Consolidation and Continuity: the Action Learning Organisation

How different is the foundation period to what follows? This depends on the extent to which the organisation is allowed to ossify.

The organisational flywheel

As shown in Figure 5.1, during the founding period, while the metastrategic design is still evolving, a feedback loop will exist between the emerging identity and the founding vision of the organisation. This becomes expressed in a configuration design and crystallised in systems of action with their own reinforcing culture. The more stable these become during periods of stability, the more they take on an identity of their own. That is, these stable systems of action, supported by a stable culture, feed back to define and reinforce both the identity of the organisation and its configuration. The organisation becomes what the organisation does—identity and metastrategy become crystallised in action.

During a period of punctuation, of discontinuity, such crystallisation can be catastrophic. The organisation's very success causes strong resistance to any equivalent dramatic change in the organisation's crystallised identity. As observed by Freeman:

> In the extreme, when inertia is very high, current technological and environmental conditions have nothing to do with explaining the current structure. Rather, one must look to those characteristics at the time of founding. [Freeman, 1984: 11]

We like to conceptualise this resistance to change in terms of the corporate flywheel. The term 'corporate flywheel' is used as a mechanical analogy of the forces of resistance that manifest when an attempt is made to change the current mode of operation of an engine. In the physical world, this resistance to change is explained by the concepts of *inertia* and *momentum*. In the corporate world 'inertia' is displayed in the apparent lack of organisational response to attempts to change its mode of operation; similarly 'momentum' is displayed in the related tendency of the organisation to preserve 'the status quo' when attempts are made to change it.

However, there is one important difference, as pointed out by Schon. Human social systems do not respond mechanically to attempts to change them—they are much more proactive, in that there is a tendency to fight to remain the same (Schon, 1971: 32). Nevertheless, although the resistance is the result of human action, the way it operates does correspond in many ways to a mechanical process.

Because the emergent metastrategic design is a worked-out version of the founding vision and identity, the two become indistinguishable in the minds of organisational members. The result is that, almost imperceptibly, the vital founding vision is forgotten and its configuration counterpart takes its place.

The configuration is embodied in the organisation's systems of action. Instead of being a means to an end, they become the right way of doing things. The organisation's identity is thus carried by its systems of action. The corporate flywheel has been put in place.

Such a flywheel has some advantages for organisations during periods of equilibrium. It gives momentum to their actions, and allows members to proceed without the continuing problem of asking why they are doing so. But when discontinuities arise, the 'right way' of doing things can become bad for the organisation, and the flywheel can then carry it into oblivion.

Transformational leaders v transactional managers: an unsatisfactory ideology

It is customary to think of the period of consolidation as one in which the founder gives way to a manager with a very different set of capabilities or, more rarely, begins to develop these new capabilities. This is, according to this narrative, the period of what Zaleznik (1977) calls 'managers' or what Burns calls 'transactional' leaders. They work by increment, continually transacting with others and maintaining the system by enabling others, by limiting options, and developing a competitive, growth-oriented culture. As Burns puts it:

> Transactional leadership is seen as the leadership we exercise in our normal lives from day to day: incremental, gradual, adjusting. Recognizing the limitation of the human mind, the inability to plan far ahead as compared, say, to a chess master, the wayward and unpredictable factors that affect all good plans, and the role of chance and serendipity, transactional leaders make short-run plans, adjust to other leaders' needs and decisions, adapt their hopes and aspirations to existing conditions, bargain and compete and manoeuvre in a continuing series of accommodations. [Burns, 1984: 153]

In this Third Blueprint model of consolidation, managers do stimulate growth and development—incrementally, through strategies of training and education.

'Organisation Development' (OD) strategies tend to be more developmentally oriented. Consider, for example, the following two excerpts from the writings of two of OD's most prominent practitioners and protagonists:

[OD is] a response to change, a complex educational strategy intended to change the beliefs, attitudes, values and structure of organisations so that they can better adapt to new technologies, markets and challenges and the dizzying rate of change itself. [Bennis, 1969: 2]

[O]rganization development is a top-management-supported, long-range effort to improve an organization's problem-solving and renewal processes, particularly through a more effective and collaborative diagnosis and management of organization culture—with special emphasis on formal work team, temporary team, and intergroup culture—with the assistance of a consultant–facilitator and the use of the theory and technology of applied behavioural science, including action research. [French & Bell, 1984: 17]

In the main, the technology is based on the assumptions and values of the Third Blueprint. It assumes that:

- The management of change is most effective when those affected by it are allowed to participate in the decision making for it.
- The most effective form of change takes place slowly over an extended period of time.
- Change is best brought about by a process of education that attempts to develop new attitudes, values and beliefs.
- An organisation and its members are free to change in any way they wish.
- There exists an overwhelming common interest that organisational members are capable of recognising, and to which they are willing to subordinate their own individual interests.
- The work group or team is the elemental building block of organisational activity.
- The legitimate target of OD is the ongoing systems of action (the teams and their intercommunication) rather than the very identity of the organisation itself.

Managers, in contrast to transformational leaders, are not supposed to concern themselves with vision: they adapt their hopes and aspirations to existing conditions. When they implement OD programs, their target is ongoing systems of action, and there is little impetus to revisit the issue of organisational identity. The organisational flywheel is left undisturbed. Despite these drawbacks, however, within the ideology of OD lie the seeds of a very different approach to managing development, implicit in French and Bell's references to 'renewal' and 'action research'.

The action learning organisation

The picture of organizational consolidation and change that is emerging in Fourth Blueprint organisations is very different from the image of the transactional manager improving current operations. It shows the participants themselves constantly concerned with reflecting on the vision, values, and mission of the organisation, experimenting with new activities, legitimating new activities in terms of that vision, and sharing that identity and spirit of empowerment with all others in the organisation. They are managers of 'learning organisations' (Senge, 1990; Nevis, DiBella & Gould, 1995; DiBella, Nevis & Gould, 1996), for this has become their major source of competitive advantage in an unpredictable world (Stewart, 1991). They gain competitive advantage not only by learning from others within their organisations but by learning from their partners in their alliances. Hamel, Doz & Prahalad (1989), for example, found that the companies that get the most out of alliances are those that set out to learn from each other.

Our analysis goes further than that, however. It suggests that companies have to become *action-learning organisations*. What is needed is a new kind of organisational learning paradigm that assists that process, one that is self-reflective and can transcend and critique its own identity, values, assumptions, and mission and that is initiated and controlled by line managers themselves. It is no accident that action learning has evoked so much interest over the past decade, for it meets this need admirably. It is, potentially, a quintessentially Fourth Blueprint technology (Limerick, 1990).

The reason why action learning is so well suited to the Fourth Blueprint is that it is *self-transcendent*, or self-reflective (Nohria & Berkley, 1994). Discontinuity requires that an organisation be able to challenge its own identity. But, paradoxically, periods of punctuated 'discontinuity' do not occur as one-shot events without historical input. Events that culminate in discontinuity occur much earlier, during periods of equilibrium. The point is made clearly by Nonaka (1988: 59):

In a system condition, an element fluctuates. It acts on the neighboring elements one after another or competes with them, and the fluctuation begins to be amplified. When a macroscopic pattern begins to emerge from such a dynamic cooperative phenomenon, a feedback to each element takes place, spontaneously, and a definite function is performed forming a stable order. When the order becomes fixed, the organic system again carries on a similar process irreversibly. [Nonaka, 1988: 59]

In other words, looking at the organisation during periods of equilibrium from a macroscopic perspective, it is possible to see a stable, deep structure. But within that, at a microscopic level, change and fluctuations are taking place. An organisation that actually encourages many such fluctuations is in a far better position to take advantage of environmental discontinuities than one that does not. First, its entire culture is tolerant of new, non-current-identity experimentation. And, second, it may have already developed a head start in some of the new strategic opportunities presented by the discontinuity. In fact, it may well create discontinuities for others. That is more or less what Weick (1987) means when he argues that the internal chaos within a firm must reflect the chaos outside it.

That this point is borne out in practice is clear from a study by Shell of long-surviving organizations, ranging from 100 to 700 years old. De Geus (1988, 1992) reports that a key factor that these organisations have in common is tolerance—their business units were allowed to experiment with and even move into businesses that were entirely different from current identity restrictions. The study found that during their histories, these organisations were able to change their corporate content entirely, often a number of times. They were ready for discontinuity.

Thus Fourth Blueprint thinking suggests that even during periods of equilibrium and consolidation the organisation has to be self-transcendent. Action learning provides a systemic process that allows it to do so. It has the capacity to turn the reactive organisation into a learning organisation, one that, to use Senge's terms, is 'continually expanding its capacity to create its future' (Senge, 1990: 14). Action learning has a number of key characteristics (Zuber-Skerritt, 1991). First, it consists of an ongoing cycle of reflection and critique, action, evaluation, reflection and critique, further action, and so on. Second, it attempts what Argyris & Schon (1974) call 'double-loop' learning. In its process of critique, it will continually reflect on and challenge the basic assumptions under-lying action—including the very identity assumptions of the system. Third, it sets up a learning community to control the process of action, evaluation, critique, action, and evaluation. That learning community consists of those responsible for the action together with informed outsiders who are capable of challenging assumptions. Fourth, it is emancipatory and empower-ing. It frees learners from their own hidden assumptions and from the hidden imperatives of others. It allows them to become proactive by experimenting, evaluating and critiquing, seeking the imperatives and opportunities of the situation, and creating new situations.

In other words, action learning depends not only on learning by reflection on experience (Daudelin, 1996), but also on learning by design and learning by self-transcendence. This can be an extremely subtle process. As Pankow (1976: 20) has so aptly put it, 'Self transcendence means the capability to change one's own point of view, and therefore the capability to view a situation in a new light, or, one might say, the ability to jump over one's shadow'. The entire technology of action learning is aimed at this capacity to jump over one's shadow. The reader who wishes to follow up the theory of action learning in more detail can consult a number of authors, including Zuber-Skerritt (1991), Revans (1982), and Passfield (1996). A paper by Limerick, Passfield & Cunnington (1992) attempts to summarise some of this literature by noting that, in general, action-learning organisations possess the following characteristics:

- *Bias for reflection-in-action*. Action enhances learning because it provides a basis for the critical dimension of reflection. Reflection is designed to develop questioning insight, the capacity to ask fresh questions in conditions of ignorance, risk, and confusion, when nobody knows what to do next (Revans, 1982). It is a mechanism for managers to reflect on their actions and the assumptions that underlie them.

- *Formation of learning alliances.* At the heart of networks and alliances is the fundamental acknowledgement that no organisation has all the skills and knowledge necessary to survive in the global market. Organisations that achieve major shifts in competitive strength through alliances build their own skills through their partners' capabilities, and systematically diffuse new knowledge throughout their organisations. The alliances that work best are those in which the partners are from a learning community.

- *Development of external networks.* Action-learning organisations recognise the social dimension of learning and the value of collaborative interdependence. Individuals are encouraged to form external networks and contribute to network development through the exchange of ideas, information, and resources. This necessarily extends the scanning capacity of the organisation and exposes it to alternative perceptions, decision processes, and actions.

- *Multiple reward systems.* An action-learning enterprise creates a wider employment contract with employees than the basic agreement about wages. It is management's role to provide continuous opportunities for employees' self-development. The challenge confronting organisations is to develop the capacity to reward both those who engage in continuous improvement within the existing identity frame, and those who challenge organisational identity.

- *Creation of meaningful information.* Information creation is a fundamental requirement for the self-renewing organisation (Nonaka, 1988). Information flows are enhanced by external and internal networks, learning alliances, and managerial reflections. The starting point for the creation of contradictions that enervate organisational renewal is a multidisciplinary, self-organising group of middle managers.

- *Individual empowerment.* Discussion on action learning continuously reinforces the need for individuals to be autonomous and empowered to take action. An example of the systematic incorporation of such opportunities in daily work at the operator and worker level is found in quality control circles.

- *Leadership and vision.* The responsibility of leaders is to ensure that there is a shared vision. That vision can come from anywhere in the organisation, and it can translate learning from a reactive to a proactive process: it usually comes from many sources at the same time: as Hamel and Prahalad (1994: 128) comment, industry foresight is a synthesis of many people's visions. So is the vision of the Fourth Blueprint organisation. Vision may also translate individual learning into an organisational action. When there is joint reflection on the meaningfulness of any event for the organisational mission as a whole, organisational renewal is more likely. What emerges is a learning system, a learning organisation.

The strategies being adopted by many of the managers of network organisations have the effect of turning them into action-learning communities. John Welch, for example, has done exactly that at GE, and it is interesting to see how he did it.

An action-learning community

In early 1981, John Welch set out at GE to 'break the company's genetic code' (Tichy, 1989: 99). He has since been working to develop a new breed of leader who could transform the organisation, develop global product and service strategies, develop strategic alliances, develop global coordination and integration, and use global staffing and development. In other words, he has been aiming at the development of Fourth Blueprint managers. As part of his strategy, he uses his corporate executive council not as a control mechanism, but as an arena for sharing experiences and new ideas. Each strategic business unit manager reports on a new, exciting development in managing his or her unit. As Welch observes, he has succeeded in turning these meetings into a business laboratory—and that is the key characteristic of the action-learning community. But he does not stop there. Central to his change strategy is GE's internal executive training centre at Crotonville. In 1981, James

Baughman, the director of Crotonville, said, 'I want a revolution to start at Crotonville. I want it to be part of the glue that holds GE together' (Tichy, 1989: 100).

Baughman responded, in effect, by turning Crotonville into an action-learning arena: 'The shift in the Crotonville mindset from a training to a workshop mentality has led to a totally new program design: an increasing number of teams attend sessions whenever possible. Participants bring with them real business problems and leave with action plans, and representatives from various GE businesses bring unresolved live cases to Crotonville for participants to help solve' (Tichy, 1989: 102). In 1989, Crotonville began to be used to head an effort to liberate middle managers at GE. Tichy reports that a series of workshops were to be used as a catalyst for mobilising 30–40,000 middle managers.

We have found similar examples in Australian organisations. Nuno D'Aquino's efforts in turning Carlton and United Breweries (CUB) into a 'lead organisation' have produced phenomenal results in efficiency, flexibility, creativity and morale. Working with a vigorous management team, he started in his Sydney-based brewery, which he transformed into an action-learning organisation. He set up a 'concept group', comprising a cross-section of managers, workers and union officials, which he sent on a world tour to pick up ideas for leading-edge organisational forms and processes. This group in turn called for ideas from the total factory, assisted by a 'learning centre'—a mobile office set up right in the middle of the brewery that could be visited by anyone with ideas or seeking development. The concept group set up action priorities such as the establishment of self-managing work groups that followed the work-flow, and created project teams to implement them. The result of these and a myriad other actions with the same objective—creating a lead organisation—was a leaner, more flexible, creative organisation. D'Aquino then turned his sights on CUB as a whole, and using the Sydney brewery as an example, led his entire organisation through a similar process.

Action learning is totally congruent both with loosely Fourth Blueprint network organisations, and with the individuals who inhabit them. It is participative and collaborative yet stresses the importance of individual critique, control and development. Thus Nuno D'Aquino has not developed an Enterprise Agreement with his unions: he drew up an Enterprise *Development* Agreement! He tells organisational participants, 'I cannot guarantee you employment—but I can guarantee you employability'. Action learning is primarily an emancipating form of organising, ideally suited to the problems of developing learning communities comprising collaborating individuals who are capable of responding to both continuity and discontinuity. It is a system of empowerment and self- transcendence.

Phase 3: Renewal—a Period of Discontinuity

The systemic use of action learning will act to reduce the frequency of massive transformation encountered by so many organisations today, for the organisation is continuously adapting to and creating change, conscious of the extent to which this challenges its identity. Even then it is possible for a major environmental discontinuity, or major forms of social shift to suddenly challenge the ongoing, evolving system—and its very identity (de Geus, 1992). This calls for a very special form of action learning that sets out to recompose and recreate the organisation, such as appreciative inquiry.

Appreciative inquiry

Appreciative inquiry is a form of social change process that comes directly out of postmodern interpretivist thinking (Cooperrider & Srivastva, 1987; Cooperrider, 1990; Hammond, 1996). It comes out of a deceptively simple, sociorationalist question: if organisations are socially constructed, why do we not build them to express and support values about which we feel passionate? This is quintessentially Fourth Blueprint thinking. We should not be prisoners of the social systems we have created—on the contrary, these systems should support our deepest values.

Unlike conventional forms of action learning, appreciative inquiry is not a problem-solving process: it sets out to create new patterns of social action, new forms of social reality:

At the heart of sociorationalism is the assumption of impermanence—the fundamental instability of social order. No matter what the durability to date, virtually any pattern of social action is open to infinite revision. Accepting for the moment the argument of the social constructionists that social reality, at any given point is a product of broad social agreement (shared meanings), and further granting a linkage between the conceptual schemes of a culture and its other patterns of action, we must seriously consider the idea that alterations in conceptual practices, in ways of symbolising the world, hold tremendous potential for guiding changes in the social order. [Cooperrider & Srivastva, 1987: 136]

Thus appreciative inquiry sets out to 'present provocative new possibilities for social action, and ... [to] stimulate normative dialogue about how we can and should organise ourselves' (Cooperrider & Srivastva, 1987: 137). It does this by involving all of the actors in a social system in four phases of inquiry:

- *Discovery*: appreciating what gives life, the best of what is: participants are asked to tell each other life-giving stories—stories about when people have experienced the organisation as most alive and effective.
- *Dream*: envisioning what might be, what the world is calling for. Despite the title, this phase is also practical, for it invites people to envision potential results and outcomes. It asks them to take their history into the future, transformed into a positive possibility. It calls for fundamental agreement about the organisation's calling—the unique contribution it can make to global well-being.
- *Design*: co-constructing what the ideal should be. This involves creating the social architecture of the organisation. It allows the collaborative construction of positive images about the future of the organisation, based on provocative propositions about what their future might be, and about how those rare moments of social excellence can become commonplace.
- *Destiny*: sustaining a pattern of social action that empowers, learns, adjusts and improvises. It is the phase that focuses on delivery, on the redesign of systems of action so that the provocative propositions can be realised.

This discussion of appreciative inquiry gives a good window into the processes of management that implement Fourth Blueprint thinking. It provides a good stepping off point for a more thorough consideration of everyday management, of what we call micro-strategy. It builds for participants an 'appreciative eye' into the organisation's systems, procedures and ways of working.

A few moments of reflection will reveal that this process invites all participants in the system to revisit the entire metastrategic cycle outlined in Figure 5.1:

- identity (discover);
- vision (dream);
- configuration (design); and
- systems of action (destiny).

Its focus is on constructing new realities, on taking the best of the past into a new shared, dreamed future. We noted earlier the enormous influence of the founder on identity and metastrategy during the first phase of organisational existence. Under Fourth Blueprint management, by the time we reach the stage of renewal, metastrategy has become a process in which the entire organisational community is involved. Of course, there are still leadership roles to be played—but leadership is not considered to be the property of a single individual or élite group at the apex of a hierarchy.

This is easier to see in a network: those at the hub become facilitators of appreciative processes that involve the whole network community in redefining identity and vision. In a post-corporate formal organisation such as GE or CUB, senior management plays a similar role. There is undeniably a residual hierarchy that can take command when circumstances require it. But in the matter of metastrategic renewal they tend to act like the hub of a network—as coaches and facilitators of self-transcendence. We will return to this issue of shared leadership in the next chapter.

Overall, there is mounting evidence that appreciative inquiry can produce profound changes in both formal organisations and networks. Cooperrider and his colleagues have used the process effectively in both small and large-scale social change programs, working with both single organisations and networks of organisations. Its history of use in Australian organisations is still relatively recent (Mellish & Brigid Limerick, 1997), but it has been used, as one example, in a Queensland school (Beerwah State High School) engaged in the process of moving towards school-based management to work towards a partnership agreement between school and community. A cohort of senior managers within the school began a process of appreciative inquiry that involved all of the school's communities, including staff, students, parents and other stakeholders. The provocative propositions that emerged from this process have been used as the basis for redefining the very identity and mission of the school, and have acted as a basis for its strategic planning. The level of energy and commitment aroused by the process, and its effect on the school's thinking, astounded even those managers who introduced the process, and who were themselves changed by it.

This glimpse of Fourth Blueprint management provides a good stepping off point for a more thorough examination of everyday management—of what we call microstrategic management.

CHAPTER 6

MICROSTRATEGY: WORKPLACE MANAGEMENT IN THE FOURTH BLUEPRINT

> *[I]n all organisations managers need both the knowledge of management of work and discipline and the knowledge and understanding of the organisation itself—its purposes, its values, its environment and markets, its core competencies.*
>
> [Drucker, 1994: 11]

IN CHAPTER 5 we looked at metastrategy—the process of determining organisational vision, identity, configuration design, and systems of action in Fourth Blueprint systems. In this chapter, we look at the ideas that underpin similar processes at the level of operational management. This second level we call *microstrategic*. It mirrors all aspects of the metastrategic cycle—vision, identity, configuration design, and systems of action—but has as its direct focus the renewal and the revitalisation of the workplace. It mirrors these aspects because Fourth Blueprint management, even at a day-to-day level, is self-reflective: it requires the continual adjustment of workplace operating systems to the identity and vision of the organisation, and permits the renegotiation of these fields of meaning by organisational participants.

We will not, within the scope of this book, examine the minutiae of operational management. More important for us is the examination of fundamental values that underlie microstrategic decision making in Fourth Blueprint systems. These values are expressed in the answers to five questions that frame Fourth Blueprint workplace management:

- What are the essential features of meaningful human work in the Fourth Blueprint organisation?
- What is the purpose of work in the Fourth Blueprint organisation?
- What is the relationship between work and the individual in the Fourth Blueprint organisation?
- How do Fourth Blueprint managers conceptualise their resources?
- What patterns of leadership are congruent with Fourth Blueprint systems?

The first three questions are deeply interrelated, and the Fourth Blueprint answers to them can be encapsulated in the notion of an *ecological perspective* on work. We will examine this in the next section, and then proceed to the two remaining questions.

MEANINGFUL WORK— AN ECOLOGICAL PERSPECTIVE

It is hard to avoid two realisations in analysing the changes that have taken place during this century in the work that humans in Western industrial countries do. The first is that much of the work of the industrial and corporate eras, or of the Second and Third Blueprints, has wrought unacceptable destruction on the earth at the same time that it has contributed to enhanced standards of living in most of the Western world. The second is that work itself has been transformed from a situation characterised largely by deprivation to one of secure and comfortable work conditions.

These two realisations lead us to consider work from a new perspective, one which is appropriately titled *ecological*. Before exploring ecological work as an essential criterion for workplace management in the postcorporate world, however, it is worth looking at images of work that dominated corporate society.

Work in Corporate Organisations

We will not spend too much time describing pre-industrial or even industrial images of work. This has been done well by others, including Braverman (1974), Oliver (1976), and Berrell (1994). We will simply note that the uncomplicated, personal relationship between people and products characteristic of pre-industrial work gave way, with the emergence of civilisations, to work with a range of new, complex and frequently contradictory meanings and purposes (Berrell, 1994), including survival, service, salvation, craft and profit, to name some of the more obvious. By the time the late industrial or corporate era arrived, there were competing ideological viewpoints about the nature of work that humans do.

One important stance is represented in Braverman's *Labor and Monopoly Capital* (1974), frequently regarded as a watershed in the development of an understanding of the relationship between work and human identity in industrial societies. Braverman contends that, compared to times when work was inextricably linked to the essence of human meaning systems, corporate work is relatively devoid of authentic human value. Central to this loss is the notion of deskilling, which Braverman views as encompassing four dimensions—loss of the right to design and plan work, the fragmentation of work into meaningless segments, the introduction of semi-skilled and unskilled labour, and the use of scientific management as a form of labour control. It has often been claimed, for example, that organisational systems based on Taylor's scientific management principles, developed in 1911 (Taylor, 1847) increased factory efficiency and stimulated economic growth in industrialised nations, but at the cost of reduced quality of worklife for factory workers.

A related issue is that of intensification, which has been interpreted by some analysts as one of the most tangible ways in which the work privileges of workers in late industrial organisations have been eroded. According to Apple (1988), for example, it has many symptoms from the trivial to the more complex—from no time even to go to the bathroom, have a cup of coffee or relax, to a total absence of time to keep up with one's field. Leisure and self-direction tend to be lost, community tends to be redefined around the needs of the labour process and, since both time and interaction are at a premium, the risk of isolation grows (105).

Related to this perspective on work in industrial organisations as inherently destructive in its effects on people, is the realisation of the tragic destruction that it is perceived by some observers to have increasingly been wrought on our earth. Technology has enabled us to bypass the checks and balances within the basic biological cycle of generation and regeneration. Berry (1988: 65) makes this point tellingly:

> Human technologies should function in an integrated relation with earth technologies, not in a despotic or disturbing manner or under the metaphor of conquest but rather in an evocative manner. [Berry, 1988: 65]

Drucker (1994) presents an alternative viewpoint to that expressed by Braverman and other critical observers of work in corporate societies. Drucker's essential point is that major occupational transformations in the course of the twentieth century (most notably from farming and live-in servants to a predominantly blue collar workforce) have been accomplished in relative peace. Furthermore, the situation of deprivation at the turn of the century (no pensions, no paid vacations, no overtime pay, no extra pay for Sunday or night work, no health or old age insurance, no unemployment compensation and so forth), had been changed by 1950 to one in which industrial workers in most countries had extensive job security, pensions, long, paid vacations, comprehensive insurance, and upper-middle-class income levels. They had also achieved political power. Thirty-five years later, however, industrial workers and their unions were in retreat. Numbers had shrunk to the extent that, in Drucker's view:

> [J]ust as the traditional small farmer had become a recipient of subsidies rather than a producer, so will the traditional industrial worker become an auxiliary employee. His place is already being taken by the 'technologist'—someone who works with both hands and with theoretical knowledge. [Drucker, 1994: 4]

So the comfort and security of the industrial worker was short-lived.

A number of observers have claimed that, the complexity of ideological viewpoints on human work notwithstanding, it has been possible to identify criteria for meaningful work in the corporate era. Crowther (1994) provided one such framework, arguing that meaningful work:

- is authentic human activity—that is, it is related to the needs of human survival;
- has productive outcomes—that is, it enhances the quality of life and the quality of the environment;
- enhances social relatedness—that is, it adds a dimension of warmth and sociability to people's lives;
- allows for political expression—that is, it allows people to articulate and assert their values and social goals; and
- is shaped by those who do it—that is, it encourages self-direction and creativity.

The problem is that this brief list of conditions for meaningful work, in addition to others that we will list below, is not being met by corporate workplaces. Indeed, the neocorporate bureaucracy, as we have seen, has taken the ills listed by Braverman to an art form and added a number of its own, including:

- short-term control systems (performance indicators) demanding responsibility without devolving decision making (pseudo devolution);
- divorcing people even further from the purpose of work by tying them up with systems and criteria for decision making;
- creating conflicting expectations for relatedness by demanding loyalty without offering reciprocal tenure or care;
- removing layers of hierarchical control and information without building horizontal bundles of communication (rendering all of Crowther's criteria above impossible to achieve);
- creating conflict for scarce resources by insisting upon competitive bidding; and
- being so concerned with accountability that people become risk-averse even when the discontinuous environment demands risk-taking.

The human costs of workplaces such as these are profound, and it is unlikely that society will be willing to tolerate them as we move into the next century. Work in the postcorporate era will need to take on a very different set of meanings and values.

Work in the Postcorporate Era

In the discussion that follows, we look at three particular features of human work that characterise the Fourth Blueprint. Before proceeding to our discussion, however, it is worth reflecting on three recent authoritative projections about human work:

- The first viewpoint is that of theorists such as Drucker (1993, 1994) who have observed that the postindustrial (postcorporate) knowledge society is one in which many more people than ever before can enjoy work-related success. His view is supported by Phil Ruthven, business forecaster with the Melbourne-based Ibis corporation. Ruthven has claimed recently that 'Full employment is possible. It could be reached soon. It should have been achieved some time ago' (Charlton, 1997: 23). Ruthven further asserts that '... we need to break the expectation that employees are owed a living by their employers and that there is a job for life. That no longer applies, if it ever did'. Where Ruthven appears to depart from Drucker is in his suggestion that employers will continue to control the workplace and the marketplace. To Drucker, in a society where the nature of work is determined by knowledge, the organisation of worklife will change dramatically from what we have known and workers will influence, if not control, the means of production.
- A second viewpoint is provided by Dale Spender (1997: 8–9) who relates her own personal experience in confronting post-corporate workplace reality:

[J]obs, as we know them, are on the way out. This doesn't mean that there is a reduction in work—it means there is a *reduction in full time, 9–5, organised jobs, with big companies.* ...

Like many people ... I now have portfolio employment. I also employ five other people, who have portfolio employment. Some of them have come from jobs that have disappeared; some have made a career choice for portfolio work (PR, film producer) ...

There is no point in educating people for jobs and work patterns that have passed. This is not to say that education is entirely vocational. But it is assuredly to say that the education system, which has been based on preparing people for the industrial age, is no longer appropriate. [Spender, 1997: 8–9]

- A third viewpoint is that of those observers who point to the immense uncertainty that the dawn of the postcorporate era poses for work as a dimension of human existence. Rifkin (1995: 13) describes this as follows:

We are being swept up in a powerful new technology revolution that offers the promise of a great social transformation, unlike any in history. The new high-technology revolution could mean fewer hours of work and greater benefits for millions ... The same technological forces could, however, as easily lead to growing unemployment and a global depression ... If ... the dramatic productivity gains of the hightech revolution are not shared ... chances are that the growing gap between the haves and the have-nots will lead to social and political upheaval on a global scale. [Rifkin, 1995: 13]

Clearly, Fourth Blueprint participants confront massive challenges in reconstructing their workplaces so that they are linked, to the greatest extent possible, to human and environmental well-being, rather than to the negative and degrading effects that some associate with industrial and corporate processes. But, as we have observed previously, participants have choice in shaping the ways that work in their organisations will be undertaken:

This developing consensus on the importance of the symbolic realm— on the power of ideas—by such independent sources embracing such diverse objectives reflects the reality of organised life in the modern world. However reluctantly, even the most traditional social thinkers are now recognising the distinctiveness of the postindustrial world for what it truly is—an unfolding drama of human interaction whose potential seems limited or enhanced primarily by our symbolic capacities for constructing meaningful agreements that allow for the committed enactment of collective life. [Cooperrider & Srivastva, 1987: 133]

We can be guided by the utilitarian, performance-oriented values of corporate blueprints, or we can attempt to actualise our dreams of contributive, supportive systems of action in our social order and in our workplace. Such systems must, at a minimum, address the following issues.

The Social Sustainability of Work

Socially sustainable work translates into a concern for society as a whole. Work is conducive to social sustainability if it serves to enhance the quality of our lives or the quality of the environment.

Socially sustainable work is possible because, in the Fourth Blueprint, organisations coexist with, and are interdependent with, others. They are boundaryless systems that draw on society for energy and life. If they deplete that energy, they cannot exist in the long run—that has been the lesson of, say, totalitarianism. But sustainability is more than just not drawing too much from the environment. The open system must put back what it takes out, and more, to sustain other systems. It must build up the physical, intellectual, affective, processual, nurturant and environmental assets of society and of the individuals within it.

Treston (1994), after considering arguments such as these, raises questions which challenge the nature of values about human work which are explicit in the Third Blueprint:

> How long will it be before the vast majority of the earth's people discover that they are an integral part of the ecological network, and not disinterested bystanders? How do we change our production goals to enable us to live more simply within a sustainable economic system? Irresponsible landcare, the production of armaments, destruction of rainforests, leaking of toxic wastes, water and air pollution … all are the consequences of destructive work. Perhaps our generation is the last generation which can reverse the downward spiral of degradation. [Treston, 1994: 26–7]

Rifkin projects an equally apocalyptic future in which the developed nations will be burdened with explosive legions of idle and angry ex-workers and the prospect of global depression and social upheaval. To some observers (Menzies, 1996; Mintzberg, 1996; Rifkin, 1995) any viable conception of work in the post-corporate era will therefore have to accept as reality a myriad interdependent and mutually sustaining 'sectors'—with the services (social, private and public) all assuming responsibility for human employment. Paquette (1997: 23), for example, has predicted 'third-sector organisations ... on a scale sufficient to provide to burgeoning armies of under and unemployed adequate opportunities for meaningful work that contributes in positive ways to community life and development'.

What emerges here is a construction of work that has limited meaning in industrial and corporate organisations which are characterised for the most part by tight boundaries and a narrow definition of their purpose. 'Employment', 'employer' and 'employee' assume meanings in postcorporate settings that did not exist in earlier blueprints. Indeed, given the declining levels of participation in Australia, and in most Western societies, of traditional forms of community service and volunteer activities (Institute of Public Affairs, 1996) it can be seen that the creation of socially sustainable work represents a challenge for Fourth Blueprint participants that is at one and the same time daunting, imposing and exciting.

Thus far, the argument for socially sustainable work has been presented as a survival issue, which it undoubtedly is. But aside from that issue, corporate conceptions of work and of the individual as the resource of the organisation (to wit, human resource management) are offensive to the new generation of collaborative individuals. The latter are, as we have seen, value driven, and they will seek to negotiate those values into the field of shared meaning that comprises their working community. Their values of generativity and care for the entire ecology are ends in themselves, and they simply will not accept the argument that work, however unpleasant in the short term, is necessary for a broader social end. (This is the argument which has been used, for example, by the Australian Prime Minister, John Howard, in resisting international demands for tighter pollution emission standards for Australia as a coal-resource dependent country.) For them, the end cannot justify the means. They are far more likely to accept Martin Luther King's dictum that the means *is* the end-in-process.

Thus, social sustainability is not only a matter for society at large, it is of vital concern to the individuals within the postcorporate world. This is more clearly seen in the issue of lifestream compatibility.

Lifestream Compatibility

As we saw in our previous chapters, we have come to the end of the era of 'the good corporate soldier', or the 'corporate citizen', in which compatibility between the organisation and the individual was a one-way street—that is, individuals became integrated into the organisation. In the Fourth Blueprint, the opposite is also the case—*the organisation must be capable of being integrated into the life of the individual.* We have acknowledged a debt to Burgess-Limerick (1995) for her concept of *lifestreaming.* She links it to a twin concept, that of *processual being.* She argues that individuals today see self not as a static structure, but rather as a lifestream, to be developed and composed on a day-to-day, year-to-year basis. They are continually in process.

Burgess-Limerick combines these two constructs—lifestreaming and processual being—with a third, *responsive agency.* We have already canvassed this notion in earlier chapters of our book. Fundamentally, it implies that, as individuals compose their life-streams on a day-to-day processual basis, they are not imprisoned or constrained by their environment—they *use* it to compose their lives. They bring work and home together into a set of relationships which are continuously evolving and which define who they are. Organisations that do not give them support in the process of developing their lifestreams will lose them, and cannot be sustainable in the long term. You will recall that this, as Deutschman (1990) pointed out, is the generation that can say No!

As Burgess-Limerick describes it, we are accustomed, in our conventional organisational mindsets, to distinguishing between home and working life (and here we are, of course, referring only to paid work). We make the assumption that the working person starts at the factory gate, and that the organisation's concern for the individual starts there too. Thus we have been concerned with issues such as 'the quality of working life', and 'career', on the assumption that working life is separable from home life and that careers are hierarchical and contained within the organisation.

It will be apparent that lifestream compatibility cannot be separated from organisational structures. The flat organisational structures found in some emerging, high performing organisations are fundamentally important to lifestream compatibility, for they give the individuals within them the capacity to participate in moulding the organisation and its systems to their own circumstances. In doing so, these organisations are able to attract and keep the individuals they need. One Australian bank, for example, found that they had lost much of their training and development investment because their women employees tended to leave when they had children. The bank went back to these women and asked: 'How do we have to *be* in order to make it possible for you to work for us?'—and changed their entire work organisation to make it lifestream compatible. A non-teaching hospital in Queensland found that it relied on mature, experienced nurses for its operations, but could not keep them as they developed families. So they did the same as the bank: they brought experienced, married nurses back into the hospital and allowed them to work the number of shifts they wanted, mutually negotiating with others the time of work. They now have a cohort of involved, committed, permanent part-time employees. Both organisations have developed processes that are socially sustainable: they are compatible with and contribute towards the society in which they exist.

But lifestream compatibility does not just mean the integration of temporary or part-time work into mainstream configuration, for such work may suit only some (Feldman, Doerpinghaus & Turnley, 1994). It means greater flexibility and management for diversity (Thomas & Ely, 1996; Hall & Parker, 1993). That diversity has to be diversity-within-community.

Communal Belonging

The attenuation of community life has been a major theme in the work of many twentieth century writers. Perhaps one of the clearest statements of the 'problem of community' in contemporary society has been provided by Nisbet, who defines 'community' as:

The product of people working on problems of autonomous and collective fulfilment of internal objectives, and the experience of living under codes of authority which have been set in large degree by the persons involved. [Nisbet, 1957: 73]

Nisbet asserts that '… the quest for community will not be denied, for it springs from some of the powerful needs of human nature—needs for a clear sense of cultural purpose, membership, status and community'.

Numerous theorists have observed that the postcorporate age has accentuated both loss of community and the social function of the workplace. Drucker (1994), for example, says that old communities—family, village, parish, and so on—have all but disappeared in the emergence of a 'knowledge society'. Their place has largely been taken by the new unit of social integration, the organisation. Where community claimed the entire person, organisation is a means to a person's ends, a tool. Drucker states that:

By definition, a knowledge society is a society of mobility. And all the social functions of the old communities, whether performed well or poorly (and most were performed very poorly indeed), presupposed that the individual and the family would stay put. But the essence of a knowledge society is mobility in terms of where one lives, mobility in terms of what one does, mobility in terms of one's affiliations. People no longer have roots. [Drucker, 1994: 12]

Perhaps Drucker is overly focusing on 'the organisation' as the primary integrator of social life. As we have seen, people today may be involved in many organisations or systems of action. But Drucker's essential point is well made: work-related systems of action provide the basis for the development of community, even if individuals identify with a number of overlapping, intersecting communities that are all part of their lifestreams.

Participants in each system of action therefore need to pay attention to the development of structures and processes that facilitate community building. This can be achieved even in highly efficient assembly lines, as Majchrzak and Wang (1996) argue:

We found that such collective responsibility could be fostered in a variety of ways: by structuring jobs with overlapping responsibilities, basing rewards on group performance, laying out the work area so that people can see one another's work, and designing procedures so that employees with different jobs are better able to collaborate.

Interestingly, the particular method or number of methods employed did not seem to matter. Process-complete departments that had adopted all four methods did not have significantly faster cycle times than those that had adopted only one or two. What did matter was whether a company had embraced any of the methods—whether the company recognised that it needed to do more than merely restructure the organisation to foster a collaborative culture. [Majchrzak & Wang, 1996: 94]

According to Majchrzak and Wang, designing jobs so that employees can at least partially perform most of the functions assigned to a department helps create a shared sense of responsibility because people understand one another's work and thus share a common language and similar constraints and objectives. More important, if a process-complete department does not make responsibilities overlap, it will end up with a set of specialised jobs by default and may inadvertently recreate the same coordination problems and high overheads that bedevil organisations with functional departments.

Educational research also contains convincing evidence of the value of countering corporate structures by moving toward 'communal' models of school organisation. Newmann and Wehlage (1995) describe the characteristics of schools which had been restructured by the school community and where enhanced student achievement across subject areas, age, and socioeconomic status was a definitive outcome:

The most successful schools were those that used restructuring tools to help them function as professional communities. That is, they found a way to channel staff and student efforts toward a clear, commonly shared purpose for student learning; they created opportunities for teachers to collaborate and help one another achieve the purpose; and teachers in these schools took collective—not just individual—responsibility for student learning. Schools with strong professional communities were better able to offer authentic pedagogy and were more effective in promoting student achievement. [Newmann & Wehlage, 1995: 3]

Power Sensitivity

The problems of social sustainability, lifestream compatibility and communal nurturance cannot be satisfactorily handled without taking a cold, hard look at the problem of power in Fourth Blueprint systems. Throughout this book we have noted the concern of many theorists and commentators that the postmodern, postcorporate era may well bring with it greater distances between the haves and the have nots, greater levels of managerial manipulation by the 'greedy organisation' (see Blackmore, 1996: 337–8) using humanist techniques of emotional recruitment, and, ultimately, social upheaval.

As one reviews the chapters above, what stands out most clearly is the tight link between managing the new organisation and empowerment. The strength of the new organisation lies in the power of each individual to participate in collaborative systems of action, and in the process of social construction. Ironically, though, the weaknesses of the new organisation lie in the shadows of these strengths. Empowerment is its strength. The assumption that all people are empowered is its weakness.

Strategic networks rest on two assumptions. First, they assume that there are not huge differences of power between participants. There will of course be differences in both the bases and the amount of power that different people have—but networks assume that if these were graphed, the gradient would be relatively flat. Indeed there is something of the flavour of the Foucauldian belief that all people have power—they just have to learn how to use it. Thus the concept of power is central to networks:

> Power is the central concept in network analysis ... Power is too often thought of as possessed unilaterally. The more typical phenomenon is that of interdependence. [Thorelli, 1986: 38]

The whole purpose and dynamic of the loosely coupled system is to facilitate empowered interdependence.

Second, strategic networks assume that all people in the organisation have considerable amounts of power. It is not sufficient for there to be few differences in power, if no one really has any power at all. That would be a sort of egalitarian power impoverishment.

Networks depend on high levels of power in the organisational community as a whole, power that can be harnessed to shape the future.

These assumptions are only partially met in modern societies. To be sure, the phenomenon of People Power has demonstrated just how much power collaborating individuals can have. Moreover, most modern societies have seen the back of the worst aspects of a stratified class structure, in which whole strata of society were disempowered. But this has just enabled another problem to become more obvious—the existence of groups of people who are disempowered by systemic discrimination based on gender, race, nationality, age, or any other axis of social differentiation—a new form of class structure, if you like. The problem of systemic discrimination is that it is very deeply embedded in the social attitudes and systems of a community, and thus very difficult to eradicate through individual action.

The fundamental problem in this whole matter of discrimination —of minority-power groups—is that the process of individual empowerment cannot handle it. It is worth repeating Staples' argument, quoted in Chapter 4:

> Individual empowerment is not now, and never will be, the salvation of powerless groups. To attain power equality, power relations between 'haves', 'have-a-littles' and 'have-nots' must be transformed. This requires a change in the structure of power. [Staples, 1990: 37]

An attack on systemic discrimination relies on a change in the structure of power in both organisations and the societies in which they are embedded. Those who participate in the management of Fourth Blueprint systems therefore have to be sensitive to the issues of power impoverishment and act both internally and externally to the organisation to handle it. Without doing so, organisations will not be socially sustainable, lifestream compatible, or community nurturant.

The problem with postcorporate organisations is that they are not well positioned to lead that attack internally. Affirmative action relies quite heavily on bodies of corporate personnel who can audit and manage affirmative action programs. For example, Griffiths (1990) found that women were only represented reasonably well in the managerial ranks of the larger organisations in Australia if these organisations had strong affirmative action programs. There is little protection for the disempowered in the flat network organisations that have very small corporate headquarters and that assume all within them are empowered.

It would be easy for Fourth Blueprint participants to wash their hands of the problem, and to pass it on to society at large. But that would run counter to the very belief system of collaborative individualism, which asserts that individuals, in collaboration with each other, can do something about most issues! So we will not insult modern organisational participants by suggesting that there are some things to which they can pay attention, and some that are the responsibility of 'others'.

So what can be done by Fourth Blueprint participants to address the issue of power equalisation in organisational systems? In part, the answer lies in developing a *participant centred paradigm of organisational management*—to move past managerialist conceptions of organisational collaboration. This issue is explored in detail in the following chapter. In part, too, the answer lies in developing and acting upon very *different conceptions of leadership*. This is addressed in the final section of this chapter. But a third leg of the answer is explored here: *the management of diversity*.

The management of diversity

The management of diversity has two objectives. The first is the recognition of the presence within the organisation of individuals and groups of individuals with a diverse range of backgrounds and experience (Thomas & Ely, 1996). The second objective is the empowerment of all those individuals and groups—the enabling of their freedom to be different and their capacity to have equal influence with others on those things that are important to their lives. Perhaps we should be talking about 'managing for diversity'. Managing for diversity and being power sensitive are essentially the same issue, and require action both within and without the organisation.

Action within the organisation

We have seen that what holds the network organisation together is a shared field of meaning—a shared set of values, norms and beliefs that surround a shared mission. That is what gives decentralised units coherence and direction. The key to managing against systemic disempowerment, therefore, is strong, clear, overt, directive policy. Paradoxically, the more decentralised a system is, the clearer its policy has to be if it is not to become decoupled.

But the management of diversity always runs against entrenched interests: there will always be those who perceive that the empowerment of others reduces their own power. So a second prong of attack requires a back-up policy with sanctions—with power. However, this leaves a third problem. The policy and sanctions cannot be aimed at just 'equal treatment'. Different groups that have experienced systemic discrimination do not start with the hypothetical 'level playing field'. Therefore equal treatment will not do, for equal treatment under conditions of disequality serves to magnify disequalities. What is required instead is *equalising* treatment—that is, a positive program of empowerment. Management programs for women managers, for example, are one method of empowering women (B. Limerick & Heywood, 1993). Overall, the fundamental shape of any approach to managing diversity has three essential, interrelated ingredients:

- clear, directive policy, based on clear values;
- the back-up of strong sanctions; and
- the back-up of empowerment programs.

Most of the internal actions that will achieve diversity were explored in the previous chapter's discussion of metastrategy, particularly the section on appreciative inquiry, and we will not revisit this material. These actions will be based on strong leadership patterns (see below) capable of projecting new meanings into the organisation. The major focus of this leadership will be on empowerment—and we have little doubt that system-wide empowerment in loosely coupled systems demands that the organisation become an action learning community. The management of diversity represents a break with the past for most societies, and demands that the diverse groups participate in inventing their own future.

Action outside the organisation

Action taken inside organisations will go some way towards the achievement of diverse, empowered groups. But in the end they will not be sufficient to change the structure of power in a society—and that is the context in which disempowerment is embedded. More direct action needs to be taken to ensure that the structures and processes of society protect the disempowered in systems of collaborative individualism. Paradoxically, the values that underpin Fourth Blueprint microstrategic management require a macro level of awareness and action.

There are obviously no easy 'quick fix' solutions for action on this scale. What we would like to do here is to emphasise that loosely coupled social structures are here to stay (and that they raise problems of protecting diversity) and to highlight the importance of opening the debate about some of the major arenas in which we will have to invent social action. The arenas we have chosen to look at are:

- the contract-arbitration processes;
- middle-range institutions;
- the legal system; and
- communication systems.

Together these represent some of the most important fields in which the battle for empowerment will be won or lost.

Contract-arbitration processes

The intervention of arbitrators such as ombudspersons, equal opportunity commissioners and the like will become an increasingly important feature of our social and organisational life if we are to achieve social diversity and empowerment. Such intervention is vitally important to the functioning of Fourth Blueprint organisations and the society of which they are a part.

If the glue that holds our organisations together is a combination of values and implicit or explicit contracts, then we will become increasingly dependent on mechanisms that can interpret those contracts within the values of the system. That is the role of the ombudsperson—to protect and interpret the contract, to reinforce the values behind it, and to protect the interests of all parties within it. This protection is becoming increasingly important for the otherwise unempowered, because many middle-range institutions, such as unions, are losing their traditional membership and their central protective role. In effect, a well-developed arbitration capacity will give the unempowered recourse to a broader base of power outside the organisation. It will give them protection from unfair dismissal, exploitation, discrimination and misdirection.

This is not an argument for a centralised arbitration system, such as that which dominates Australian industrial relations. It is an argument that proposes that decentralised enterprise bargaining and access to arbitration are not mutually exclusive—they should both be asserted at the same time. More than that, it is an argument for the development of a broad system of alternative dispute resolution (ADR) accessible by the underempowered.

Typically, in Western countries, the development of a range of such arbitrators is being undertaken 'on the run' to meet the exigencies of situational pressures. In Australia alone, the various states and territories differ broadly in the array of arbitrators available, and in their powers and responsibilities. Certainly, situations are different, and arbitration networks will continue to be different. ADR is in its infancy, and as yet remains largely the domain of corporate players. What is required in most Western societies is a more deliberate review of the role of arbitration in our organisations (and society generally), and a more comprehensive, proactive development of systems of protective arbitration.

The transformation of middle-range institutions

The development of collaborative individualism and the emergence of arbitration mechanisms does not reduce the need for middle-range organisations such as unions and political parties. On the contrary, it underlines the importance of their existence in the management of diversity. But it will require a massive transformation in their perceptions of the role they play and in the services they offer. Just as central offices in organisations have yielded operational control to decentralised line managers, but substituted high levels of facilitation, advice and responsiveness to the autonomous units, so middle-range institutions require a parallel transformation.

Unions, for example, will continue to experience pressures towards decentralisation to the shop-floor level, with leaner, policy-oriented headquarters. But the transformation is more profound than that. They will be under pressure, at both levels, to de-emphasise their operational role in organising labour, for empowered individuals will organise themselves.

Instead of relying on the obligations of citizenship of the union, they will have to provide improved services to their clients. They will have to act as pressure groups in developing national policy on issues such as contract relationships and minority group interests. As a last resort, though, they will undoubtedly find it necessary to resort to the use of countervailing power—to strikes. But they will find that they cannot deal with complexity and discontinuity by attempting to 'own' and represent all issues; they will have to network with other diasporas and pressure groups, such as the green movement, the grey power movement, and feminist and ethnic interest groups to achieve broader objectives.

Unions are not the only institutions finding themselves under such pressures. Churches have fewer members, but are experiencing more pressure to comment on social values and events and to link across to other global and local value-oriented diasporas.

Political parties, too, find their membership allegiances diminishing and an increasing need to link across to broader pressure groups such as the green movement. Nevertheless, political parties will have an enormous role to play in providing coherence in 'solar system' political networks. Wayne Swan, Director of the Australian Labor Party's successful campaigns in the 1989 and 1992 Queensland, and the 1990 federal, elections, reflected this changing role when he argued that:

> The lesson from the federal election particularly is that the electorate is becoming far more critical, far more willing to change its vote ... Fewer people are tied to their votes for the rest of their life, which puts more pressure on the parties to perform. You can't behave in the old way. You have to be a lot more reflective and sensitive to communities than before. [quoted in the *Sunday Mail*, April 1, 1990: 11]

Faceless managerialism in our social institutions will not handle this problem. Political parties have to develop broad patterns of leadership that sets out to recognise the needs of diverse groups, and that empowers them to meet those needs.

Legislation and the legal system

Decentralised, diverse, social and organisational systems rely on a user-friendly legal system, one that is responsive to different, rapidly changing social values and circumstances, and one that services the negotiative, contractual processes in which individuals are involved.

The protection of unempowered individuals relies heavily on at least two factors. The first is a clear set of anti-discrimination and anti-exploitation national values enshrined in law. The second is the capacity of unempowered individuals to access the law by banding together and empowering themselves. The right to undertake joint 'class' actions seems vital to this capacity, and the Australian states and territories will find themselves under increasing pressure to facilitate such action.

A changed role such as this will require that the legal system, too, becomes an open, permeable, responsive part of broader social networks, with expertise and a fundamental interest in sociopolitical philosophies and action systems. In Australia, for example, a prominent jurist, Fitzgerald, led a commission of inquiry that revolutionised the state of Queensland's police system. He was then appointed by a new government to head an inquiry into the environmental exploitation of Fraser Island. He has not played a passive, interpretive part in either role. He was an active transformer, advancing views on the relationship between the state and the police force, and on environmental issues—views that reflect the implacable demands of the broader communities of individuals.

It could be argued that a more overt political concern has always been part of the legal system, despite its oft-claimed impartiality. Apoliticism is a profoundly political stance. But our new loosely coupled societies cannot afford the detached 'gentlemen's club' into which many Western legal professions have withdrawn. Collaborative individualism demands a much more proactive, critical, and ethically and socially reflective empowering legal system.

Communication systems

One of the central themes of this book has been a focus on the key role of communication technology in enabling the emergence of loosely coupled systems by empowering the individual. In the main, that focus has looked at micro-communication systems such as electronic mail and computer control systems. Just as fundamental to the broader social system in which collaborative individualism is embedded, is the role of the media. The media are important in at least three ways. First, they allow dispersed individuals to experience different possibilities and to share new visions. For example, communist authorities in eastern Europe were simply unable to prevent their communities accessing televised and printed images of a different world. The US attempted to initiate change in Cuba by beaming ordinary sit-com programs across in order to create an awareness of a different dream. Not surprisingly, Cuban authorities jammed these broadcasts and threatened to retaliate in kind.

A second role of the media is to provide communication between decentralised individuals as they mobilise their efforts into joint action. That was the role of the media in East Berlin in 1990, and in Russia during the abortive coup of 1991. The failure of the coup leaders to control the media proved decisive. In the same way, media access is just as important for individuals within organisations. In Australia, for example, faculty staff at universities have used the media to combat national educational policies, or to mobilise efforts to overturn hierarchically determined policies and procedures.

The third and less obvious role of the media is to act in an informal *auditing* role for the unempowered in organisations. Few institutions are able to focus on broad, diffuse networks of action as effectively as the press. It is playing an increasingly important role in penetrating various organisations on behalf of individuals or groups who would otherwise have few ways of monitoring their contractual relationships with others. It is becoming more active in issues such as discrimination, unfair dismissal, consumer relationships, uncovering strategic alliances and counter-alliances and the like.

These three roles alone underline the importance of the freedom of the press to Fourth Blueprint systems, and to the dangers of concentration of media ownership in the hands of a few. The media play an essential power balancing role—but could easily become the source of imbalance. By providing knowledge and large-scale communication, they are capable of empowering the individual—but, captured by one interest group, they could imprison individuals and groups of individuals.

There is little doubt that the issue of media freedom and concentration, already alive, will become even more vital in the next few decades as we struggle to empower and protect a diverse range of individuals.

These issues are clearly not the only important contextual issues that will be raised by the acceleration of loosely coupled systems. The ramifications that we are experiencing of technological, educational, political and social change are profound. We have focused briefly on a few issues that have central importance to the problem of power balancing, of controls and checks, within collaborative individualism, for that presents a *sine qua non* for collaborative systems. If we cannot solve that problem, collaborative individualism will not mature into a stable paradigm.

In sum, work which meets the challenges of the Fourth Blueprint has the following interrelated characteristics:

- it is socially sustainable;
- it supports the lifestreams of individuals;
- it nurtures communal belonging;
- it is power sensitive; and it embraces and manages diversity.

Taken together, these characteristics imply a meaning system in relation to human work that is peculiar to the Fourth Blueprint. It is a meaning system which is pervaded by ecological concern for the quality of worklife, and also for the applications of the work that humans do in the external world. In developing our framework for microstrategy, this ecological concern is of fundamental importance.

Resources In The Fourth Blueprint Workplace—A Processual Perspective

The issue of organisational resources in Fourth Blueprint organisations is tightly related to the ecological, processual model of the workplace developed above. Fourth Blueprint management requires a number of conceptual shifts:

- from people as resources to organisations as resources;
- from inputs as resources to processes as resources; and
- from knowledge as a resource to knowledge technology as a resource

Resource Management in Earlier Blueprints

We are all reasonably familiar with the conventional resource models of the corporate blueprints. They derive from a conceptualisation of the organisation as a 'thing' (a corporation) which is designed to meet the goals of its owners and architects. In doing so, it has a number of 'resources', including people (human resources), money (financial resources) and materials (material commodities). Not unexpectedly, these typify management training programs, where courses tend to be ascribed specialised functional titles like 'financial administration', 'HRM' and 'asset management'.

In corporate blueprints, then, resources are construed as inputs that have to be acquired, developed and maintained. Human resource management (HRM), for example, implies that people are resources of the organisation. They have to be managed according to something like the following well-known framework:

- *acquisition* (for example, recruitment, selection, induction);
- *development* (for example, career development, organisational development, professional development);
- *motivation* (for example, job design, performance appraisal, professional recognition and reward); and
- *maintenance* (for example, conflict resolution, safety and health). [Robbins, Low & Mourell, 1986]

Equivalent classification systems abound for other resource elements. A model such as this is entirely incongruent with Fourth Blueprint organisations, which turn most of its elements on their head.

Resources in the Fourth Blueprint

When systems of action are stable, it is easy to reify them—to see the organisation as an entity that owns and uses resources. The organisation in turn is the property of its owners (the shareholders). Indeed, this is the legal model that underpins much of our corporate law. But this model begins to creak at the seams when it is applied to loosely coupled systems such as networks. Who 'owns' a network, an alliance? The answer, of course, is its participants—it has no existence outside of the social reality they have created. (We are reminded of our earlier discussion of Drucker's contention that 'in the knowledge society the employees—that is the knowledge workers—own the tools of production'.) In the Fourth Blueprint, this same line of thinking clearly applies to loosely coupled postcorporate organisations.

Organisation as a Resource

A basic tenet of the Fourth Blueprint, then, is that the organisation does not have people as a resource, people have the organisation as a resource. They can alter it, mould it, redefine it, restructure it at will—it exists in their world of shared meaning, and is expressed in systems of action that are seen to be temporary and linked to the shared objectives of the working community. As we write, it becomes increasingly more difficult to speak of 'the organisation' as an 'it'. What is owned by people is a *process*—a process of collaboratively adding value for a client, thereby serving a range of disparate needs of the working community and its constituencies. It is this process that can be moulded and reshaped at will, and it is the resource of the participants. It is more accurate to talk of the *process of organising* than of 'the organisation'. But such language is clumsy: we have therefore chosen to continue to talk about 'the Fourth Blueprint organisation' when we mean the systems of action and processes that support collaborative action.

From Inputs as Resources to Processes as Resources

So what are the critical resources of those in the collaborative community? Strictly speaking, a resource is the means of producing an outcome. The resources from this perspective are the *processes* used to collaboratively add value. Thus, within the Fourth Blueprint it is not money that is the resource—it is *financial management*, the learned processes of acquiring, maintaining and using money, that is the resource that has to be acquired, nurtured and maintained. That is, the primary resource of collaborative systems is knowledge (see, for example, Inkpen (1996)).

Knowledge Technology as a Resource

To be accurate, it is not even knowledge that is the resource of the collaborative participants—it is the knowledge of how to use knowledge, or knowledge technology, as we prefer to think of it. In general terms, the importance of knowledge as a key resource in the emerging Fourth Blueprint is summed up by Drucker (1994) as follows:

> The market researcher needs a computer. But increasingly this is the researcher's own computer, and it goes along wherever he or she goes. The true 'capital equipment' of market research is the knowledge of markets, of statistics, and of the application of market research to business strategy, which is lodged between the researcher's ears and is his or her exclusive and inalienable property. ... The industrial worker needed the capitalist infinitely more than the capitalist needed the industrial worker ... In the knowledge society the most probable assumption for organisations—and certainly the assumption on which they have to conduct their affairs—is that they need knowledge workers far more than knowledge workers need them. [Drucker, 1994: 10]

The implication, according to Drucker, of knowledge becoming the key organisational resource is that there is a world economy, and it is the world economy, rather than the national economy, that is in control: 'Every country, every industry, and every business will be in an increasingly competitive environment. Every country, every industry, and every business will, in its decisions, have to consider its competitive standing in the world economy and the competitiveness of its knowledge competencies'. Hayes & Pisano (1994: 86) come close to meeting Drucker's criteria in arguing that '... a company should think of itself as a collection of evolving capabilities'. But it is the knowledge of *how to evolve capabilities* that is the key.

Drucker's phrase 'knowledge competencies' is equivalent to our concept of knowledge technology. It is not knowledge itself that is the resource, the means of producing the output. The resource is the history of learning of the participants about how to acquire and use changing knowledge bases. Some of this technology is brought in by each participant. But much of it is developed in concert with the others—it is an interactively generated and sustained process of knowledge management, tailored to the system of action they have created.

The question of how an organisation's knowledge resources can be fully used in the Fourth Blueprint workplace is complex. Our conclusion is that it is a process which must be recognised as multidimensional. We find helpful the three-stage model proposed by Huber (1991):

- *knowledge acquisition*—the development or creation of skills, insights, relationships;
- *knowledge sharing*—the dissemination of what has been learned;
- *knowledge utilisation*—the integration of learning so it is broadly available and can be generalised to new situations.

Huber refers to the assimilation and utilisation process as 'organisational memory'. He asserts that relatively little is known about this process in which knowledge becomes institutionally available, as opposed to being the property of select individuals or groups. Certainly, the problem is that individuals come from other intersecting systems of action with their own language and culture. Schein (1996), for example, concludes that organisations will not learn effectively until their subcultures discover that they use different languages and make different assumptions about what is important, and until they learn to treat the other cultures as valid and normal.

Our experience suggests that Schein is right. Elsewhere, we have described the phenomenon of 'parallel talk' (Limerick, Passfield & Cunnington, 1994: 29) in which those involved in strategic change processes talk *next* to, or *parallel* to, one another. In this sense, they exhibit characteristics not unlike those of some young children in a playground who do not play *with* one another, they play *next* to one another. Part of the challenge of developing knowledge technology is that of learning to talk to each other so that differences can be used. As Mintzberg and his colleagues show, the knowledge of how people connect can often be surprising. 'Collaboration can be a pain in the ass' (Mintzberg et al, 1996: 71), but knowing how people connect is a key organisational resource.

Finally, the importance which Fourth Blueprint organisation places on processes of collaborative individualism and networked alliances facilitates the maximal use of knowledge sources. Kanter (1995) makes this point tellingly in an interview with Richard Hodgetts. She asserts that where local economies exhibit collaborative advantage in the world economy, a key factor is the distinctive excellence that applies in three specialities which she describes as makers, traders and thinkers. She concludes that:

> No local economy is in a secure position without distinctive excellence in one skill and the ability to use the other two. ... So what I'm saying is that whether you are a thinker, maker, or trader, you have to leverage your competence. You can't confine it to an industry per se because that's too narrow. [Kanter, 1995: 64]

Thus, knowledge in Fourth Blueprint organisations is *enabling* because it facilitates the development of value-addedness and collaborative advantage; it is *distinctive* because it reflects a unique organisational vision; and it is *processual* because it emphasises 'knowledge of how to use knowledge'. This technology, used as part of a self-transcendent microstrategic cycle, is a potent force for change.

Technological Integration as Force for Change

In discussing the research which led to her highly influential publication, *World Class: Thriving Locally in the Global Economy* (1995), Kanter summed up the central role which technology plays in the Fourth Blueprint workplace. In the interview with Hodgetts, she said:

> I define globalisation in terms of two things: increased cross-border activity as well as technology that permits instantaneous communication. I think these are the two most important phenomena that are part of what we call globalisation. In turn, these help create forces that start the globalisation cascade effect. [Kanter, 1995: 57]

While the obvious point is that technology enables us to exploit the value chain (Rayport & Sviokla, 1995), Kanter's point is that technology in its emerging forms is more than hardware, software, or combinations of the two—it is an integrative force which accords new meanings to time and space. Again from the interview with Hodgetts, she argues that:

> Greater international activity on the part of one company in one industry starts having impact on other companies in other industries. One of these is rapid resource mobility. Resources are not nearly as space-bound as they once were. Capital now flows much more freely, and ideas flow very freely, in part because of the instantaneous communication. ... A second force is simultaneity. Today more things occur at the same time in various parts of the world. ... Another is the growing tendency of companies to treat the world as one world. So the array of products available across countries is becoming more and more similar. [Kanter, 1995: 57]

The development of integrative knowledge technology transforms the very system of action in which it is used, and provides new possibilities for defining the identity, scope and interactive nature of the collaborative community. Riffel and Levin (1997) have drawn attention to the dilemma that this poses for educational institutions caught on the cusp of the postcorporate era:

> Computer studies is one of the few areas in which teachers accept that some students will know more than they do. The changes in power relations, in roles and skills needed to be successful in a new environment, could be dramatic, but whether these opportunities will be seized is yet an open question. [Riffel & Levin, 1997: 60]

Perhaps the bottom line is that it is now well within the realm of possibility to imagine community schools and colleges in which teachers have access via the net to internationally-approved curriculum frameworks; students have 24-hour on-line enrolment access to globally accredited courses; the personal 'home page' constitutes a source of identity that cuts across boundaries of age, gender, ethnicity, politics, geography and numerous other variables; courses are offered by non-credentialled experts; the 'cyber coffee shop' is the central social venue of middle schools and high schools; and teachers are networked inter-systemically and cross-systemically within their discipline areas. We are on the cusp of an educational future that may know none of the constraints of compulsory attendance, hours of operation, location or credentialling that have characterised schooling for the past century. Indeed, when Peter Drucker (1994) stated that in the postcorporate world the school will be 'society's centre', *but not tied to any particular country or system of education*, he appears to have had in mind a view of education that is defined in large part by technological access. Thus, the challenge posed by Riffel and Levin (1997) for schools might be posed for all organisations striving to enter the Fourth Blueprint; it is to use new forms of technology, not to reinforce existing hierarchical and social relationships, but as a basis for reinventing them.

The capacity of postcorporate technologies to develop and enhance communal identity and create 'on line' communities is also a distinctive feature of the Fourth Blueprint. For example, Armstrong and Hagel (1996) report that electronic communities meet four types of consumer needs:

- *communities of transaction,* which primarily facilitate the buying and selling of products and services, and deliver information related to those transactions;
- *communities of interest,* which bring together participants who interact extensively with one another on specific topics;
- *communities of fantasy,* where new environments, personalities, or stories can be created; and
- *communities of relationship* around certain life experiences that often are very intense and can lead to the formation of deep personal convictions.

Dale Spender (1997) provides the following illuminating observations of ways in which advances in technology in Fourth Blueprint organisations contribute to reshaping the concept of individual identity to individual in community identity:

> The personal home page is the electronic equivalent of the diary or journal; it will be the electronic identity—the means of self presentation and promotion—in the digital environment.

Putting a home page on the World Wide Web, and upgrading it each day, is much the same activity as was putting pen to paper for the old journal entry. However one difference is—and it is a very big difference—that whereas the journal was private, the Home Page is there for all the millions of cybercitizens to read.

Creating a home page is all about creating an on-line identity. You have to think pretty carefully about who you are—and how you want the cyberworld to see you. And then you have to be pretty good at putting it all out there. It takes both technical know how—and a great deal of creativity. [Spender, 1997: 27]

Thus, technology is a pervasive, integrating force which, by its very existence, engenders new communication systems, changes power relationships, and has the potential to eliminate traditional lines of vertical and horizontal demarcation and organisational boundaries.

The challenge of developing processual resources is not an easy one, as the following example illustrates:

Developing Processual Resources in a Secondary College

An example of the challenge faced by Third Blueprint organisations as they attempt to change over to Fourth Blueprint conceptions of resources is that of a medium size secondary college with a well-developed market niche, now under pressure to establish alliances with a range of offshore educational institutions. Responsibility for all aspects of governance is vested in the School Council, which comprises the principal and an equal number of school staff and community members. Commonwealth and state grants for capital works complements a student fees system for which the principal and bursar are responsible. The school teaches the state curriculum but has been alerted to the growing preference of some parents for internationally approved, competency-based programs in vocational areas. The school also engages extensively in a range of high profile, extracurricular activities which are monitored carefully by alumni and parent advisory bodies. A Board decision has recently been made to encourage all newly enrolling Year 7 students to purchase their own individual laptop computers. At the principal's initiative, a joint venture has been undertaken with the local municipal authority to create a community recreational facility on college property. Most recently, however, the effects of drought and a declining community population have raised questions about amalgamations with some schools in the area, possibly extending to include technology-based course offerings with a TAFE college in a nearby town.

It is apparent from situations such as this that educational organisations coming out of the late corporate era can and must establish means of reconceptualising their resources. In managing resource issues, they need to ensure strong links between their metastrategic vision and their processes for operational design and action. In doing so, their total identity and vision will change. They will view themselves as located in contexts of multi-employers (ranging across offshore, Commonwealth, state and local educational authorities), as catering to multi-sectors (employment, community welfare, postcompulsory institutions, to name a few), and as part of the global economy.

LEADERSHIP: A MULTIPLE ROLE PERSPECTIVE

We have left one of the thorniest issues in Fourth Blueprint microstrategy until last. It is thorny because it flies in the face of one of our most dearly held hierarchical concepts—that of 'the leader'. The critical reader will have noted that, as we moved in our discussion from First to Third and then to Fourth Blueprint thinking, we began to change our terminology about influence relationships in organisations. As Hassard (1994) and others have argued, the only way we can know the world is through shared language. Our language perforce has changed as the nature of the social reality we have been describing has changed.

Thus, in our discussion of First and Second Blueprint systems, we spoke easily about the role of the CEO as the prime mover and shaper of organisational identity and configuration. When we moved on to the Third Blueprint we spoke about the CEO and 'those at the strategic apex' of the organisation. By the time we moved on to Fourth Blueprint metastrategy, we began to focus on the role of the founder, or the hub, in initiating the identity, vision and configuration design of the organisation. But we then turned our attention to all organisational participants in describing the process of negotiating, maintaining and renewing the organisation through such processes as appreciative inquiry. We began to see the role of managing the organisation as not confined to an organisational leader, nor to an élite: it is the task of all participants.

What makes this discussion particularly difficult and potentially confusing is that while we have stressed participant involvement in 'shared fields of meaning', our examples have given clear evidence of the impact of individuals like Welch and D'Aquino on the renewal of organisations. How can such clear evidence of the powerful impact of leaders on Fourth Blueprint organisations coexist with a focus on all participants as the architects of the new organisation?

The answer to this paradox lies in the fact that our discussion draws on a very different tradition of thinking about leadership than the mainstream leader–follower paradigm—that of shared leadership, or, more accurately, *multiple leadership roles*.

From 'the Leader' to Multiple Leadership Roles

Any examination of mainstream, malestream leadership theory will show that it is predicated on the model of leader–followers. That is, it is assumed that in any well-functioning system there is a leader who inspires or influences his (usually) followers. These images are part of our historical consciousness, embedded in 'great man', situational and/or contingency models of leadership. The leader is the person who is attractive by dint of the possession of charisma, or who can choose the right leadership style for the situation.

Interestingly enough, even the recent discussions of transformational leadership perpetuate such a model. Typical of fairly early assertions on transformational leadership is that of Levinson and Rosenthal:

> Strong leaders are necessary, particularly for organisations that must undergo significant change. Not good managers, or executives, but strong leaders. [Levinson & Rosenthal, 1984: 289]

This was paralleled by Burns' distinction between the transformational leaders and the transactional leaders, to which we referred disparagingly in Chapter 5.

> Instead of the incrementally oriented, systems maintaining, transactional leader, transformational leaders ... seek to engage with not only passing and relatively superficial desires of followers but with their most fundamental wants and needs, which in the interaction of such leaders and followers are converted into hopes and aspirations and ultimately into expectations, entitlements, and demands on leadership. [Burns, 1984: 153]

So deeply linked to our hero heritage are these images that writers can wax lyrical about them:

> The central issue of path-finding is not influence or persuasion, nor is it reasoning or systematic analysis. The key word here is *mission*. The path-finding part of managing is the homeland of the visionary, the dreamer, the innovator, the creator, the entrepreneur and the charismatic leader. [Leavitt, 1987: 10–11]

Clifford and Cavanagh are even more enthusiastic:

> Life can be lonely and frustrating for a visionary with a cause in a crowd of the dispassionate and uninterested. What distinguishes the best founders and leaders is how they transform their personal commitment and obsession into institutional obsession and energy.

> Part and parcel of the temporal leadership of the winning chief executive is his or her success in instilling among others in the organisation the same meaning the enterprise has for its leaders;

because, most importantly, what distinguishes the high performance companies from the also-rans is the meanings—beyond a place to get a pay-cheque, these enterprises provide for those who populate them.

But more important than sheer enthusiasm is their commitment to and understanding of the values ... many, many acts—symbolic and substantial—build meanings for these companies ... [Clifford & Cavanagh, 1985: 234]

Not all writers agree that such leadership is a feature of the leader's personality. Bass and Avolio, for example, believe that such leadership can be taught and developed in people, although their circumstances are more likely to have acted as the teacher. Bass suggests that transformational leaders 'are "twice-born" individuals who endure major events that lead to a sense of separateness, or perhaps estrangement, from their environments' (Bass, 1990: 9). Moreover, they are characterised by 'energy, self-confidence, determination, intellect, verbal skill, and strong ego ideals' (Bass & Avolio, 1990: 26).

This paradigm is echoed by many of the practitioner heroes of our Western society. General Norman Schwarzkopf, for example, uses an unblushing First Blueprint paradigm when he asserts that leadership is 'motivating people to do what they don't want to do' (Schmidt, 1997, 32). He summarises his views on leadership with two rules: 'when put in charge, take command', and 'do the right thing'. Lee Iacocca, the former Ford and Chrysler chairman, takes the same line: 'Leadership can be very lonely, but one person must lead and get people to do things they don't want to do' (Schmidt, 1997: 32).

The problem with these images is not that they are wrong: it is that they are only partly right. They ignore a whole alternative stream of leadership research and theory that goes right back into the 1950s. To understand this alternative paradigm, we invite you to undertake the following steps.

• Stop thinking about leadership as the quality of some individual. Think of it instead as *facilitative behaviour*—as behaviour that facilitates collective action towards a common goal. It is not hidden behaviour; it is recognised and expected by others in the system—it is a role.

- Now ask yourself: How is that *behaviour distributed* in the groups you have experienced? Is it normally:
  (a) carried out by one person in the group?
  (b) randomly distributed between members of the group? or
  (c) distributed between a number of members of the group, depending on the situation?

When we have workshopped that question amongst groups of managers, very few have opted for alternative (a). Most have chosen (c). That is, even from our own experience, the notion of 'the leader', Iacocca's 'one person', is a nonsense: leadership behaviour is distributed between many members of groups.

The results of research into this area lead to the same conclusion. Without exception, every single study that has specifically looked at the distribution of leadership behaviour in groups has found that it is never in the hands of just one person (see even the earliest of studies by Benne & Sheats, 1948; Bales, 1950; Parsons, Bales & Shils, 1953; Bales & Slater 1955; Slater, 1955; Zaleznik, 1963; and Limerick, 1976). More recent work, particularly that of Belbin (1993) on team roles, leads to the same conclusion: it is more accurate to think of different leadership roles in a group than to think of 'the leader'.

Why should leadership behaviour be distributed between different members of a social system? Or, to put the question the other way around, why can one member not use all the leadership behaviours in a group? The answer is: because many of the behaviours are incompatible. If one person tried to use them at the same time they would cause confusion or lose credibility. Thus, it is possible to identify different roles, or patterns of behaviour, which reflect different, balancing, contradictory needs in a system. At least three axes of role formation have been identified:

1. process and content roles;
2. convergent and divergent roles; and
3. task and maintenance roles.

- *Process and content roles.* As early as 1976, Limerick found that process/content distinctions served as one axis for leadership role differentiation. Process leaders normally have structural authority in a group—that is, they are the boss, or the chairperson. Their job is to use that authority to set the agenda, control and facilitate processes and commit the group to action. It is not a passive, secretarial role: on the contrary, it is a demanding, challenging role which seeks out commitment to high goals, and takes command where necessary and asks challenging questions.

It is such a visible command role that you can understand why Schwarzkopf and Iacocca would see it as the whole of leadership. But it is not: process leaders ask the challenging questions, but do not provide the answers themselves (Heifetz & Laurie, 1997). First, if they did, they would soon convince the others that they need not be there at all: we have known for a long time that autocratic leaders who use groups have lower productivity than those who do not bother to do so! (Likert, 1961). Second, if they tried to lead the content as well, they would soon confront authority dilemmas. When the chair of a group, or the boss, says 'We must do this...' does it mean 'We must ... (command, or commitment to action)'? or 'We must do this if we want to do the job properly (advice)'? When others in the group do not know, they tend to play it safe, assume it is a command and, since the speaker is the boss, go along with it. Thus, process leaders who get into content (the solution, what we ought to do) actually suppress the number and range of ideas that come out of a group. This is suicidal for groups in an unpredictable environment. Monsanto's CEO, Robert Shapiro, sums up what we regard as a Fourth Blueprint view of leadership in relation to the organisation's microstrategic functions:

People give more if they can figure out how to ... contribute what they can contribute out of their own authentic abilities and beliefs. [Magretta, 1996: 87]

Good process leaders therefore stimulate and work along with *content* leaders in the group. These are recognisable as the 'wise owls' of the group, who can express the group's consensus on content. This, in turn, provides a sound basis for the process leader's commands or commitment to action. Process and content leadership roles are synergistic—they produce more leadership, not a watered-down shared version of leadership.

- *Convergent and divergent leadership roles.* There are at least two kinds of content leadership roles: those that exemplify or express the group's convergence or consensus, and those that contribute by blowing it apart. One person cannot credibly do both—one person cannot fight for consensus and keep throwing out the wild ideas at the same time. While the two needs, convergence and divergence, are contradictory, they are both needed. Thus effective Fourth Blueprint groups achieve a balance between the exemplar and challenger leadership roles.
- *Task and maintenance roles.* Bales and his colleagues (1970) found that behaviours which pursue task solution (content) roles, and behaviours that help maintain the group's social cohesion are often incompatible. It is hard to win an argument and be the best-liked person at the same time. So in the groups they studied, Bales and his colleagues found two complementary leadership roles—the task leader (the person recognised as having the best ideas), and the maintenance leader (the person recognised as the best liked in the group). Both, they argue are necessary for group effectiveness.

These are just some of the studies that recognise the emergence of multiple leadership roles in groups. Some, of course, overlap. Bales's 'task leaders' are similar to Limerick's (1976) 'content leaders'. There is still a great deal to be learned about the multiple leadership roles and how they interact, and, as the focus moves away from transformational leadership to shared leadership and a communitarian, communal view arising from the feminist literature (Rogers, 1988; Shakeshaft, 1995), no doubt a greater understanding will emerge. But the basic lesson is clear: leadership is an organisational quality, not the property of an individual (Ogawa & Bossert, 1995). It is likely that Fourth Blueprint organisations will require and will stimulate a high density of divergent roles—they not only need the capacity to commit themselves to action, and often very quickly, but their discontinuous environment and loosely coupled nature exacerbate the need for different ideas, for consensus, and for social maintenance. In this respect, Lakomski's conclusion is appropriate:

> [T]he conception of leadership, as currently debated in both TA (transactional) and TF (transformational) guises, raises a number of

difficulties ... More participative structures which incorporate the knowledge of all may yet make the best sense in terms of facing the challenges posed by an inherently uncertain and unpredictable future. [Lakomski, 1995: 223]

A second lesson is also clear—'great' people do not do all of the things all of the time (*role fusion*); they do the right thing at the right time (*role flexibility*). People in Fourth Blueprint systems are members of very different systems of action in which they may play different roles. And change, even in one system, is so discontinuous that they may have to give up one kind of contributing role and play another as circumstances change. Our training programs will have to focus more on role flexibility, and less on the ideology of transformational leadership. We assume that there is some sort of normal curve in our capacity to play different kinds of roles. Some will have little flexibility: they will have to learn how to maximise the contribution of their narrow strengths in a wider variety of systems. Most can develop some flexibility—and the more, the better. Some will be very flexible, and they will be able to play a wide range of roles.

We will still need good, strong, challenging process leaders like Welch and D'Aquino. And like those two, they will have to have the confidence to work synergistically with the diversity of leadership roles within organisations. Perhaps the image of Ricardo Semler, tearing up the rule-books at Semco, searching for complementary leaders by inviting all workers to budget and strategy meetings and having his own possibly stupid, potentially costly mistakes prevented by workers (Schmidt 1997, 32–3), provides a clear picture of leadership in Fourth Blueprint post-corporate systems.

Of course, process leadership is so visible and so obvious because it is normally exercised at the top of the apex in the residual hierarchy of postcorporate formal organisations. Thus, we will still tend to see the heads of those systems as charismatic, transformational leaders. It is not hard to, because, as Gronn points out, it fulfils the 'promise of the hero. This promise is that it is the actions of individual leaders who make a difference'(1995: 14). But we will also be aware of the diversity of leadership with which the heroes have collaborated, and aware that our attributions of charisma are probably just that—attributions that take place after the action (Lakomski, 1995). In postcorporate networks processes, leadership is less obvious because there is no hierarchy. But we will still build narratives and legends around the different, diverse, important leaders in these complex systems.

Those who approach leadership from within the newer paradigm often tend to talk of 'shared leadership' or 'leadership density'. But such phrases might suggest that there is a limited quantum of leadership that is shared out, or that there is a high density of the same kind of leadership in effective groups. We prefer, therefore, to use phrases such as *multiple leadership roles* which reflect the existence of different kinds of leadership roles in a group, and which imply a capacity to act together to produce *more* leadership (not to share it). Similarly, we use terms like *leadership diversity* which suggest that effective social systems have a density of diverse leadership roles. That is, as Senge (1997) has asserted, the task of the participants—to build 'a community of leaders'.

MICROSTRATEGIC MANAGEMENT: THE NEED FOR A PARADIGM SHIFT

As this chapter has progressed, it will have become clear that the key to understanding microstrategic management in Fourth Blueprint systems does not lie in a more detailed examination of different operational techniques of management. Nor does it make much sense to attempt to describe a structural blueprint that can be used as a guide for managerial action. What has impressed us in researching the shape of new organisations is just how different they are, and how creatively they have used the material of their own contexts to compose workable systems of action. CUB used concept groups and learning centres, Beerwah State High school focused on appreciative inquiry groups, Welch turned GE into a management laboratory. The Fourth Blueprint is not a structural blueprint. Rather it is a process blueprint. For despite these differences, as this discussion has progressed, a distinctive image of Fourth Blueprint management at work has emerged. As a conclusion to this chapter, it is worth teasing out the most salient aspects of that image.

Everyone a manager. In the Fourth Blueprint system, managers are not a defined hierarchical élite. Anyone who is contributing to collaborative processes is managing and is a manager. That is, everyone, at times, is a manager. So when we refer to a 'Fourth Blueprint manager' we are referring to any participant who is focusing on collaborative processes. This is easy to see in a network—all the participants are its managers. The picture is a bit muddier in postcorporate organisations, where there is a residual hierarchy of people who would be 'managers' in corporate organisations. And of course they are still managers in post-corporate organisations where they have distinctive process leadership roles. But so are most of the other participants: if the span of control is one manager to 90 people, the message is clear. One manager cannot manage 90 people. So who is going to manage them? They are going to manage themselves! All participants are managers.

The situation is even more radical than that. Even 'outsiders' may be managers. As Mellish, from Mellish and Associates Consultants, argues, contemporary managers often subcontract part of the process leadership role to consultants, who ask the challenging questions and push for commitment to action. In a diverse, fast-moving world there is not much room for discussing the niceties of who should be called a manager.

Managing appreciatively. Fourth Blueprint managers (participants) are constantly working with diverse constituencies, attempting to manage meaning. That is, they are constantly trying to facilitate shared fields of meaning that allow collaboration. Yet, in doing so, they assert difference and eschew homogenisation of ideas and agendas—they focus instead on the creative design of systems of action that will satisfy the diverse participants. Of course there are problems to be solved, and Fourth Blueprint managers have to be able to react quickly. But in the general scheme of things, the solving of problems within current systems takes a back seat to designing better systems for the future. As the current idiom goes, it is no good driving into the future with one's eyes fixed on the rear-view mirror.

Managing the organisation as a resource. Fundamental to Fourth Blueprint managers' action is the understanding that the organisation is the participants' resource. They focus on the growth and development of its knowledge technology resources—its capacity to learn, and its capacity to use knowledge.

Managing horizontally. Whereas the focus of corporate management is on hierarchical coordination, the day-to-day concerns of Fourth Blueprint managers revolve around the horizontal connections that make up the value chain of which they are a part. This, as we have seen, requires very professional management competencies from all its participants, covering areas as critical as just-in-time technology, quality management, technological integration, and the like. The focus of the Fourth Blueprint manager, unlike the corporate counterpart, goes way beyond the conventional boundaries of the organisation to include current and potential allies. The hallmark of such managers is their determination to erase, not erect, boundaries.

Managing reflectively and holistically. Fourth Blueprint managers are constantly moving through the metastrategic cycle, relating what they are doing to the core values and evolving identity of the organisation as whole. Because they are aware of the constructedness of action, they are less likely to carry bureaucracies in their minds with sets of rule designed to protect a perceived identity. On the contrary, it is because they perceive identity to be problematic that they spend so much time on the management of meaning.

Managing ecologically. Because of this holistic approach, Fourth Blueprint managers focus centrally on the long-term sustainability of their organisation within its community. Indeed, public and private managers alike—school principals, teachers, managers of CUB—tend to see their organisation as a resource of the community.

Clearly, many of the management competencies and techniques developed in earlier blueprints are still relevant and useful—but they have to be taken into a new paradigm and reframed. There *are* new skills to be learned in managing beyond hierarchy—skills in horizontal coordination, technology management, the management of meaning, and creativity in composing new social systems. As Peters said, transforming a system does not require doing one thing 400 per cent differently, it requires doing 400 things one per cent differently. But what ties all of these actions together and gives them transformative force is a *mindset, a paradigm* that integrates and gives new meaning to them, that brings them into alignment so that their combined effect is capable of creating new, more effective, more satisfying social systems. The essence of the Fourth Blueprint is a new paradigm, and we now turn to a deeper understanding of that paradigm.

CHAPTER 7

THE FOURTH BLUEPRINT: TOWARDS A PARTICIPANT BASED PARADIGM OF ORGANISATIONAL MANAGEMENT

> *We are losing ourselves as fields of dreams. We believe that to regain the balance we must create alternative ways of working and living together.*
>
> [Kofman & Senge, 1993: 220]

IT IS IMPOSSIBLE to become immersed in the literature and practice of the new management without coming to the conclusion that the dominant paradigm in management theory today is fast becoming irrelevant to the majority of the working population. Moreover, it holds limited promise for throwing light on organisational problems of the future. It is true that there have been significant changes in the values, concerns and methodologies of management theory over the past decade as the field has moved towards more holistic concerns with cultural and strategic change. Nevertheless, while the world in which people work is being reconfigured by the discontinuities of postmodernism, the ageing, male, corporatist paradigm that underlies management theory and science remains firmly in place.

The reader who has had the fortitude and stubbornness to stay with us thus far will be aware that this book can be treated at two levels of analysis. At the more overt level it sets out to describe changes in social and economic patterns, and the changes in management mindsets and processes that accompany them. But at a deeper level of analysis the reader will sense that the book represents a journey in ways of understanding organisational life. As we undertook the task of understanding postcorporate organisation, we found that our focus, as well as our assumptions about the nature of reality, of knowledge and of science, were changing. With it, our language also changed, for language is our means of knowing reality.

In describing First, Second and Third Blueprint corporate organisations, we found it relatively easy to talk about 'the organisation', 'managers', the 'organisation's values' and the like. But as we tried to talk about Fourth Blueprint organisations, this sense of comfort disappeared in the face of virtual organisations, the sheer impermanence of patterns of social action, the extent to which social 'reality' was constructed by the participants, the problematic nature of individual and social identity and the understanding that, despite fields of shared meaning, there were multiple realities for multiple participants.

We have been able to draw on some assistance in conducting this journey. There are developing theoretical perspectives that focus on the constructivity of social action in fields as disparate as disorganised capitalism, postmodernism, feminism, constructivism, interpretivism, and the new management. However, in the field of management these perspectives have been largely disregarded by mainstream theorists, researchers and practitioners. They have been largely ignored (disorganised capitalism, interpretivism), marginalised into their own journals (feminism and postmodernism), and/or trivialised (the new management) by the mainstream, malestream management tradition, despite the increasing emphasis placed on managing diversity. We found that the concerns of these other movements hold much more relevance and promise for understanding postcorporate organisational processes than does our current management paradigm, but they require focused interpretation.

We have not only interpreted them, we have taken considerable liberties with them. We have used their basic concepts and insights without fully expounding on their theoretical frameworks. The views expressed here are ours, not those of any of the schools of thought mentioned above!

We have not set out to develop, and do not claim to have developed, a fully fledged empirically justified theory of organisational action in this book. Rather, we have accepted the sociorationalist, interpretivist position that theory should not be judged on the extent to which it corresponds with observable facts. Rather, as Cooperrider and Srivastva (1987) argue, the emphasis for evaluating good theory becomes 'To what extent does this theory present provocative new possibilities for social action, and to what extent does it stimulate normative dialogue about how we can and should organise ourselves?' (137).

Gergen (1992) makes essentially the same point: theory is to be judged by its 'pragmatic value'. Our model of the Fourth Blueprint and, within it, our model of collaborative individuals working through metastrategic cycles to create new social identities and actions, sets out to contribute to such provocative theory. The process of building towards such theory is not complete, and never will be. But, informed by many of the newer developments and theoretical debates in management (see, for example, Hassard, 1994) and by contemporary models of postcorporatism, we can begin to discern the shape of a new paradigm for management theory. In this final chapter we attempt to make that paradigm more accessible by teasing out some of the fundamental changes in focus and in the basic theoretical assumptions that underlie our exposition of Fourth Blueprint thinking. We are attempting to open doors to new organisational theory.

FROM CORPORATISM TO POSTCORPORATISM

The Traditional Focus on Corporatism

Management theory has been overwhelmingly concerned with the formal corporation. A perusal of almost any textbook or journal on management will reveal a single-minded preoccupation with medium to large sized, more or less hierarchical, organisations. A subject such as organisational behaviour (OB) focuses on human behaviour but it draws on the traditions of psychology for an understanding of individual, interpersonal and group behaviour. What distinguishes it from mainstream psychology is its contextualisation in, and limited relevance to, *the formal organisation*. It is true that OB attempts to be broadly interdisciplinary in drawing on the complementary insights of the other social sciences, but it is nevertheless also true that the insights that are considered important, or considered at all, are typically those that relate to the formal corporate organisation. The same is true for most other management disciplines.

Consider, for example, the following list of more or less randomly selected management concerns and applications:

- organisational commitment;
- job satisfaction;
- quality of *working* life (emphasis added);
- transformational leadership;
- cultural change;
- the learning organisation;
- job evaluation;
- organisation design;
- performance indicators;
- inter-group conflict (within organisations);
- participation;
- organisational excellence;
- one-minute management; and
- self-governing workgroups.

Each is heavily contextualised within the framework of the formal corporation. Almost any title from a recent management book or journal added to this list would carry the same message: the key concerns of management are those that are relevant to the corporate organisation. It might be argued that this is fair enough. After all, most people work for large organisations, don't they? And most management graduates will go into corporations, won't they? And in any case, that is what is important for our economic growth, isn't it?

The problem is that, as we saw in Chapter 1, the real answer to any of these questions is 'No!'. A huge proportion of people in the postcorporate world of disorganised capitalism work for themselves or in small businesses. Many, if not most MBA graduates are going into similar fields. And the importance of small business to economic growth is only just being grasped by governments that have traditionally been concerned with big business, big unions and big government.

The implications of socioeconomic reconfiguration for management theory are profound. For the postmodern individual who works for Jill Smith's photographic shop, the management concerns and applications listed above are largely irrelevant. For example, the concept of 'organisational commitment' is meaningless: the individual may get on well with Jill and/or coworkers, but there is no 'organisation' phenomenological correlate in their relationship.

Even those caught in neocorporate bureaucracies are frequently so turned off, or so injured, by the experience that they have outered and for them phrases like 'organisational commitment' are a laugh. For the consultant or outworker, concepts such as job satisfaction (as opposed to life satisfaction), quality of working life (as opposed to the quality of life), job evaluation, intergroup conflict and transformational leadership are either meaningless or require comprehensive reframing. For the unemployed and disempowered, all of these concepts are irrelevant. *If management theory is to be of any significance at all in such a world, it will have to change its focus from the corporatism of a bygone era to one that is grounded in postmodern, disorganised capitalism.* It will also have to change from its focus on business and government organisations to a focus on the service sector, too. As Paquette (1997: 10) points out:

> Developed societies are at a crossroads. Before them lies the possibility [of] a better life for all through encouragement of 'third sector' activity, rebalancing of emphasis and effort among private, public and non-profit sectors, and a revaluing of human contribution to the community. [Paquette, 1997: 10]

This is not to suggest that we should ignore the world of corporate behaviour. Large corporations will continue to exist and to represent an important stream of socioeconomic activity. But management theory will have to see them as part of the larger milieu of disorganised capitalism, and develop frameworks that can handle their changed intra- and extra-organisational processes. The Fourth Blueprint represents not an approach to understanding small business, but a holistic approach to understanding behaviour in a world in which individuals, small businesses, networks and diasporas, as well as corporations, organise their activity both severally and jointly.

A book such as this, therefore, that sets out to document the thinking behind, and the practices of, postcorporate management, demands also a different, postcorporatist, paradigm for the management of collaborative effort. Such a paradigm must enable a shift in focus from the corporation to the total, complex organisational ecology.

Towards a New Paradigm

A new paradigm of organisational action grounded in postcorporatism will have to reflect changes in the focus (What do we study?), the ontology (What is the nature of reality?), and the epistemology (What is the nature of knowledge?) of management theory.

A CHANGE OF FOCUS

From Large to All

We cannot continue to confine the focus of management and business schools to the corporate world of medium and large organisations, when a large proportion of workers are outside them, and when they form just part of a larger organisational ecology. To be sure, small business courses and research exist within most business schools, but, except in the work of Porter (1990) and others working on value chains, they are separated and marginalised from mainstream management. They are different courses, and they have a largely different focus—often a focus on entrepreneurial behaviour. Indeed, one major reason that they are not included in mainstream management courses is that their concerns and issues are so different from those of the prevailing paradigm that it would be clumsy to try to include them. At almost every point one would have to say parenthetically, 'Of course in small businesses ...'. What one would then put into the rest of the sentence is a moot point, because relatively little research has been done on small businesses. But, to the extent that small and large businesses are kept apart both conceptually and in research, graduates cannot hope to understand behaviour in the complex atomised yet interrelated ecology of disorganised capitalism. The task is not an easy one: it is to find a paradigm that can be used to shape an understanding of behaviour in the total ecology in which individuals and organisations of all sizes compete and collaborate. The concept that dominates this book, of loosely coupled, multiple systems of action arrayed along a value chain, goes some way to contributing to such a paradigm.

From Hierarchy to Horizontalism and Loose Coupling

The management theory paradigm was largely constructed in an era in which large corporations were tightly integrated hierarchies. Many of its concepts have limited relevance to the loosely coupled (structurally) networks of disorganised capitalism. The critical point is that the study of behaviour in networks cannot be handled satisfactorily as an add-on to studies of corporate behaviour. Many corporations themselves have also moved from hierarchy to horizontalism, from boundaries to organisations without walls. They have been interpenetrated by, and form part of, the dynamics of disorganised capitalism. The task that now confronts management theory is to redefine the term 'organisation' to include the total ecology of organised activity and to develop a language that recognises and makes focal the interconnectedness of that ecology. It is likely, for example, that terms such as 'systems of action', or 'social architecture' which may straddle formal organisational boundaries, hold more promise for handling diffuse organisational ecologies than does our conventional structural terminology.

From the Small Group to the Diaspora

We are accustomed to limiting the study of interpersonal relationships to dyads and small groups, and to relegating large-number groups to a conceptual dustbin called 'crowds'. But modern forms of organising, using hi-tech information systems backed up by information management systems, are producing groups and teams of anywhere from 20 to 100 members. The process of appreciative inquiry is based on an acceptance of large numbers of loosely coupled individuals being involved in the change process. We have not yet begun to understand the dynamics and leadership patterns of large, organised, task-oriented groupings such as these. Unfortunately, the problem confronting management theory today is even more complex than that: it is to understand the dynamics and influence patterns of diasporas—of dispersions of people who share the same values and who partake in the same social action. These diasporas are becoming basic structural units within and between organisations. For example, in large organisations the most influential sub-cultures are often not those within different departments or units. They are groupings, like different age cohorts, that straddle the organisation and extend into broader social arenas. Conventional concepts of group cohesiveness, leadership and teamwork will require significant reframing if they are to capture the dynamics of such groupings. Without doubt, we require a new language for looking at the interaction–influence processes of such virtual organisations. Again, concepts such as collaborative individualism, the death of membership, and loose coupling, together with an understanding of the role of technology in allowing diasporas to become social actors by creating systems of action, go some way to helping us move out of the straightjacket of corporate thinking.

From Males to Multiplicity and Diversity

The problem is not so much that management theory has focused on male participants in organisations—there have been studies of female participants. The more fundamental problem has been that such studies have taken place within the paradigm of the formal, hierarchical, malestream organisation. Much of the current work that focuses on women in organisations from within the management theory perspective treats subjects such as EEO and affirmative action as band-aids and palliatives to handle the worst aspects of male power systems—and uses malestream research techniques to do so. Yet one of the most consistent messages coming out of the new management is that, in order to deal with the postmodern era, organisations will have to learn to use different intelligences—the intelligences of all their participants. What is required are organisational configurations that are more compatible with *women's ways of being*—indeed, with multiple ways of being and multiple realities. A number of feminist authors has begun to address this problem, but their work is marginalised in the management literature, and rarely cited or integrated into it. Undoubtedly, their perspectives have much to offer in understanding lifestream and social sustainability issues in modern organisational forms.

From the Factory Gate to Lifestream

One of the most persistent critiques of management theory traditions that has been launched by sociologists pertains to the tendency to treat as important only that behaviour which starts at the factory gate. Feminist research and scholarship has done much to fill that gap by focusing on the relationship between home and work. As Burgess-Limerick (1995) points out, this work will have to be developed even further if it is to cope with the experiences of, say, women owner-managers of small businesses. Primarily, it will have to abandon the oppositional dichotomy between home and work, and recognise the extent to which these are part of the broader 'lifestream' of the individual. As we saw in Chapter Five, the postmodern individual does not see her context (home and/or work) as constraining, but rather as part of a world that can be shaped by appropriate positioning, redefining and experimentation. Under these conditions, Burgess-Limerick argues, concepts of self-as-entity are highly problematic, and a more processual paradigm is required, one that focuses on the ways in which individuals use context to compose self and negotiate their lifestreams. That is, as we saw in Chapters 3 and 4, management theory will have to move from a paradigm of constrained agency (agency constrained by context) to one of responsive agency (agency using context). Overall, the holistic, processual, proactive language and ontological assumptions of this kind of analysis are far more congruent with an era of postmodern, disorganised capitalism than are the rather quaint notions of corporate citizenship and the good organisational soldier (Organ, 1988) that still permeate so much management theory.

From a Reactive Outward–Inward Focus to Holism

The more holistic paradigm reflected in lifestream concepts will also have to be echoed at the level of the organisation. Typically, the assumption underpinning studies of organisation–environment relationships is one of constrained agency. Thus the premise of management theory's much loved contingency theory is that organisational behaviour is contingent upon environmental variables. This is sometimes accompanied by the parenthetical observation that the organisation can also, of course, act upon the environment. But this observation tends not to be built into the contingency theory paradigm. The alternative notion of responsive agency, not based on oppositional dichotomies, would suggest that organisational and environmental action are part of a broader stream of processes in which the boundaries between organisation and the environment are constantly shifting. They act on and shape the environment as they shape themselves. Within these processes, organisational actors play a proactive role in experimenting with and redefining organisation–environment boundaries, processes and relationships. Within such a milieu, as Millett found in his study of change in educational institutions, the concept of organisational identity is highly problematic. Key actors within organisations during periods of change are in a constant process of defining and redefining—of composing—organisational identity (Millett, 1995).

From Management to the Participant

Management studies take an overwhelmingly managerialist approach to behaviour in organisations: they focus almost exclusively on the problems of a managerial élite in managing organisations. The most obvious problem of such a perspective is that it can lead to what Etzioni many years ago called the 'manipulative charge' (Etzioni, 1964). That is, management theory can be seen to be the servant of managers in helping them to manipulate workers (Ehrensal, 1995). The manipulative possibilities inherent in concepts such as organisational commitment, empowerment, job evaluation and the like, are obvious enough and have been widely explored, particularly within the class-based dialectic of the radical, neo-marxist critique. But that is not the issue central to this book. In order to capture the perspective adopted here, it is necessary to move away from the considerations of management and the worker and to reframe the issue entirely.

Imagine, instead, a book on *how to manage the organisation—from the point of view of the individual joining it*. Such a book would take an entirely different perspective. For example, it would be concerned not with the problem of organisational commitment, but with the issue of how the individual can manage organisational systems of action so that they support lifestream issues and objectives and social processes. From such a perspective, the notion of organisational commitment may be highly problematic for the individual.

Our book has been a journey towards this perspective, as we move from the easy managerialist assumptions of corporatism into the impermanent world of the collaborative individual and of metastrategic processes in which vision and identity are negotiated social outcomes. This different perspective, approaching issues in behaviour in organised effort from the viewpoint of the participant, is perhaps the most fundamental shift required for the study of organised postcorporate action. It turns most of the assumptions of management theory and its sub-disciplines on their head. When viewed from the perspective of the individual joining an organisation, topics such as organisational commitment, transformational leadership, control, cultural change, job evaluation and the like take on entirely different meanings, and the behavioural questions associated with them have to be framed in a very different way. Yet this is quintessentially what is required of a management paradigm that has the capacity to handle post-modernism. It has to be able to handle the problems of managing for *all* in the organisation, and to do so without simply extending the concerns of a managerial élite in a hierarchical system to everyone else. When management is participant-based, it is *different from hierarchical manipulative management concerns.*

Moving towards a focus on the participant is not an argument for phenomenological reductionism. Processes of organising behaviour cannot be fully understood from the experience of any one individual. It is, instead, an argument for adopting multiple perspectives but without any implicit ordering of those perspectives into a hierarchy of assumed salience for under-standing organised behaviour. It is an essentially constructionist argument that focuses on the ways in which individuals, acting together, construct organisations to meet their own lifestream needs.

From High Performance to Social Sustainability

An approach such as this makes the normal managerial tele-ological assumption that organisational action is to be judged by its impact upon organisational 'performance' look outdated.

In general, most management research and theory has focused on concepts of organisational effectiveness that are deeply embedded in notions of high performance—a trend that has culminated in the currently popular notion of the 'high performing organisation'. Such concepts are easier to maintain within a paradigm which assumes fairly sharp, stable boundaries to formal organisations and which assumes that organisations are teleologically defined. But this paradigm becomes problematic in a world in which organisational and environmental processes and action are inseparable aspects of larger streams of events. Under these conditions, one of the key considerations for the workability of social action processes is the extent to which they are sustained by, and sustain, the social matrix in which they are embedded. Thus, as we concluded in the previous chapter, the 'effective organisation' is at a minimum a socially sustainable organisation. Its performance must be judged in terms of its reciprocal contributive relationships with its environment.

The high performance concept is also easier to maintain in a paradigm which assumes that the teleology of the organisation is to be defined from the point of view of one group of participants. There is an inevitable value judgement to be made in any definition of organisational effectiveness. But the point being made here is that a new paradigm is required that does not define effectiveness in terms of the values of just one constituency, or even of multiple constituencies. Organisational effectiveness, in a system of fluid reciprocal action, is to be defined in terms of the interacting, changing values and desired outcomes of all the actors as they mutually sustain each other. The emphasis is on the paradigm: as Shapiro, CEO of Monsanto, interviewed by Magretta (1997) comments:

> I'm fascinated with the concept of distinctions that transform people … For me, sustainability is one of those distinctions. Once you get it, it changes how you think. [Magretta, 1997: 88]

Porter and van der Linde make the same point:

> It is not at all surprising that the debate pitting the environment against competitiveness has developed as it has. Indeed, economically destructive struggles over redistribution are the norm in many areas of public policy. But now is the time for a paradigm shift to carry us forward into the next century. [Porter & van der Linde, 1995: 134]

A CHANGE OF ONTOLOGY, EPISTEMOLOGY AND METHODOLOGY

The ontology of any paradigm (its views on the nature of reality), its epistemology (its views on the nature of knowledge) and its methodology (how issues are to be researched and understood) are deeply interrelated. The past few decades have seen a number of vigorous critiques of the dominant positivist research paradigm.

Perhaps one of the most trenchant of the early attacks on positivism was that of Goffman:

> I claim as a defence that the traditional research designs thus far employed in this area have considerable limitations of their own ... The variables that emerge tend to be creatures of research designs that have no existence outside the room in which the subjects are located, except perhaps briefly when a replication or a 'continuity' has been performed under sympathetic auspices and a full moon ... Concepts have not emerged that reorder our view of social activity. Frameworks have not been established into which a continuously larger number of facts can be placed. Understanding of ordinary behavior has not accumulated; distance has. [Goffman, 1971: xvii]

Goffman's comments are worth noting because while he criticised positivism for focusing on variables and constructs rather than on a more holistic process, he left the ontological assumptions of realism intact. He wanted to continue the search for 'facts', but he wanted to do so from a more 'ethological' point of view, with 'unsystematic, naturalistic observation' (xvii).

In the past decade or so, many management researchers have more or less met the challenge of this critique by moving towards more holistic, case study based research, and by including in their repertoire 'grounded' approaches such as those of Glaser and Strauss (1967), and Strauss and Corbin (1990). What has been more difficult to handle has been the attack on realism itself. This attack has been sustained by a number of traditions, including neoMarxist critical theory, action theory, phenomenology, ethnomethodology and, more recently, feminism and interpretivism.

There is no intention within this book to rehash what is now becoming a rather boring argument between proponents of positivistic and qualitative methodologies. But it must be recognised that the narrow focus on positivism that dominates most management journals, texts and teaching offers limited leverage on the issues raised in this book. All of the alternative paradigms to which we have referred have something to offer in meeting the newer focus of the Fourth Blueprint. Ethnomethodology provides higher levels of holism in analysis and offers more leverage on both process issues and diffuse organisational ecologies such as networking. Critical theory and action theory move past managerial manipulation towards understanding the impact of class and power relationships upon social action: they move decisively past the factory gate. Phenomenology and interpretivism help complete the move from manager to participant, and provide leverage on the constructedness of social process and social institutions. Feminist perspectives offer an opportunity to move away from malestream assumptions about both organisational configurations and individual experience, and view these through a different lens.

Even these comments, however, do little justice to the richness of the opportunities offered by methodologies and paradigms that lie outside the dominant management paradigm. Perhaps one of the most interesting of the new methodologies canvassed in this book is appreciative inquiry. With its interpretivist ontology and action research methodology, it offers what we regard as refreshingly provocative insights into the process of composing social action.

A Focus on Actor Rather than Variable

It is ironic that management theory, with so many of its roots in organisational psychology and organisational behaviour, should, of all disciplines, remain wedded to a paradigm that treats people as variables within causal systems. A system that treats human beings or human behaviour as independent, moderating or dependent variables is unlikely to throw much light on the agentic processes by which people construct their lives and their behaviour. The problem is compounded by OB's propensity to explain what goes on *inside* the individual in terms of more variables—the hypothetical constructs (such as 'attitude' or 'intelligence') that enable causal generalisations to be made. Perhaps the task of inventing processual language is just too forbidding: it is far easier to explain why a person stays in an organisation in terms of a construct called 'organisational commitment', than to explore the ways in which individuals compose their lives, or to interpret the often contradictory meanings that organisations come to have for them in doing so. Yet Goffman's critique remains valid: to the extent that we treat people as variables, we do not increase understanding, we increase distance.

Why should management theorists remain so bound to such an unlikely paradigm? Perhaps it is because most of them are located in management schools where they teach managers, as opposed to teaching *about* management. Under these conditions, the charge of critical theorists—that management theory's penchant for positivism is related to its need to teach managers how to manipulate those variables called people—is uncomfortably close to the bone. When David Limerick was workshopping these ideas amongst his colleagues, he put to them the possibility of writing a book about managing the organisation from the point of view of someone joining it. The response of one of them was immediate: 'But you won't be able to sell the book!'.

Workers do not buy books and pay for research; managers do. At least that was true until the advent of disorganised capitalism. The increasing attendance at management schools of empowered knowledge workers and of those who intend to be self-employed will put the easy managerialist assumption under pressure even within management schools. Management teachers will have to come to terms with the participant-as-agent/actor rather than the participant-as-dependant variable. The research traditions that offer most hope for this shift are those that tend to start with the phenomenology and action of the individual and which therefore focus on individual agency within a lifestream context. *That* will bring us closer to understanding people.

A Focus on Process Rather than Structure

In order to move towards an understanding of the participant as agent, it will be necessary to adopt methodologies that focus on process rather than structure. In a world in which organisational systems of action were stable and bounded, structural models of organisation had considerable relevance and utility. Individuals and their behaviour could be seen as variables within them. However, in a world in which the only stable locus of activity is the individual, and where that individual is changing and is involved in changing multiple systems of action, structural paradigms become so cumbersome that they lose utility. The researcher must then start with a focus on individuals and the ways they construe and construct social action. That is, the research paradigm must become more process oriented.

This represents one of the greatest methodological challenges for management studies. One of the most difficult issues confronting us is the overwhelming lack of useful process terminology and concepts. Qualitative research methodologies are by their very nature process oriented. Grounded theory, for example, searches for 'core social processes', and one of its most critical stages comes when descriptive content categories are translated into processual language. Yet anyone who has conducted or supervised such research is uncomfortably aware that at that stage strange concepts and terminologies are invented on the run. The researcher faces the dilemma of either inventing new terminology and being accused of jargon, or using everyday words and being accused of misusing the English language. Phrases such as 'the saturated self' (Gergen, 1991), a social 'with' (Goffman, 1972), or 'responsive agency' (Burgess-Limerick, 1995) take a great deal of explaining.

This issue, however, must be confronted. We must move from a structural 'design' to an 'action' perspective (Nohria & Berkley, 1994). If we are to develop truly process-oriented theory that helps us to understand behaviour, we must develop concepts, language and taxonomies that assist in understanding the subtleties of behavioural processes. Thus, to pick on one of the above examples, we must begin to differentiate between concepts such as 'unmitigated agency', 'constrained agency', 'dialectical agency', and 'responsive agency' if we are to improve our understanding of women who own small businesses (Burgess-Limerick, 1995). Yet, as Burgess-Limerick points out, the very use of such phrases, which have been developed within feminist traditions, helps to make them inaccessible to malestream readers, and it becomes easy to dismiss them as 'girl stuff'. Organisational behaviourists will have to learn not only to tolerate such different concepts, but to embrace them, move towards their insights, and explain them to their own readers.

Contextualisation Rather than Universalism

One of the greatest difficulties with the positivist model of organisations is that it is so unselfconscious. Any doctoral thesis that uses interpretivism has to justify it, usually in a complete chapter on qualitative research. Any thesis that uses positivism simply uses it. That is true, of course, of most dominant paradigms. But what aggravates the problem in the field of management is its drive towards universalism—towards constructs, models and theories that are true for all people who work in organisations. The average American malestream textbook on management presents its models without any attempt to contextualise its perspective on job satisfaction, participation, and the like, within the cultural milieu of the malestream United States. The intellectual colonies of the new world have tended to accept this decontextualised view of behaviour without much complaint. Australia, for example, is plastered with a number of American management textbooks that have been 'Australianised' through the addition of a few Australian examples.

This is becoming increasingly problematic in a global organ-isational world. A few years ago, for example, David Limerick attended a conference on the 'Learning Organisation' held by Peter Senge and Chris Argyris in Brussels. During a tea-break that followed one of his sessions, Senge noted that he was having great difficulty gaining acceptance of his concepts by many of the European women in the audience. One of these women had been particularly scathing in asking how he expected female workers to participate with male bosses in learning how to get rid of their (the disempowered women's) jobs. Even Senge's useful concepts have to be contextualised within the European pluralist tradition. The assertion that learning organisations bring about high degrees of consensus and equity does not give much comfort to a person embedded in the European pluralist, conflicted, class based social structure. But an even more severe problem confronted Senge. The people he was confronting were *women* who were acutely aware, from the point of view of women-as-agents, of the meaning of what he was saying. The concept of 'participation' had very different meanings within their lifestreams. Argyris faced the same problem by reporting in his session that his generalisations were gender-free. The vigorous reaction of the women in the audience might have given him alternative data, but within the context of the seminar he was not able to explore their reactions in any depth.

Any attempt to understand behaviour from a processual point of view must be contextualised. The issue is not so much one of understanding behaviour *in* context; it is one of understanding behaviour *with* context (Burgess-Limerick, 1995). People-as-agents position themselves within context, redefine it, shift the boundaries between self and context, experiment with it and use its possibilities to craft self and compose their lifestreams (Kondo, 1990). To understand agency, one must understand context, for in process agency and context are inseparable. This is particularly so in examining processes of organising (and organised) action. Postmodernism, ironically, in pointing to the atomism of social structure, has to account in particular for processes of collaboration. It does so by placing the individual firmly within social context: it is a thesis of interdependence, not one of independence or dependence. Thus a concept such as 'relational self' (that is, I construct who I am in relation to various others) is quintessentially a concept within the postmodern paradigm.

Such a view can be pushed towards an extreme of relativism in which only the idiographic is a valid description and we become reluctant to make any generalisations at all. From within its own epistemology this is a defensible enough position, and there is without doubt a great deal to be gained from in-depth process oriented studies with a sample of one. But the argument here is intended to be broader than that. There is every reason for studies to take place that identify the broader nomothetic dimensions of context across multiple cases, and that examine processes within them. But these issues of context will be used differently from the usual positivist intent of prediction: they will be used to construct models and theories which facilitate new social action. The validity of such models will be judged in terms of criteria other than prediction, and will include alternatives such as warrantability, persuasiveness, generativity and the like. If a theory is good enough, all behaviour will be predictable—in retrospect!

Participant as Researcher

Perhaps the most fundamental change in the research paradigm required of management theory is a reform of power relationships in the research process itself. Such a change is necessary on pragmatic grounds because the empowered, agentic participant in postmodern work processes is unlikely to tolerate the role of 'subject'—just consider for a moment the power implications of that common OB research term! However, as Brigid Limerick, Burgess-Limerick and Grace (1996) and Burgess-Limerick (1998) point out, it is also necessary for more fundamental reasons. Research that starts with the agent generates interpretive theories that are the outcomes of collaboration between the 'researcher' and the participant. In effect, the participant becomes a collaborative researcher.

The most urgent areas for reform are in the fields of experimental research and experimental field research, which are dominated by the notion of participant-as-variable or participant-as-subject. Perhaps because so much of this research is carried out in situations where there are large power differentials (such as in research carried out by organisational behaviourists on behalf of management, or on paid student participants), it has been easier to treat the person in the organisation through an I–it, as opposed to an I–thou, relationship. However, an understanding of the person-in-process requires a joint exploration of the meanings of that process. A number of researchers have noted that subjective data are valid data in OB research. But the argument here requires a more radical shift than that; it asserts that the individual's *interpretations and explanations* of subjective experience are *required* for adequate theory formation. The participant is not only co-researcher but co-theorist, and the researcher is co-learner (Burgess-Limerick, 1998).

Consideration of this view suggests that it is not only in the area of experimental research that reform is required—it is also needed in more holistic, qualitative, ethnomethodological studies such as those that focus on cultural change. The nature of social anthropology itself is shifting dramatically because of exactly this set of considerations: empowered social groups will not accept the power assertions of the colonial 'observer'. Postmodern society, too, will not accept the researcher as colonial observer. Nor will it accept the researcher as colonial interpreter and theorist. In any case, the interpretations, to be persuasive and warrantable ('valid') and to provoke social action, require the collaborative interpretations of participants. Thus the management researcher will have to adopt a different positioning to the one that dominates the field today. The position is one of co-researchers who bring to the process a set of skills, knowledge and experiences that facilitates the participant co-researchers' understandings of themselves in process.

TOWARDS SOCIALLY SUSTAINABLE ORGANISATIONS

In the final analysis, the most significant aspect, and impact, of the new paradigm on which the Fourth Blueprint is based is its rejection of the notion of a dichotomy between description and prescription, between theory and action. Rather, it argues for theory and understanding *through* action. The purpose of research, the purpose of theory, is to facilitate action on the issues about which we feel passionate, and to learn from that action. In reviewing their paradigm of appreciative inquiry, Cooperrider and Srivastva (1987) argue that:

> [T]he core impact of sociorationalist metatheory is that it invites, encourages, and requires that students of social life rigorously exercise their theoretical imagination in the service of their vision of the good. Instead of denial, it is an invitation to fully accept and exercise those qualities of mind and action that make us uniquely human. [Cooperrider & Srivastva, 1987: 140]

No one knows what lies ahead of us—that is the very nature of discontinuity. No-one, as Hamel (1996) points out, can see the end from the beginning. No-one really has a picture of what the former Soviet Union will look like in the future. In the same way, the organisational communities in which Welch and D'Aquino played key leadership roles did not know what kinds of organisations would develop when they began their organisational trans-formations. But they were led by a broad, overarching, shared vision, a clear set of shared values with a tantalisingly elusive image of a future social system based on those values, and by a shared confidence that they had the skills to deal with evolving reality. More than that, they had the confidence that they would be able to *create organisations that could invent their own reality*, based on their own values. They knew that they could create emancipated, collaborative organisations that could invent and learn from their own social action. They could create action-learning communities.

In the final analysis, the new Fourth Blueprint organisation is a value-driven system. It rejects the hopeless, selfish anarchism of the New Right, with its capitulation to some 'invisible hand' in determining its values, just as surely as it rejects the imperatives of centralised systems. The new organisation stresses inter-dependence as implacably as autonomy, and recognises that at the heart of interdependence lie not only shared interests, but shared, transcendental values and meanings.

This is the key issue that confronts participants in loosely coupled, empowered organisations. They have to be responsive to, and responsible for, inventing and operating systems that reflect not only the values of those in their own organisations, but also those in the broader society of which they are a part. Whether they accept social responsibility or not is, in a sense, irrelevant: they will be *held* responsible for their social acts by the increasingly empowered, collaborative individuals of the societies in which they exist, and who can influence whether their organisations prosper or die.

Marilyn Ferguson notes that Huxley was profoundly optimistic about individuals at the margin of society, while he was pessimistic about 'collective humanity' (Ferguson, 1980: 52). As it turns out, the achievement of individualism has indeed been the easier part of the equation. Inventing stable systems of collaboration that express our dearest values is the hard part. But it is also the most critical to our progress. As Kofman and Senge (1993: 22) argue:

> We are losing ourselves as fields of dreams. We believe that to regain our balance we must create alternative ways of working and living together. We need to invent a new more learningful model for

business, education, healthcare, government, and family. This invention will come from the patient, concerted efforts of communities of people invoking aspiration and wonder. [Kofman & Senge, 1993]

We do not share Huxley's pessimism about coming to grips with collective action. Like others who are attempting to grapple with loosely coupled, empowered systems, we are frustrated by the impossible task of trying to imagine and talk about a discontinuous future in a language that is taken from the past. Like them, we find it relatively easier to express the transcendental values, the world view, the vision, that represent our future—difficult though that is—than to imagine the social system that reflects them. But, like them, we are attempting to collaborate with others in inventing new organisational forms, in developing new competencies to handle them, and a new language for talking about them.

That process of social entrepreneurship, of collaboratively inventing a new organisational future, looks to be a great deal of fun. Let us get on with it.

BIBLIOGRAPHY

Andrews, E. L. (1989). 'The New Minimalists'. *Venture*, 11, pp. 37–9.

Ansoff, H. I. (1988). *The New Corporate Strategy*. New York: John Wiley & Sons.

Apple, M. (1988). 'Work, Class and Teaching' in Ozra, J. (ed). *Schoolwork: Approaches to the Labour Process of Teaching*. Milton Keynes: Open University Press.

Argyris, C. (1964). *Integrating the Individual and the Organisation*. New York: Wiley.

—— & Schon, D. A. (1974). *Theory in Practice: Increasing Professional Effectiveness*. San Francisco: Jossey–Bass.

Armstrong, A. & Hagel, J. III. (1996). 'The Real Value of On-Line Communities'. *Harvard Business Review*, May–June, pp. 134–41.

Australian Teaching Council (1995). *What Do Teachers Think?* Leichhardt, ACT.

Auty, G. (1997). 'Erosion from Within'. *The Weekend Review*, Jan 25–6, p. 13.

Bales, R. F. (1950). *Interaction Process Analysis: Methods for the Study of Small Groups*, Cambridge, Mass.: Addison-Wesley.

—— (1970). *Personality and Interpersonal Behavior*. New York: Holt, Rinehart & Winston.

—— & Slater, P. E. (1955). 'Role Differentiation in Small Decision-making Groups'. In C. A. Gibb (ed 1969). *Leadership*. Harmondsworth: Penguin Books, pp. 255–76.

Baritz, L. (1977). *The Servants of Power*. Westport: Greenwood Press.

Barnard, C. I. (1948). *Functions of the Executive*. Cambridge, Mass.: Harvard University Press.

Barthes, R. (1986). *The Rustle of the Language*. New York: Hill & Wang.

Bass, B. M. (1990). 'From Transactional to Transformational Leadership: Learning to Share the Vision'. *Organizational Dynamics*, 18, Winter, pp. 19–31.

Bass, B. M. & Avolio, B. J. (1994). 'Shatter the Glass Ceiling: Women May Make "Better Managers"'. *Human Resource Management*, Vol. 33, No. 4, pp. 549–60.

—— (1990). 'Developing Transformational Leadership: 1992 and Beyond'. *Journal of European Industrial Training*, 14(5), pp. 21–7.

Bateman, T. S. & Organ, D. W. (1983). 'Job Satisfaction and the Good Soldier: The Relationship between Affect and Employee "Citizenship"'. *Academy of Management Journal*, 26(4), pp. 578–95.

Bateman, T. S. & Strasser, S. (1984). 'A Longitudinal Analysis of the Antecedents of Organisational Commitment'. *Academy of Management Journal*, 27(1), pp. 95–112.

Beare, H. (1995). *What is the Next Quantum Leap for School Systems in Australia? The 1994 Currie Lecture. (ACEA Monograph Series.)* Hawthorn: Australian Council for Educational Administration.

Benne, K. D. & Sheats, P. (1948). 'Functional Roles of Group Members'. *Journal of Social Issues*, 4 (2), pp. 41–9.

Bennis, W. G. (1969). *Organisation Development: Its Nature, Origins and Prospects*. Reading, Mass.: Addison-Wesley.

—— & Nanus, B. (1985). *Leaders: The Strategies for Taking Charge*. New York: Harper & Row.

Bergin, M. & Solman, R. (1992). 'Senior Administrators' Responses to System Wide Restructuring'. In F. Crowther & D. Ogilvie (eds). *The New Political World of Educational Administration*. Hawthorn: Australian Council for Educational Administration.

Berrell, M. (1994). 'The Nature of Work: An Introduction'. In F. Crowther, B. Caldwell, J. Chapman, G. Lakomski & I. Ogilvie (eds). *The Workplace in Education: Australian Perspectives*. Sydney: Edward Arnold.

Berry, T. (1988). *The Dream of the Earth*. San Francisco: Sierra Club Books.

Bertrand, J. & Robinson, P. (1985). *Bertrand—Born To Win*. (As told to Patrick Robinson.) Sydney: Corgi/Bantam.

Blackmore, J. (1987). 'Educational Leadership: A Feminist Critique and Reconstruction'. In J. Blackmore & J. Kenway. *Gender Issues in the Theory and Practice of Educational Administration and Policy*. Proceedings of the National Conference, Deakin University, Victoria, Dec, pp. 168–200.

—— (1996). 'Doing "Emotional Labour" in the Education Market Place: Stories from the Field of Women in Management'. *Discourse: Studies in the Cultural Politics of Education*, Vol. 17, No. 3, pp. 337–49.

Borys, B. & Jemison, D. B. (1989). 'Hybrid Arrangements as Strategic Alliances: Theoretical Issues in Organisational Combinations'. *Academy of Management Review*, 14(2), pp. 234–49.

Boudette, N. E. (1989). 'The Nineties: Networks to Dismantle Old Structures'. *Industry Week*, 238(2), pp. 27–31.

Bovee, C. L. & Thill J. V. (1995). 'Communicating Successfully in an Organisation'. *Business Communication Today* (4th ed). N.Y.: McGraw Hill, pp. 2–25.

Braverman, H. (1996). *Labor and Monopoly Capital: The Degradation of Work in the Twentieth Century*. New York: Monthly Review Press.

Brown, T. L. (1990). 'Fearful of "Empowerment"'. *Industry Week*, 18 June, p. 12.

Brusco, S. (1982). 'The Emilian Model: Productive Decentralisation and Social Integration'. *Cambridge Journal of Economics*, 6, pp. 167–84.

Burgess-Limerick, T. (1993). 'A Work–Home Mesh? Understanding the Lives of Women who Own Small Businesses'. *Feminism and Psychology*, 3(3), pp. 306–62.

—— (1995a). *Lives-in-Process. The Lifestream Narrative of Women who Own Small Businesses*. Unpublished paper, Brisbane.

—— (1995b). *Lives-in-Process: Women who Own Small Businesses*. Unpublished PhD thesis. Griffith University, Brisbane.

—— (1998) 'Researcher as Learner: Negotiating Responsive Agency'. *Feminism and Psychology*, 8(1), pp. 111–22.

Burke, J. E. (1984). 'Johnson & Johnson: Philosophy and Culture'. A videotape prepared by F. J. Aguilar. Boston: Harvard University.

Burns, J. M. (1978). *Leadership*. New York: Harper & Row.

—— (1984). *The Power to Lead: The Crisis of the American Presidency*. New York: Simon & Schuster.

Burns, T. & Stalker, G. M. (1961). *The Management of Innovation*. London: Tavistock.

Charan, R. (1991). 'How Networks Reshape Organizations—For Results'. *Harvard Business Review*, Sept–Oct, pp. 104–15.

Charlton, P. (1997a). 'Back to Work: A Blueprint for the Future'. *The Courier Mail*, Brisbane, Aug 9, p. 23.

—— (1997b). 'The Great Divide'. *The Courier Mail*, Brisbane, March 15, p. 23.

Chusmir, L. (1985). 'Motivation of Managers: Is Gender a Factor?'. *Psychology of Women Quarterly*, 9, pp. 153–9.

Clifford, D. K. & Cavanagh, R. E. (1985). *The Winning Performance*. New York: Bantam Books.

Coase, R. H. (1937). 'The Nature of the Firm'. *Economica*, 4, pp. 386–405.

Coates, J. F., Jarratt, J. & Mahaffe, J. (1989). 'Workplace Management 2000: Seven Themes Shaping the US Workforce and its Structure'. *Personnel Administrator*, 34(12), pp. 50–5.

Collins, J. C. and Porras, J. I. (1996). 'Building your Company's Vision', *Harvard Business Review*, Sept–Oct, pp. 65–77.

Conger, J. A. (1989). 'Leadership: The Art of Empowering Others'. *The Academy of Management Executive*, 3(1), pp. 17–24.

—— & Kanungo, R. N. (1988). *Charismatic Leadership: The Elusive Factor in Organisational Effectiveness*. San Francisco: Jossey–Bass.

Connell, R. W. (1985). *Teacher's Work*. Sydney: Allen & Unwin.

Cooper, R. & Burrell, G. (1988). 'Modernism, Postmodernism and Organisational Analysis: An Introduction'. *Organization Studies*, 9(1), pp. 91–112.

Cooperrider, D. & Srivastva, S. (1987). 'Appreciative Inquiry in Organisational Life'. *Research in Organisational Change and Development*, Vol. 1, pp. 129–69.

Covey, S. R. (1990). *The Seven Habits of Highly Effective People: Restoring the Character Ethic*. Melbourne: Australian Business Library.

Crowther, F. (1994). 'The Work We Do and the Search for Meaning'. In F. Crowther, B. Caldwell, J. Chapman, G. Lakomski & D. Ogilvie (eds). *The Workplace in Education: Australian Perspectives*. Sydney: Edward Arnold.

Cunnington, B. (1987). 'Studies in the Silicon Forest of Oregon and Silicon Valley of California'. Unpublished notes and papers.

—— (1990). 'So You Want to be a World Class Manufacturer: Perhaps you had Better Change your Mind'. Paper presented to the Fifth International Conference of Manufacturing Engineering, Wollongong, 11–13 July.

—— (1991a). 'The Collaborative Organisation'. Paper presented to the Annual Conference of the Australia and New Zealand Association of Management Educators, Bond University, Gold Coast, 5–9 Dec.

—— (1991b). 'Managing in Times of Discontinuity: The Role of Strategic Alliances'. National Engineering Management Conference, Adelaide, 10–11 Oct. Available in the Institution of Engineers, Australia, Preprints of Papers (National Conference Publication No 91/20), pp. 30–5.

—— & Limerick, D. (1987). 'The Fourth Blueprint: An Emergent Managerial Frame of Reference'. *Journal of Managerial Psychology*, 2(2), pp. 26–31.

—— & Trevor–Roberts, B. (1986). 'Educating General Managers for Tomorrow: Have We Got it Right?'. *Business Education*, 17(4), pp. 37–47.

Cyert, R. & Goodman, P. S. (1997). 'Creating Effective University–Industry Alliances: An Organisational Learning Perspective'. *Organizational Dynamics*, Spring, pp. 45–57.

Dalton, G., Perry, L. T., Younger, J. & Smallwood, N. (1996). 'Strategic Restructuring'. *Human Resource Management*, Vol. 35, No. 4, Winter, pp. 433–52.

Daudelin, M. (1996). 'Learning from Experience through Reflection'. *Organizational Dynamics*, Winter, pp. 36–48.

de Chardin, T. P. (1959). *The Phenomenon of Man*. New York: Harper.

de Geus, A. P. (1988). 'Planning as Learning'. *Harvard Business Review*. Mar–Apr, pp. 70–4.

—— (1992). *Keynote Address to the EMFD–Forsyth Group Dialogue on Learning Organizations*. Nov, Brussels: EMFD–Forsyth Group.

Delbecq, A. & Weiss, J. W. (1988). 'The Business Culture of Silicon Valley: Is it a Model for the Future?'. In J. W. Weiss (ed.). *Regional Cultures, Managerial Behaviour and Entrepreneurship: An International Perspective*, Westport: Greenwood Press, pp. 23–41.

Derrida, J. (1973). *Speech and Phenomena*. Evanston: Northwestern University Press.

Deutschman, A. (1990). 'What 25-year Olds Want'. *Fortune*, 27 Aug, pp. 22–8.

DiBella, A., Nevis, A. & Gould, J. (1996). 'Understanding Organizational Learning Capacity'. *Journal of Management Studies*, Vol. 33, No. 3, May, pp. 361–79.

Doyle, F. P. (1990). 'People-Power: The Global Human Resource Challenge for the '90s'. *Columbia Journal of World Business*, 25(1 & 2), pp. 36–45.

Doz, Y. & Prahalad, C. K. (1988). 'A Process Model of Strategic Redirection in Large Complex Firms'. In A. Pettigrew (ed.). *The Management of Strategic Change*. Oxford: Basil Blackwell.

Driver, M. J. (1985). 'Demographic and Societal Factors Affecting the Linear Career Crisis'. *Canadian Journal of Administrative Studies*.

Drucker, P. (1942). *The Future of Industrial Man: A Conservative Approach*. New York: Day.

—— (1965). *The Future of Industrial Man*. New York: New American Library.

—— (1969). *The Age of Discontinuity*. New York: Harper & Row.

—— (1980). *Managing in Turbulent Times*. New York: Harper & Row.

—— (1989a). 'Peter Drucker's 1990's: The Futures that Have Already Happened'. *The Economist*, 313, pp. 19–20.

—— (1989b). *The New Realities*. London: Mandarin.

—— (1993). *Post-Capitalist Society*. HarperCollins: New York.

—— (1994). 'The Age of Social Transformation'. From *The Atlantic Monthly*, Nov. http://www. theatlantic.com/issues/a5dec/chilearn/drucker.html.

Dunphy, D. C. & Stace, D. A. (1988). 'Transformational and Coercive Strategies for Planned Organisational Change'. *Organisation Studies*, 9(3), pp. 317–34.

Ehrensal, K. N. (1995). 'Discourses of Global Competition'. *Journal of Organizational Change Management*, Vol. 8, No. 5, pp. 5–16.

Ehrich, L. C. & Limerick, I. B. (1989). *The Dilemma of Management Programs for Women*. Brisbane: Leadership Centre, Brisbane College of Advanced Education.

Eisenstein, H. (1985). 'The Gender of Bureaucracy: Reflections on Feminism and the State'. In J. Goodnow & C. Pateman (eds). *Women, Social Science and Public Policy*. Sydney: George Allen & Unwin, pp. 105–15.

Eriksen, H. L. (1985). 'Conflict and the Female Principal'. *Phi Delta Kappan*, 67(4), pp. 288–91.

Elkington, J. (1994). 'Towards the Sustainable Corporation'. *California Management Review*, Vol. 36, No. 2, Winter, pp. 90–100.

Etzioni, A. (1964). *Modern Organisations*. Englewood Cliffs: Prentice-Hall.

Fallows, J. (1989). *More Like Us; Making America Great Again*. Boston: Houghton Mifflin.

Fayol, H. D. (1956). *General and Industrial Management*. C. Storrs (trans.). London: Pitman.

Feldman, D., Doerpinghaus, H. & Turnley, W. (1994). 'Managing Temporary Workers: A Permanent HRM Challenge'. *Organizational Dynamics*, Autumn, pp. 49–63.

Ferguson, M. (1980). *The Aquarian Conspiracy: Personal and Social Transformation in the 1980's*. Los Angeles: J. P. Tarhcer.

—— (1985). 'The Mandate of Our Collective, Real Self'. In L. Zonneveld & R. Muller (eds). *The Desire to be Human*. Wassenaar: Mirananda, pp. 162–70.

Fletcher, B. R. (1990). *Organisation Transformation Theorists and Practitioners*. New York: Praeger.

Follett, M. P. (1949). *Freedom and Coordination: Lectures in Business Organisation by Mary P. Follet*. London: Management Publications Trust.

Fombrun, C. & Astley, W. G. (1983). 'Beyond Corporate Strategy'. *Journal of Business Strategy*, 3(4), pp. 47–54.

Foucalt, M. (1973). *Madness and Civilisation*. New York: Vintage Books.

—— (1977). *Language, Counter-memory, Practice*. Ithaca, New York: Cornell University Press.

Fox, A. (1966). *Industrial Sociology and Industrial Relations*. London: Her Majesty's Stationery Office.

Freeman, J. (1984). 'Entrepreneurs as Organisational Products'. Paper presented at the 1984 business/academic dialogue, Karleller Centre, University of Arizona.

French, W. L. & Bell, C. H. Jnr (1984). *Organization Development—Behavioural Science Interventions for Organization Improvement* (3rd edn). Englewood Cliffs: Prentice-Hall.

Fromm, E. & Maccoby, M. (1970). *Social Character in a Mexican Village*. Englewood Cliffs: Prentice-Hall.

[Fry, Art] 'An Interview with Post-it Notes Inventor Art Fry'. *Journal of Business Strategy*, 9(2), pp. 20–4.

Galbraith, J. R. (1977). *Organization Design*. Reading, Mass.: Addison-Wesley.

Gantth, H. L. (1910). *Work, Wages and Profit*. New York: Engineering Magazine Company.

—— (1916). *Industrial Leadership*. New Haven, Conn.: Yale University Press.

—— (1919). *Organizing for Work*. New York: Harcourt Brace Jovanovich.

Garten, J. (1997). 'Can the World Survive the Triumph of Capitalism?'. *Harvard Business Review*, Jan–Feb, pp. 144–50.

Gazzaniger, M. S. (1983). 'Right Hemisphere Language Following Brain Bisection: A 20-year Perspective'. *American Psychologist*, 38, pp. 525–37.

Geldof, R. (1986). *Is That It?*. London: Penguin Books.

Gergen, K. J. (1991). *The Saturated Self: Dilemmas of Identity in Contemporary Life*. USA: Basic Books.

—— (1992). 'Unbundling our Binaries—Genders, Sexualities, Desires'. *Feminism & Psychology*, 3 (3), pp. 447–9.

Ghoshal, S. & Bartlett, C. A. (1990). 'The Multinational Corporation as an Interorganizational Network'. *Academy of Management Review*, 15(4), pp. 603–25.

—— (1995). 'Changing the Role of Top Management: Beyond Structure to Processes'. *Harvard Business Review*, Jan–Feb, pp. 86–96.

Ghousal, S. & Mintzberg, H. (1994). 'Diversification and Diversifact'. *California Management Review*, Vol. 37, No. 1, pp. 8–27.

Gilmore, F. F. (1973). 'The Changing Nature of Policy Formation'. In B. Taylor & K. MacMillan (eds). *Business Policy: Teaching and Research*. New York: John Wiley & Sons, pp. 3–64

Glaser, B. G. & Strauss A. L. (1967). *The Discovery of Grounded Theory: Strategies for Qualitative Research*. Chicago: Aldine.

Goffman, E. (1971). *Relations in Public: Microstudies of the Public Order*. London: Allen Lane/The Penguin Press.

Goldbaum, E. (1988). 'New Alliances: Share the Work and the Rewards'. *Chemical Week*, 143(27), pp. 19–33.

Gould, S. J. (1989). 'An Asteroid to Die For'. *Discover*, Oct.

—— & Eldredge, N. (1986). 'Punctuated Equilibrium at the Third Stage'. *Systematic Zoology*, 35 (1), pp. 143–8.

Greider, W. (1997). *One World, Ready or Not: The Manic Logic of Global Capitalism*. New York: Simon & Schuster.

Griffiths, I. Y. C. (1990). 'Organisation Structures and Women in Management'. Unpublished PhD thesis, Griffith University, Brisbane.

Gronn, P. (1995). 'Greatness Revisited: The Current Obsession with Transformational Leadership'. *Leading and Managing*, Vol. 1, No. 1, Autumn, pp. 14–27.

Gulick, L. & Urwick, L. (eds) (1973). *Papers on the Science of Administration*. New York: A.M. Kelley.

Hall, D. T. & Parker, V. A. (1993). 'The Role of Workplace Flexibility in Managing Diversity'. *Organizational Dynamics*, Summer, pp. 5–18.

Hall, R. (1988). *Attaining Manufacturing Excellence*. Homewood: Dow Jones–Irwin.

Hamel, G., Doz, Y. L. & Prahalad, C. K. (1989). 'Collaborate with Your Competitors—and Win'. *Harvard Business Review*, Jan–Feb, pp. 133–9.

Hamel, G. & Prahalad, C. K. (1994). 'Competing for the Future'. *Harvard Business Review*, July–Aug, pp. 122–8.

—— (1996). 'Strategy as Revolution'. *Harvard Business Review*, July–Aug, pp. 69–82.

Hargreaves, A. (1994). 'Changing Work Cultures of Teaching'. In F. Crowther, B. Caldwell, J. Chapman, G. Lakomski & D. Ogilvie (eds). *The Workplace in Education: Australian Perspectives*. Sydney: Edward Arnold, pp. 39–51.

—— (1994a). *Cultures of Teaching*. Visiting Scholar Address to Australian Council of Educational Administration Conference, Brisbane, pp. 1–26.

Harman, F. C. & Jacobs, G. (1985). *The Vital Difference: Unleashing the Powers of Sustained Corporate Success*. New York: AMACOM.

Harris, T. George. (1993). 'The Post-Capitalist Executive: An Interview with Peter F. Drucker'. *Harvard Business Review*, May–June, pp. 114–22.

Hart, S. L. (1997). 'Beyond Greening: Strategies for a Sustainable World'. *Harvard Business Review*, Jan–Feb, pp. 66–76.

Harvey-Jones, J. (1988). *Making it Happen*. London: Collins.

Hassard, J. (1994). 'Postmodern Organizational Analysis: Toward a Conceptual Framework'. *Journal of Management Studies*, Vol. 31, No. 3, May, pp. 303–24.

Hax, A. C. & Majluf, N. S. (1984). *Strategic Management: An Integrative Perspective*. Englewood Cliffs: Prentice-Hall.

Hayes, R. & Pisano, G. (1994). 'Beyond World Class: The New Manufacturing Strategy'. *Harvard Business Review*, Jan–Feb, pp. 77–86.

Heifetz, R. A. & Laurie, D. L. (1997). 'The Work of Leadership'. *Harvard Business Review*, Jan–Feb, pp. 124–34.

Heller, R. (1984). *The Supermanagers*. New York: E.T. Dutton Inc.

Henley, W. E. (1907). 'Invictus'. *Oxford Book of English Verse*. Oxford: at the Clarendon Press.

Hickman, C. R. & Silva, M. A. (1987). *The Future 500: Creating Tomorrow's Organisations Today*. New York: NAL Books.

Higgins, J. M. & Vincze, J. W. (1989). *Strategic Management* (4th edn). New York: The Dryden Press.

Hirschhorn, L. & Gilmore, T. (1992). 'The New Boundaries of the "Boundaryless" Company'. *Harvard Business Review*, May–June, pp. 104–15.

Hodgetts, R. (1995). 'A Conversation with Rosabeth Moss Kanter'. *Organizational Dynamics*, Summer, pp. 57–69.

Hodgson, C. A. (1985). 'Women in State Leadership'. *Vocational Educational Journal*, 60(7), pp. 40–1.

Hofer, C. W., Murray, E. A. Jnr, Charan, R. & Pitts, R. A. (1980). *Strategic Management: A Casebook in Policy and Planning*. Minnesota: West Publishing.

Hollingworth, P. (1997). 'Clearer Policies Needed'. *The Sunday Mail*, Brisbane, Apr 6, p. 65.

Hough, M. & Payne, J. (1997). *Creating Quality Learning Communities*. Melbourne: Macmillan Education Australia.

Huber, G. (1991). 'Organisational Learning: The Continuing Processes and Literature'. *Organisation Science*, 2, pp. 88–115.

Huberman, M. (1995). 'Networks That Alter Teaching: Conceptualizations, Exchanges and Experiments'. *Teachers and Teaching: Theory and Practice*, Vol. 1, No. 2, pp. 193–211.

Inkpen, A. (1996). 'Creating Knowledge through Collaboration'. *California Management Review*, Vol. 39, No. 1, Fall, pp. 123–40.

Institute of Public Affairs (1996). 'The Plight of Voluntary Organisations'. *L.P.A. Review*, Vol. 48, No. 2, pp. 5–6.

Jahoda, M. (1979). 'The Impact of Unemployment in the 1930s and the 1970s'. *Bulletin of the British Psychological Society*, p. 32.

James, W. (1905). *Psychology*. London: Macmillan & Co.

Jantsch, E. J. & Waddington, C. H. (eds) (1976). *Evolution and Consciousness: Human Systems in Transition*. Reading, Mass.: Addison-Wesley.

Jarillo, C. J. (1988). 'On Strategic Networks'. *Strategic Management Journal*, 9, pp. 31–41.

—— & Ricart, J. E. (1987). 'Sustaining Networks'. *Interfaces*, 17(5), pp. 82–91.

Johnson, R. A., Kast, F. E. & Rosenzweig, J. E. (1967). *The Theory and Management of Systems*. New York: McGraw-Hill.

Johnston, R. A. & Lawrence, P. R. (1988). 'Beyond Vertical Integration—The Rise of the Value-adding Partnership'. *Harvard Business Review*, July–Aug, pp. 94–101.

Jones, P. d'A. (1965). *The Consumer Society: A History of American Capitalism*. London: Penguin.

Jones, R. T. (1996). 'The Challenge of World Class Training'. *Address to the VICAD Second National Conference*, Melbourne, Oct 15.

Kami, M. J. (1979). 'Revamping Planning for this Era of Discontinuity'. In R. J. Allio & M. W. Pennington (eds). *Corporate Planning Techniques*. New York: AMACOM, pp. 147–52.

Kanter, R. M. (1978). 'Work in a New America'. *Daedalus*, Winter, p. 107.

—— (1989a). *When Giants Learn to Dance: Mastering the Challenges of Strategy, Management and Careers in the 1990's*. London: Simon & Schuster.

—— (1989b). 'Becoming PALs: Pooling, Allying and Linking Across Companies'. *Academy of Management Executive*, 3(3), pp. 183–93.

—— (1989–90). 'Navigating the 90s'. *Best of Business Quarterly*, 11(4), pp. 80–5.

—— (1990). 'When Giants Learn Cooperative Strategies'. *Planning Review*, 18(1), Jan/Feb, pp. 15–22.

—— (1991). 'Transcending Business Boundaries: 12,000 World Managers View Change'. *Harvard Business Review*, 69, May–June, pp. 151–91.

—— (1994). 'Collaborative Advantage: The Art of Alliances'. *Harvard Business Review*, July–Aug, pp. 96–108.

—— (1995). *World-Class: Thriving Locally in the Global Economy*. New York: Simon & Schuster.

Kaplan, R. S. & Norton, D. P. (1996). 'Using the Balanced Scorecard as a Strategic Management System'. *Harvard Business Review*, Jan–Feb, pp. 75–85.

Katz, R. L. (1970). *Management of the Total Enterprise*. Englewood Cliffs: Prentice-Hall.

Keen, P. G. W. (1991). 'Redesigning the Organization Through Information Technology'. *Planning Review*, 19(3), pp. 4–9.

Kelley, R. E. (1985). *The Gold Collar Worker*. Reading, Mass.: Addison-Wesley.

Kiechel, W. (1990). 'The Organisation that Learns'. *Fortune*, 12 March, pp. 75–7.

Kilmann, R., Saxton, M. J., Serpa, R., et al (1985). *Gaining Control of the Corporate Culture*. San Francisco: Jossey-Bass.

Kim, W. & Mauborgne, R. (1997). 'Fair Process: Managing in the Knowledge Economy'. *Harvard Business Review*, July–Aug, pp. 65–75.

Kipling, R. (1958). *Rudyard Kipling's Verse: Definitive Addition*. London: Hodder & Stoughton.

Koestler, A. (1975). *The Act of Creation*. London: Picador.

—— (1978). *Janus: A Summing Up*. London: Picador.

Kofman, F. & Senge, P. M. (1993). 'Communities of Commitment: The Heart of Learning Organizations'. *Harvard Business Review*, Autumn, pp. 5–23.

Koidin, M. (1996). 'Leary Takes Final Trip—Inner to Outer Space'. *The Chronicle*, Australian Associated Press, p. 13.

Kondo, D. K. (1990). *Crafting Selves: Power, Gender and Discourses of Identity in a Japanese Workplace*. Chicago: University of Chicago Press.

Kotter, J. P. (1995). 'Leading Change: Why Transformational Efforts Fail'. *Harvard Business Review*, March–Apr, pp. 59–67.

Kuhn, T. S. (1962). *The Structure of Scientific Revolutions*. Chicago: University of Chicago Press.

Kumar, N. (1996). 'The Power of Trust in Manufacturer–Retailer Relationships'. *Harvard Business Review*, Nov–Dec, pp. 92–106.

Larocque, L. (1995). 'Symposium on School–University Collaboration'. *The Canadian Administrator*, Vol. 34, No. 5, pp. 1–8.

Lakomski, G. (1995). 'Leadership and Learning: From Transformational Leadership to Organisational Learning'. *Leading and Managing*, Vol. 1, No. 3, Spring, pp. 211–25.

Lampel, J. & Mintzberg, H. (1996). 'Customizing Customization'. *Sloan Management Review*, Fall, pp. 21–30.

Lasch, C. (1995). *The Revolt of the Élites and the Betrayal of Democracy*. New York: W. W. Norton.

Lash, S. & Urry, J. (1987). *The End of Organized Capitalism*. Oxford: Basil Blackwell.

Lawrence, N. & Bunk, S. (1985). *The Stump Jumpers*. Sydney: Hale & Iremonger.

Lawrence, P. R. & Lorsch, J. W. (1967). *Organisation and the Environment: Managing Differentiation and Integration*. Boston: Division of Research, Harvard University Graduate School of Business Administration.

Learned, E. P., Christensen, C. R., Andrews, K. R. & Guth, W. D. (eds) (1969). *Business Policy: Text and Cases*. Homewood: R. D. Irwin.

Leavitt, H. J. (1987). *Corporate Pathfinders*. New York: Viking Penguin Inc.

Levinson, H. (1996). 'A New Age of Self Reliance'. *Harvard Business Review*, July–Aug, p. 161.

—— (1996). 'Capitalism with a Safety Net?'. *Harvard Business Review*, Sept–Oct, pp. 173–80.

—— (1996). 'When Executives Burn Out'. *Harvard Business Review*, July–Aug, pp. 152–63.

—— & Rosenthal, S. (1984). *CEO: Corporate Leadership in Action*. New York: Basic Books.

Levy, J. (1983). 'Language, Cognition, and the Right Hemisphere: A Response to Gazzaniger'. *American Psychologist*, 38, pp. 539–41.

Liedtka, J. M. & Roseblum, J. W. (1996). 'Shaping Conversations: Making Strategy, Making Change'. *California Management Review*, Vol. 39, No. 1, Fall, pp. 141–57.

Likert, R. (1961). *New Patterns of Management*. New York: McGraw-Hill.

Lim, H. (1981). 'Japanese Management: A Skill Profile'. *Training and Development Journal*, 35(10), pp. 18–21.

Limerick, B. (1995). 'Gendered Career Paths in Education'. In B. Limerick & B. Lingard (eds). *Gender and Changing Educational Management*. Rydalmere: Hodder Education.

——, Burgess-Limerick, T. A. & Grace, M. (1996). 'The Politics of Interviewing: Power Relations and Accepting the Gift'. *Qualitative Studies in Education*, Vol. 9, No. 4, pp. 449–60.

—— & Crowther, F. (1997). 'Leader Development Through Problem-based Learning'. *Australian Journal of Higher Education (Zeitschrift für Hochshuldidaktik)*, Vol. 39, Summer.

—— & Heywood, E. (1993). 'Training for Women in Management: the Australian Context'. *Women in Management in Australia*, 8(3), pp. 23–30.

——, Heywood, E. & Daws, L. (1994). *Mentoring: Beyond the Status Quo? Mentoring, Networking and Women in Management in Queensland*. Brisbane: Queensland University of Technology Report for the Department of Industry, Business and Regional Development.

—— & Lingard, R. (eds) (1995). *Gender and Changing Educational Management*. Sydney: Hodder Education.

——, Passfield R. & Cunnington, B. (1994). 'Transformational Change: Towards an Action Learning Organisation'. *The Learning Organisation*, Vol. 1, No. 2.

Limerick, D. (1989). 'Boomers vs Yuppies: The Educational Implications of Cohort Culture Conflict'. Paper presented to the Annual Conference of the Australian and New Zealand Association of Management Educators, Auckland, New Zealand, 4–6 Dec.

—— (1990). 'Managers of Meaning: From Bob Geldof's Band Aid to Australian CEOs'. *Organizational Dynamics*, 18, Spring, pp. 22–33.

—— (1991). 'Foreword'. In O. Zuber–Skerritt, *Action Research for Change and Development*. Aldershot: Gower–Avebury.

—— & Cunnington, B. (1987). 'Management Development: The Fourth Blueprint'. *Journal of Management Development*, 6(1), pp. 54–67.

—— & Cunnington, B. (1989). 'Management Development: A Look to the Future'. *Management Decisions*, 27(1), pp. 10–13.

——, Cunnington, B. & Trevor–Roberts, B. (1984). *Frontiers of Excellence: A Study of Strategy, Structure and Culture in Fifty Australian Organisations*, Spring Hill, Queensland: AIM Queensland Division.

Loden, M. (1985). *How to Succeed in Business without Being one of the Boys*. New York: Times Books.

Lomax, P. & Darley, J. (1995). 'Inter-School Links, Liaison and Networking: Collaboration or Competition?'. *Educational Management and Administration*, Vol. 23, No. 3, pp. 148–61.

Louis, M. (1985). 'An Investigator's Guide to Workplace Culture'. In P. J. Frost, L. F. Moore, M. R. Louis, C. C. Lundberg & J. Martin (eds). *Organizational Culture*. Beverly Hills: Sage, pp. 73–93.

Lovelock, C. & Yip, G. S. (1996). 'Developing Global Strategies for Service Businesses'. *California Management Review*, Vol. 38, No. 2, Winter, pp. 64–86.

Lukes, S. (1973). *Individualism*. Oxford: Blackwell.

Lundberg, C. (1985). 'On the Feasibility of Cultural Interventions in Organisations'. In P. J. Frost, L. F. Moore, M. R. Louis, C. C. Lundberg & J. Martin (eds). *Organizational Culture*. Beverly Hills: Sage, pp. 169–85.

Lyons, T. F., Krachenberg, A. R. & Henke, J. W. (1990). 'Mixed Motive Marriages: What's Next for Buyer–Supplier Relations?'. *Sloan Management Review*, 31(4), pp. 29–36.

Lyotard, J. F. (1984). *The Postmodern Condition*. Manchester: Manchester University Press.

Mackay, H. (1993). *Re-inventing Australia. The Mind and Mood of Australia in the 90's*. Sydney: Angus & Robertson.

Magretta, J. (1996). 'Growth through Global Sustainability: An Interview with Monsanto's CEO, Robert B. Shapiro'. *Harvard Business Review*, Jan–Feb, pp. 79–88.

Majchrzak, A. & Wang, Q. (1996). 'Breaking the Functional Mind-set in Process Organizations'. *Harvard Business Review*, Sept–Oct, pp. 93–9.

Manter, M. A. (1989). 'A Chance for Freedom'. *Personnel Administrator*, 34(12), pp. 64–70.

Manz, C. C., Keating, D. E. & Donnellon, A. (1990). 'Preparing for an Organizational Change to Employee Self-management: The Managerial Transition'. *Organizational Dynamics*, 19, Autumn, pp. 15–26.

Marshall, C. (1987). 'Using Sociolinguistics for Exploring Gender and Culture Issues in Educational Administration'. Paper presented to the Annual Meeting of the Educational Research Association Special Interest Group, Research on Women in Education. Portland, Oregon, 12–14 Nov.

Martin, B. (1981). *A Sociology of Contemporary Cultural Change*. Oxford: Basil Blackwell.

Matthes, K. (1992). 'Empowerment: Fact or Fiction?' *HR Focus*, March, pp. 1–6.

Maxcy, S. (ed) (1994). *Postmodern School Leadership: Meeting the Crisis in Educational Administration*. Westport, Connecticut: Praeger.

Mayo, E. (1933). *The Human Problems of an Industrial Civilization*. New York: Macmillan.

McCune, J. (1996). 'The Face of Tomorrow'. *Journal of Business Strategy*, Vol. 16, No. 3, pp. 50–5.

McKinney, J. & Garrison, J. (1994). 'Postmodernism and Educational Leadership: The New and Improved Panoption'. In S. Maxcy (ed.). *Postmodern School Leadership: Meeting the Crisis in Educational Administration*. Westport, Connecticut: Praeger.

Mellish, E. & Limerick, B. (1997). *Appreciative Consultation: The Consulting Perspective: Reclaiming our Imaginative Competence*. Brisbane: Paper presented at A.H.R.I. National Conference.

Menzies, H. (1996). *Whose Brave New World? The Information Highway and the New Economy*. Toronto: Between the Lines.

Miles, R. & Snow, C. (1995). 'The New Network Firm: A Spherical Structure Built on a Human Investment Philosophy. *Organisational Dynamics*, Spring, pp. 5–17.

Millet, B. (1994). *Identifying a Model of Institutional Change: the Transition from College of Advanced Education to University*. Unpublished PhD thesis. Brisbane: Griffith University.

Mills, C. Wright (1951). *White Collar—The American Middle Class*. New York: Oxford University Press.

Mintzberg, H. (1993). 'The Pitfalls of Strategic Planning'. *California Management Review*, Fall, pp. 32–47.

—— (1994). 'The Fall and Rise of Strategic Planning'. *Harvard Business Review*, Jan–Feb, pp. 107–14.

—— (1996). 'The Myth of "Society, Inc."'. *Report on Business*, Oct, pp. 113–17.

—— (1996a). 'Musings on Management'. *Harvard Business Review*, July–Aug, pp. 61–7.

——, Dougherty, D., Jorgensen, J. & Westley, F. (1996). 'Some Surprising Things about Collaboration: Knowing How People Connect Makes it Work Better'. *Organizational Dynamics*, Summer, pp. 60–71.

Mitchell, C. (1996). *The Three Rs: Roles, Rhetoric and Educating Engineers to Resolve Environmental Conflict*. Brisbane: Paper presented at the 1st Queensland Environmental Engineering Conference, The Institution of Engineers, Australia, and Griffith University, Nov.

Modic, S. J. (1988). 'Strategic Alliances: A Global Economy Demands Global Partnerships'. *Industry Week*, Oct, pp. 46–52.

Mohrman, S. A., Mohrman, A. M. & Cohen, S. G. (1995). *Designing Team Based Organisations: New Forms for Knowledge Work*. San Francisco: Jossey-Bass.

Morris, E. (1987). 'Vision and Strategy: A Focus for the Future'. *Journal of Business Strategy*, 8(2), pp. 51–8.

Mroczkowski, T. & Hanaoka, M. (1989). 'Continuity and Change in Japanese Management'. *Human Resources*, Winter, pp. 39–52.

Mulford, W. (1996). 'Do School Principals Make a Difference? Recent Evidence and Implications'. *Leading and Managing*, Vol. 2, No. 3, pp. 155–69.

Murphy, J. (1988). 'Making Sense of Postmodern Sociology'. *The British Journal of Sociology*, 39(4), pp. 600–14.

Naisbitt, J. (1982). *Megatrends: Ten New Directions for Transforming Our Lives*. New York: Warner Books.

—— (1994). *Global Paradox: the Bigger the World Economy the More Powerful Its Smallest Players*. Sydney: Allen & Unwin.

—— & Aburdene, P. (1985). *Reinventing the Corporation: Transforming Your Job and Your Company for the New Information Society*. New York: Warner Books.

—— & Aburdene, P. (1990). *Ten Directions for the 1990s—Megatrends 2000*. New York: William Morrow & Co. Inc.

Nevis, E., DiBella, A. & Gould, J. (1995). 'Understanding Organizations as Learning Systems'. *Sloan Management Review*, Winter, pp. 73–85.

Newmann, F. & Wehlage, G. (1995). *Successful School Restructuring: A Report to the Public and Educators*. Center on Organisation and Restructuring of Schools, University of Wisconsin, Madison.

Nisbet, R. (1953). *The Quest for Community*. New York: Oxford University Press.

Nohria, N. & Berkley, J. (1994). 'An Action Perspective: The Crux of the New Management'. *California Management Review*, Summer, pp. 70–92.

Nonaka, I. (1988). 'Creating Organizational Order Out of Chaos: Self-renewal in Japanese Firms'. *California Management Review*, 30 (3), Spring, pp. 57–73.

Normann, R. & Ramirez, R. (1993). 'From Value Chain to Value Constellation: Designing Interactive Strategy'. *Harvard Business Review*, July–Aug, pp. 65–77.

Ogawa, R. & Bossert, S. (1995). 'Leadership as an Organizational Quality'. *Educational Administration Quarterly*, Vol. 31, No. 2, May, pp. 224–43.

Ogilvy, J. (1995). 'The Economics of Trust'. Book review in *Harvard Business Review*, Nov–Dec, pp. 46–7.

Ohmae, K. (1985). *Triad Power*. New York: Free Press.

Ohno, T. (1983). 'Foreword'. In Y. Monden, *Toyota Production System*. Atlanta: Industrial Engineering and Management Press.

Oliver, D. W. (1976). *Education and Community: A Radical Critique of Innovative Schooling*. Berkeley: McCutchan Publishing Corporation.

Olson, P. D. (1990). 'Choices for Innovation-minded Corporations'. *Journal of Business Strategy*, 11(1), pp. 42–6.

Organ, D. W. (1988). *Organisational Citizenship Behaviour: The Good Soldier Syndrome*. Lexington, Mass.: Lexington Books.

Orton, J. D. & Weick, K. E. (1990). 'Loosely Coupled Systems: A Reconceptualisation'. *Academy of Management Review*, 15(2), pp. 203–3.

Ozra, J. & Walker, L. (1995). 'Women in Educational Management: Theory and Practice'. In B. Limerick & R. Lingard (eds). *Gender and Changing Educational Management*. Sydney: Hodder Education, pp. 34–43.

Pankow, W. (1976). 'Openness as Self-transcendence'. In E. Jantsch & C. H. Waddington (eds). *Evolution and Consciousness: Human Systems in Transition*. Reading, Mass.: Addison-Wesley, pp. 16–36.

Paquette, J. (1997). 'Education and Vocationalism in the Age of the "Death of Work"'. *Journal of Educational Administration and Foundations*, Vol. 12, No. 1, pp. 10–29.

Parsons, T., Bales, R. F. & Shils, E. A. (1953). *Working Papers in the Theory of Action*. New York: Free Press.

Pascale, R. T. (1978). 'Zen and the Art of Management'. *Harvard Business Review*, March–Apr, pp. 91–110.

—— (1990). *Managing on the Edge*. New York: Simon & Schuster.

Patton, P. (1988). 'Giving up the Ghost'. In L. Grossberg, A. Curthoys, T. Fry & P. Patton (eds). *It's a Sin: Essays on Postmodernism, Politics and Culture*. Sydney: Power Publications, pp. 88–95.

Pearce, J. A. (1982). 'The Company Mission as a Strategic Tool'. *Sloan Management Review*, 23(3), pp. 15–24.

Peters, T. J. (1987). *Thriving on Chaos: Handbook for a Management Revolution*. New York: Knopf.

—— (1988). 'Facing up to the Need for a Management Revolution'. *California Management Review*, 30(2), pp. 7–28.

—— (1990). 'Get Innovative or Get Dead'. *California Management Review*, 33(1), pp. 9–26.

—— & Waterman, R. H. (1982). *In Search of Excellence: Lessons from America's Best-run Companies*. New York: Harper & Row.

Pettigrew, A. M. (1986). 'Is Corporate Culture Manageable?'. Keynote address, Sixth Annual Strategic Management Society Conference on Cultures and Competitive Strategies, Singapore, 13–16 Oct.

Pickett, L. (1992). 'The Road to the Future—Les Pickett Interviews Professor Quinn Mills'. *Training and Development Australia*, 10(1), pp. 5–10.

Piore, M. & Sabel, C. (1984). *The Second Industrial Divide*. New York: Basic Books.

Porter, M. (1990). *Competitive Strategy: Techniques for Analysing Industries and Competitors*. New York: Free Press.

—— & van der Linde, C. (1995). 'Green and Competitive: Ending the Stalemate'. *Harvard Business Review*, Sept–Oct, pp. 120–34.

Powell, W. W. (1990). 'Neither Market nor Hierarchy: Network Forms of Organization'. *Research in Organisational Behavior*, 12, pp. 295–366.

——, Koput, K. & Smith-Doerr, L. (1996). 'Interorganisational Collaboration and the Focus of Innovation: Networks of Learning in Biotechnology'. *Administrative Science Quarterly*, 41, pp. 116–45.

Quinn, J. B. (1980). *Strategies for Change: Logical Incrementalism*. New York: Irwin.

Raelin, J. (1997). 'Action Learning and Action Science: Are they Different?'. *Organizational Dynamics*, Summer, pp. 21–34.

Raynolds, E. H. (1987). 'Management Women in the Corporate Workplace: Possibilities for the Year 2000'. *Human Resource Management*, 26(2), pp. 265–76.

Rayport, J. & Sviokla J. (1995). 'Exploiting the Virtual Value Chain'. *Harvard Business Review*, Nov–Dec, pp. 75–85.

Reich, R. B. (1983). *The Next American Frontier*. New York: Times Books.

Revans, R. W. (1982). *The Origins and Growth of Action Learning*. Bromlet: Chartwell Bratt.

Rice, E. & Schneider, G. T. (1994). 'A Decade of Teacher Empowerment: An Empirical Analysis of Teacher Involvement in Decision Making, 1980–1991'. *Journal of Educational Administration*, Vol. 32, No. 1, pp. 43–58.

Richman, T. (1988). 'Make Love Not War'. *Inc.*, Aug, pp. 56–60.

Riffel, J. & Levin, B. (1997). 'Schools Coping with the Impact of Information Technology'. *Educational Management and Administration*, Vol. 25(1), pp. 51–64.

Rifkin, J. (1995). *The End of Work. The Decline of the Global Labor Force and the Dawn of the Post-market Era*. New York: Putnam's Sons.

Rizzo, A. & Mendez, C. (1988). 'Making Things Happen in Organisations: Does Gender Make a Difference?'. *Public Personnel Management*, 17(1), pp. 9–20.

Robbins, S., Low, P. & Mourell, M. (1986). *Managing Human Resources*. Sydney: Prentice-Hall Australia.

Rodrik, D. (1997). 'Has Globalization Gone Too Far?'. *Californian Management Review*, Spring, Vol. 39, No. 3, pp. 29–53.

Rogers, J. L. (1988). 'New Paradigm Leadership: Integrating the Female Ethos'. *Initiative*, 51, Fall, pp. 1–8.

Rose, M. (1975). *Industrial Behaviour: Theoretical Development Since Taylor*. London: Allen Lane.

Rosenberg, N. (1982). *Inside the Black Box: Technology and Economics*. Cambridge: Cambridge University Press.

Rothschild, W. E. (1988). 'Who are Your Future Competitors?'. *Journal of Business Strategy*, 9(3), pp. 10–14.

Rouleau, L. & Clegg, S. R. (1992). 'Postmodernism and Postmodernity in Organization Analysis'. *Journal of Organizational Change Management*, 5(1), pp. 8–25.

Sabel, C. F. (1989). 'Flexible Specialisation and the Re-emergence of Regional Economies'. In P. Hierstand & J. Zeitlin (eds), *Reversing Industrial Decline*. Oxford: Berg, pp. 17–70.

Salancik, G. (1995). 'Wanted: A Good Network Theory of Organization'. *Administrative Science Quarterly*, 40, pp. 345–9.

Scheff, J. & Kotler, P. (1996). 'How the Arts can Prosper through Strategic Collaborations'. *Harvard Business Review*, Jan–Feb, pp. 52–62.

Schein, E. H. (1983). 'The Role of the Founder in Creating Organisational Culture'. *Organizational Dynamics*, 12(1), pp. 13–28.

—— (1990). 'Career Stress in Changing Times: Some Final Observations'. *Prevention in Human Services*, 8(1), pp. 251–61.

—— (1995). *Building the Learning Consortium*. Working paper 10.005. Cambridge, Mass.: MIT Organizational Learning Center.

—— (1996). 'Three Cultures of Management: The Key to Organisational Learning'. *Sloan Management Review*, Fall, pp. 9–20.

Schmidt, L. (1997). 'Touring Gurus Serve up Uncommon Sense'. *Business Review Weekly*, Aug 18, pp. 32–3.

Schoemaker, P. (1995). 'Scenario Planning: A Tool for Stategic Thinking'. *Sloan Management Review*, Winter, pp. 25–40.

Schon, D. A. (1971). *Beyond the Stable State*. New York: Random House.

Scotrail (1985). *Climbing the Mountain*. Glasgow: Scotrail.

Senge, P. M. (1990). *The Fifth Discipline: The Art and Practice of the Learning Organisation*. New York: Doubleday/Currency.

—— (1997). 'Communities of Leaders and Learners'. *Harvard Business Review*, Sept–Oct, pp. 30–1.

Shakeshaft, C. (1987). *Women in Educational Administration*. California: Sage.

—— (1995). 'Gendered Leadership Styles in Educational Organisations'. In B. Limerick & R. Lingard (eds). *Gender and Educational Management*. Hodder Education: Sydney.

Sheppard, B. & Brown, J. (1996). 'Taylor High: An Emerging Learning Organisation' *The Canadian Administrator*, Vol. 36, No. 3, Dec, pp. 1–6.

Silverman, D. (1970). *The Theory of Organisation: A Sociological Framework*. London: Heinemann Educational.

Simons, R. (1995). 'Control in an Age of Empowerment'. *Harvard Business Review*, March–Apr, pp. 80–8.

Sinclair, A. (1995). 'The Seduction of the Self-Managed Team and the Reinvention of the Team-as-Group'. *Leading and Managing*, Vol. 1, No. 1, pp. 79–92.

Slater, P. E. (1955). 'Role Differentiation in Small Groups'. In A. P. Hare, F. Borgatta & R. F. Bales (eds). *Small Groups*. Alfred Knopf, pp. 498–515.

Smircich, L. (1983). 'Concepts of Culture and Organisational Analysis'. *Administrative Science Quarterly*, 28, pp. 339–58.

Spender, D. (1997). *From the Factory System to Portfolio Living: Access, Equity and Self-promotion in the 21st Century*. Canberra: Paper presented to Australian Council for Educational Administration Annual Conference, July.

Staples, L. H. (1990). 'Powerful Ideas About Empowerment'. *Administration in Social Work*, 14(2), pp. 29–42.

Statham, A. (1987). 'The Gender Model Revisited: Differences in the Management Styles of Men and Women'. *Sex Roles*, 16(7), pp. 409–29.

Steketee, M. (1996). 'Public Servant or Party Slave?'. *The Weekend Australian*, Apr 5, p. 23.

Stevens, M. (1988). 'A Nobel View'. *Best of Business Quarterly*, 10(2), pp. 9–13.

Stevenson, H. & Moldoveanu, M. (1995). 'The Power of Predictability'. *Harvard Business Review*, July–Aug, pp. 140–3.

Stewart, T. A. (1991). 'Brainpower'. *Fortune*, 123(21), pp. 41–56.

Still, L. (1988). *Becoming a Top Woman Manager*. Sydney: Allen & Unwin.

Strauss, A. & Corbin, J. (1990). *Basics of Qualitative Research: Grounded Theory Procedures and Techniques*. Newbury Park, Calif.: Sage.

Sullivan, T. A. (1990). 'The Decline of Occupations'. In M. T. Hallinan, D. M. Klein & J. Glass (eds). *Change in Societal Institutions*. New York: Plennum Press, pp. 13–31.

Summer, C. E. (1980). *Strategic Behavior in Business and Government*. Boston: Little, Brown & Company.

Swartz, P. (undated). *Peter Drucker: A Conversation with Peter Swartz*. http://www.mag.keio.ac.jp/-po.tcap.html.

Taylor, F. W. (1947). *The Principles of Scientific Management*. New York: Harper & Row.

Teece, D. & Pisano, G. (1987). 'Collaborative Arrangements and Technology Strategy'. Paper presented at the Conference on New Technology and New Intermediaries, Centre for European Studies, Stanford University.

Tersine, R. J. (1980). *Materials Management and Inventory Systems*. New York: Elsevier North Holland.

Thomas, D. & Ely, R. (1996). 'Making Differences Matter: A New Paradigm for Managing Diversity'. *Harvard Business Review*, Sept–Oct, pp. 79–90.

Thompson, A. A., Fulmer, W. E. & Strickland, A. J. (1989). *Readings in Strategic Management* (3rd edn). Homewood: BPI Irwin.

Thompson, A. A. & Strickland, A. J. (1990). *Strategic Management: Concepts and Cases* (5th edn). Homewood: BPI Irwin.

Thorelli, H. B. (1986). 'Networks: Between Markets and Hierarchies'. *Strategic Management Journal*, 7(1), pp. 37–51.

Thurow, L. (1996). 'The Future of Capitalism: How Today's Economic Forces Shape Tomorrow's World'. *New York Times*, 14 Apr.

Tichy, N. (1983). 'The Essentials of Strategic Change Management'. *Journal of Business Strategy*, 3(4), pp. 55–67.

—— (1989). 'GE's Crotonville: A Staging Ground for Corporate Revolution'. *Academy of Management Executive*, 4(2), pp. 99–106.

Toffler, A. (1981). *The Third Wave*. London: Pan Books/Collins.

—— (1985). *The Adaptive Corporation*. London: Pan Books.

Tomasko, R. M. (1987). 'Running Lean, Staying Lean'. *Management Review*, 76(11), pp. 32–8.

Toynbee, A. & Ikeda, D. (1989). *Choose Life: A Dialogue*. Oxford: Oxford University Press.

Treston, K. (1994). 'Work and Spirituality'. In F. Crowther, B. Caldwell, J. Chapman, G. Lakomski & D. Ogilvie (eds). *The Workplace in Education: Australian Perspectives*. Sydney: Edward Arnold.

Tucker, R. B. (1987). 'You, Inc.'. *Success!*, Apr, pp. 58–9.

Tushman, M. L., Newman, W. H. & Romanelli, E. (1986). 'Convergence and Upheaval: Managing the Unsteady Pace of Organizational Evolution'. *California Management Review*, 29, pp. 29–44.

Tushman, M. L. & O'Reilly, C. A. III. (1996). 'Ambidextrous Organizations: Managing Evolutionary and Revolutionary Change'. *California Management Review*, Vol. 38, No. 4, Summer, pp. 8–30.

Udy, S. H. (1970). *Work in Traditional and Modern Society*. Englewood Cliffs: Prentice-Hall.

Ulrich, D. & Wiersema, M. F. (1989). 'Gaining Strategic and Organizational Capability in a Turbulent Business Environment'. *The Academy of Management Executive*, 3(2), pp. 115–22.

van Biema, M. & Greenwald, B. (1997). 'Managing our Way to Higher Service Sector Productivity'. *Harvard Business Review*, July–Aug, pp. 87–95.

Vitousek, P. (1997). 'Stopping Biological Invasions Before They Do Lasting Damage'. *The Chronicle of Higher Education*, Jan 17, Vol. XLIII, No. 19, pp. B4–5.

Wall, S. & Wall, S. (1995). 'The Evolution (Not The Death) of Strategy'. *Organizational Dynamics*, Autumn, pp. 7–19.

Waterman, R. H. Jnr (1987). *The Renewal Factor*. New York: Bantam Books.

——, Waterman, J. A. & Collard, B. A. (1994). 'Toward a Career-Resilient Workforce'. *Harvard Business Review*, July–Aug, pp. 87–95.

Weick, K. E. (1976). 'Educational Organizations as Loosely Coupled Systems'. *Administrative Science Quarterly*, 21, pp. 1–9.

—— (1979). 'Cognitive Processes in Organizations'. In B. Staw (ed.). *Research in Organisations: Vol 1*. JAI Press, pp. 41–74.

—— (1982). 'Management of Organisational Change Among Loosely Coupled Elements'. In P. S. Goodman et al (eds). *Change in Organisations*. San Francisco: Jossey-Bass, pp. 375–408.

—— (1985). 'The Significance of Corporate Culture'. In P. J. Frost, L. F. Moore, M. R. Louis, C. C. Lundberg & J. Martin (eds). *Organisational Culture*. Beverly Hills: Sage, pp. 381–9.

Weidenbaum, M. (1996). 'The Chinese Family Business Enterprise'. *California Management Review*, Vol. 38, No. 4, Summer, pp. 141–56.

Weimer, G., Knill, B., Modic, S. J. & Potter, C. (1988a). 'Integrated Manufacturing VI—Strategic Alliances; An International Strategy'. *Automation*, 35(11), IM2–IM30.

—— (1988b). 'Integrated Manufacturing VI: Strategic Alliances Make Marketing and Manufacturing an International Game'. *CAE*, 7(11), IM2–IM30.

Whipp, R., Rosenfeld, R. & Pettigrew, A. (1989). 'Managing Strategic Change in a Mature Business'. *Long Range Planning*, 22(6), pp. 92–9.

Whyte, R. (1992). 'The Regional Director in a Restructured World: A Case Study of Accommodation'. In I. Crowther & D. Ogilvie. *The New Political World of Educational Administration*. Hawthorn: Australian Council for Educational Administration.

Woodburn, T. L. (1979). 'Corporate Strategic Planning in South African Organisations'. Unpublished PhD thesis. University of Witwatersrand, Johannesburg.

Wren D. A. (1972). *The Evolution of Management Thought*. New York: Ronald Press.

Yankelovich, D. (1981). *New Rules: Searching for Self Fulfilment in a World Turned Upside Down*. New York: Random House.

Yeung, I. & Tung, R. (1996). 'Achieving Business Success in Confucian Societies: The Importance of Guanxi'. *Organizational Dynamics*, Autumn, pp. 54–65.

Zaleznik, A. (1963). *Role Development and Interpersonal Competence*. Cambridge, Mass.: Division of Research, Harvard Business School.

—— (1977). 'Managers and Leaders: Are They Different?'. *Harvard Business Review*, 55(3), pp. 67–78.

—— (1989). *The Managerial Mystique*. New York: Harper & Row.

—— (1990). 'The Leadership Gap'. *Academy of Management Executive*, 4(1), pp. 7–22.

Zonneveld, L. & Muller, R. (1985). *The Desire to be Human*. Wassenaar: Mirananda.

Zuber–Skerritt, O. (1991). *Action Learning for Change and Development*. Aldershot: Gower–Avebury.

REFERENCES

Aburdene, P., 8
Akers, J., 128
Andrews, E., 90
Andrews, K., 39, 146
Ansoff, H., 57, 59, 60, 82, 148
Apple, M., 190
Argyris, C., 34, 83, 180, 248
Armstrong, A., 73, 217
Astley, W., 172
Auty, G., 24, 25
Avolio, B., 132, 222
Bailey, W., 106
Bales, R., 121, 223, 225
Baritz, L., 32
Barnard, C., 33
Barnett, cited in Powell et al., 69
Barthes, R., 12
Bartlett, C., 46
Bass, B., 132, 222
Bateman, T., vii, 107
Baughman, J., 183
Bauman, S., 110, 112
Beare, H., 54, 56, 163
Belbin, M., 223
Bell, M., 177
Benne, K. D., 223
Bennis, W., 34, 153, 177
Bergin, M., 113
Berkley, J., 178, 247
Berrell, M., 190
Berry, T., 191
Bertrand, J., 41
Blackmore, J., 133, 201
Borys, B., 27, 46, 89, 90, 94
Bossert, S., 225
Boudette, N., 62
Bovee, C. L., 92
Braverman, H., 190, 191, 192
Brown, T., 140
Bruggere, T., 160, 161
Brusco, S., 74
Bunk, S., 173
Burgess-Limerick, T. A., 26, 130, 131, 197, 239, 247, 249, 250

Burke, J., 168, 169
Burns, J., 125, 176, 221
Burns, T., 37, 38
Burrell, G., 12
Carroll, J., 20
Cavanagh, R., 221, 222
Charan, R., 55, 64, 66, 148
Charlton, P., 20, 193
Christensen, C., 39, 146
Chusmir, L., 132
Clegg, S., 14
Clifford, D., 221, 222
Clinton, B., 119
Coase, R., 72
Coates, J., 8
Collins, J. C., 160
Conger, J., 139
Connell, R., 136
Cooper, R., 12
Cooperrider, D., 184, 185, 186, 194, 233, 251
Corbin, J., 244
Covey, R., 111
Crowther, F., viii, 6, 75, 192
Cunnington, B., v, vi, vii, ix, 122, 130, 180, 214
Cyert, R., 69
Dalton, G., 149
D'Aquino, N., 161, 162, 170, 183, 184, 220, 226, 251
Darley, J., 77
Daudelin, M., 180
de Chardin, T., 16
de Geus, A. P., 179, 184
Delbecq, A., 65, 138
Derrida, J., 12
Deutschman, A., 13, 101, 110, 114, 130, 197
DiBella, A., 178
Doerpinghaus, H., 198
Donnellon, A., 140
Doyle, F., 8, 112, 139
Doz, Y., 135, 178
Driver, M., 136

Watson, T., 169
Wehlage, G., 26, 200
Weick, K., 43, 45, 46, 143, 179
Weidenbaum, M., 70
Weimer, G., 77, 78, 93
Weiss, J., 65, 138
Welch, J. Jnr, 1, 16, 65, 66, 80, 155, 180, 220, 226, 251
Whipp, R., 173
Whyte, R., 113

Wiersema, M., 8, 159
Wran, N., 123
Wren, D., 32, 33
Yankelovich, D., 36
Yeung, I., 71
Yip, G. S., viii, 92
Zaleznik, A., 94, 95, 125, 176, 223
Zonneveld, L., 16
Zuber–Skerritt, O., 179, 180

INDEX